Lilly & Ian

Lilly & Ian

MOUSE & DRAGON

Ian T. Walker

PARTRIDGE
A Penguin Random House Company

Library of Congress Control Number:		2015944369
ISBN:	Hardcover	978-1-4828-3220-4
	Softcover	978-1-4828-3219-8
	eBook	978-1-4828-3221-1

Print information available on the last page.

To order additional copies of this book, contact
Toll Free 800 101 2657 (Singapore)
Toll Free 1 800 81 7340 (Malaysia)
orders.singapore@partridgepublishing.com

www.partridgepublishing.com/singapore

Contents

Introduction...ix

BOOK ONE

Lilly's profile 1

About myself and my ideal match 1

Hello dear Ian.. 2

Hi Lilly 4

Lilly & Ian Mouse & Dragon 5

Kingsford Smith Airport Sydney June 30, 2012 5

China, 2012 8

Mouse and Dragon Join the Fire Brigade 27

Mouse and Dragon Go To War...37

Mouse Has a Birthday... 42

Mouse and Dragon Buy a Car..58

For a Long Time 73

Lost in the Smog of Beijing.. 77

The Yellow Room... 80

Mouse and Dragon 84

Mouse and Dragon Go Fishing.. 86

Mouse and Dragon Bake a Cake...91

Mouse and Dragon Go Shopping..102

The Balloon Ride 110

Mouse and Dragon Find an Audience 117

Guangzhou airport 119

Australia 121

Tyalgum, New South Wales 123

My Dear Ian 124

BOOK TWO

Mouse and Dragon Go To Sea 127

China, 2013 132

Shenyang 136

The Water Tunnel 156

The Grandmother's lore 159

Benxi 165

Mouse and Dragon Find a Super Market 190

The Park, Shenyang 200

Family 205

Beijing Exhibition 213

Beijing 215

Exhibition 220

Mother's house 237

China June 6 2013 244

Mouse Finds the Source 255

This book is dedicated to Chun Li

Introduction

"Hey come and look at this!" called my friend from the other room five months ago, back in Australia, he was asking me to look at something on the computer and there a beautiful young woman was looking back at us.

"Yanzhi is her name." He said, "I write to her often, she lives in China. Isn't she beautiful!" and she was. "You must try." He said, knowing that I had just returned from three months travel in India at the end of a dilapidated ten year relationship with an old school and family friend.

To us unfortunately that relationship had died years before but I had promised her a trip to India as a friend. Now my friend was pressuring me to look at these ladies on the net, so reluctantly I did. He said I must choose a mouse or a rat which was the astrological star-sign, the magic first breath, which would be most compatible.

The first woman I saw was Lilly, masseuses and doctor. I was stunned. I had never seen a woman as beautiful, staring back out, looking at me, only me! I sat there for some time looking at her then at others, scrolling through their birth dates and hopeful faces. My friend urged me to write a small paragraph about myself and join.

"No." I said and he disappeared. I kept coming back to Lilly's face, back and back, nobody in the one hundred and fifty faces or so that I looked at seemed as acutely aware, sincere and wondrous.

When I saw her birth date I rubbed my eyes in disbelief. I wrote to her immediately and sent a small note expressing my absolute joy.

My friend signed me up in a flash altering a few words of my profile which he wrote. The next morning thirty six women were waiting to speak to me, all very good looking and all very young. But my heart had already gone to Lilly.

Would anybody impress me as much? I could not take my eyes off her. Her face hovered above the screen, already I could see deep into her soul. I was amazed. And at that instant I knew my life had changed!

Through that network, over a four month period we wrote over eighty letters to each other.

After perhaps the third letter we knew we would meet.

This book begins at Sydney airport while sitting waiting to board a flight to Shanghai, China and then on to Shenyang where Lilly lived.

Lilly's profile

About myself and my ideal match:

If the young girls are cool Coca-Cola, then I am a cup of coffee. The more you taste it, the more flavoursome and mellow you will feel.

I'm 50 years old. But I have never been pessimistic about my age. Age has not left marks on my face. On the contrary, more experience in life makes me more mature, intelligent and charming!

I'm very outgoing, humorous, romantic, honest, caring and sincere. I'm young at heart.

I like swimming, jogging, dancing and exercising. I always look energetic and happy.

I have many friends. When they are with me, they always feel happy too.

Life is colourful, but I still feel lonely at heart. Although my family and my friends can give me care and help, they can't share the rest of life with me. What I really need is a special man who will hold my hands and spend life with me together! I hope he is a kind-hearted, compassionate and sincere man. Are you the one I'm looking for? Do you want to taste this special coffee?

I'm waiting for you here.....

Hello dear Ian,

It is so nice to hear from you! That's what I have been waiting for eagerly since I replied to your Cupid Note! Your letter brought me a big smile and good mood! I hope this good beginning will take us to a bright future full of surprise!

So your friend introduced you to join this website? Please say hello to him and tell him I thank him very much! I feel very lucky to have met you on this website dear Ian!

I'm glad to know you think I'm beautiful and intelligent! Thanks for your compliments, I'm really pleased. From your letter and your profile, I feel you are a man who is kind and sincere.

That's good! Because I am the same. What's more, I am outgoing, humorous, soft, caring, understanding, loving, romantic, honest, dedicated and faithful. Of course you cannot just tell this from my physical appearance. It is said a woman is just like a book. The more you learn, the more you are attracted to her. I am such a kind of woman, are you ready to concentrate on me?

I like it here in Shenyang which is in the north east part of China. I work as a masseuses and acupuncturist in a clinic. I love my job, because I can make people healthier and stronger.

So you are retired? In your profile, you write you are an environmentalist, artist/painter, writer/publisher.

Wow, you must be a very intelligent, competent and versatile man! Which one is your main job? Could you tell me more about your jobs? Thanks a lot!

Well, the place where you live sounds very beautiful, with sea, beach, creek and forest around.

Like you, I also love nature a lot. I love the blue sky, the fresh air, the huge mountains, the green trees, the colourful flowers, the beautiful beach and the lovely animals. I live in a big city with large population. Wherever I go, it is always so crowded and noisy here. There is traffic jam very often. To be honest, I'm really tired of this busy life. I prefer to live in the countryside or in a small town.

I have always been dreaming of living a simple, peaceful and happy life with my beloved one at such a place!

So you have two sons? How old are they? I also have a son. He is 26 years old. He has his own life and he doesn't live with me. He comes to see me on festivals.

Well, I smiled when you said we had met before. Maybe we met in our previous life. I would certainly love to meet you again! When we have known each other well and when time is ripe,

I hope you will come to China to visit me. It will be my greatest pleasure to be your private guide, your friend or maybe more when you come. I will welcome you with open arms!

Did you attach any photo to me? But I didn't see one. Could you please send them to me next time? Thank you very much!

Dear Ian, we have found each other from so far away and from millions of people. It is because we were meant to find. I cherish this chance that we met here very much! I do hope we will have a bright future!

I am eager to know more about you. Please tell me more about you and your life. If you have any questions, please just ask me. I will open my heart and be honest to you!

Have a great day!

Take care!
Look forward to your letter!

Sincerely yours,

Lilly
XXXXXXXXXXXXXXOOOOOOOOOOOOOOOO

Hi Lilly,

I hope you received some photographs, my fingers became a little stuck in the key board in my haste to send them. I have read your words a thousand times and stay up late biting my finger-nails writing to you in the rain, about the rain.

Today I vacuumed the whole house thinking you would not like the dust. I have to fix the house as best I can, one day you will come over here for sure.

I found Shenyang on my phone, but it did not get me there. It is late now, the small insects are chirping, squeaking. They don't need mobiles or computers to love, they only know one note too, quite boring for us, so we write many words in our love songs, each word different and wonderful, happy and sad, with all the mystery. Like dark coffee Lilly and I laugh......It was nice to hear of your family and to, in a way, meet them. You are the only girl! You must be their star, sun and moon. How lucky they are! And you to be so proud of them. And your wonderful mother how she has struggled and won, for you have her strength. How lucky for your mother that she had you. And lucky for you to be able to help.

I work non-stop for myself too, that is my life. My life is my work, my work is my play and that is where I meet you too.....

Lilly & Ian
Mouse & Dragon

Kingsford Smith Airport
Sydney
June 30, 2012

As I look across the aisle at the Australian tourist shop, even though I have some feathers stuck in my shoes, I feel alone in a sea of bleating sheep whose wool. Koala Bears fear and flee as sheep devour by green degrees, alas their dying trees!

Airport wisdom, the rising red sap of those special trees evaporates into blossom scents with sunny sweet smelling yellow eyes, those eucalyptus flowers migrating and pollinating arid lands beyond these shores.

This flat island engaged in dust and fossil-gore is burnt by the sun where Caribou dances to the bark of didgeridoo and corroboree. Rolling in the ash of years whose seeds have washed you through.

We humble sheep obey your love, your leaves and rain, these ancient ankles, feet, toes, both webbed and clawed, clasp together with the joy of being – where no fear dares to tread – to cavort and marry into the great human family.

China, I will bring Australia to you.

People stoop and bend, their leaves fluttering in the breeze, peering endlessly into their symphonic mobile phones. Their money-hole as deep as their thoughts about the distance. Eyes shimmer and fingers skin the catch.

Their waves to sense the rush of life between their wobbly legs as time swings back and forward hypnotising them to feel financially rubbery between the ears.

Our keepers - how can you leave and abandon us to live within this fear you have wrought on us? Why do you use us to suckle for yourselves and not give back to our Earth? We are your slaves still, for you abduct our souls into your belly of egoistic wealth.

"More!" you shout while we cry in our sleep with the pain of getting nowhere. Yet you say we are your reflections!

Misty window, glazed vision, mobile disaster for our feelings. Where is the earth about our bare feet? The electric universe starves us for time's happiness is only for an instant. We are taught to be slaves, slaves of Reason; that is the ointment which attracts and distracts. Perhaps as I grasp for words, it is gravity which sets my feathers on fire and Reason which extinguishes the flame?

Aboard the plane, the babble continues, softly now the music lulls before the bird, scared from the bushes, takes flight. The eyes flash like flickering mobiles. These leaves so sweet rest in a mulch. This giant winged seed-pod full of blood, is pumped by a soaring heart and soon will take off in a great wind.

The green carpet floats below, valleyed with splintered chips of rock-cliffs exposed, whose decaying fangs maw the landscape. Where ancient sieves spin and twist and erode the sands. Where man walked with his stone tools and chased the hunger from his gut and called the bird.

Those fiery hills, my childhood home, now mature with the dark hair of trees.

And scents deep within her valleys, where shadow lies and cloud protects so many secrets of love.

The land is old, the white hair of cloud unshaven, pushes up from crevasses deep.

Snaking black rivers pass salt-sprinkled houses where modern man watches his television and starts his tractor-dragon, another slave of slaves.

The plane curettes the sky and below the dome scrapes the skin off the Earth.

Why do we need to sleep? The world goes on before, endless – with no beginning and no end. The soup we came from breathes deeply, still within us. Our sleep is fragmented by sunlit splinters of joy. The particles that we are zoom throughout the universe, communicating with the stars which breathe beauty in and out. These fortunes are forever changing and happiness knows just where they go.

Aloft and in a breeze the steel dragon melts the sky. It boils the seas and shatters the flesh as though frozen. How can she/we keep giving birth to these horrid ogres of oil, coloured black within the veins of what change?

In our time how many people sleep soundly, unsure of wealth and criminality? What laws create the laws to create? These days the pen like a shaft of wood gouges inward beneath the skin, the challenge of the word.

That information - love, will it ever come to know itself or glaze itself over like a transparent sea with humility or will it like an angry wave, swamp the sharp stones and laughing wash us away? Inventions of the mind, the electric soul, give us your patents and your cosmic breath that I may breathe upon a bosom and then within another galaxy gape upon her navel-womb much the same as here.

Will love destroy this planet, or will the imagination fly off to live again?

Is that your folly, to pillage and destroy and then move on? Or is it as you say, "Creation moving forward?"

China as a living fossil, may I uncover your womb of love and feast upon that wealth of tide born from other planets. Your wisdom is the pit of fools unless garnered within an Earthly being, for the crying child, innocent and free, will always desperately hope to live like every dream to an infinite age.

Give us your love, eternal and we, the people, will grow wealthy and tall, our wise eyes beyond the mobile, beyond the chip and far into that universe, our home. You are the monster and we the frail ones. Let us over populate and devour you with love!

Lilly, my dream, how can words explain how my heart reaches out for you with anticipation? How my eyes see you all the time? Why must I sleep and close my eyes and not be with your touch, your words? For those dreams of you are in the waking gone. As I fly to meet you over the great slippery ocean, I wrap all my thoughts in the charms of eternal love. And China, such a pumping heart will touch me deeply as I will extract from her in the sharing, essences of our being.

Should this plane fall from the sky into the sea, would carry my dream under your waves.

For now awake, you are my drowning in a red fermenting sea.

China, 2012

Silence at last, the engines have slowed. The steel dragon has repented and lost its roar.

Without sound we glide above the cloud, which cakes as ice on the windows. My very first sight of China is through a pale patchy, misty sky. I silently watch as the square buildings of an industrial landscape slip by. The people whisper quietly and then the bump of the soft landing arouses the crew.

Shanghai airport, void of soft edges. Artificial trees leap out of the concrete and strangle the air. The leaden smell of it wafts into chemical whiffs far beyond the clean.

I am guided to my destination by sweet smiling faces, some blankly refuse to speak. I stand in a queue for hours and watch their quickened runs, their dainty steps and frilly skirts. Their funny hats and high heeled shoes. The roof is massive and blue like the deep sky. From it plunge white supports like shooting stars, their cold white metal fingers pointing down at us.

Now I am directed somewhere else for I was misdirected originally. Perhaps I am late and my heart beats for my love. The directions are vague and the way very long. Eventually out of sheer luck I find my gate. It is surrounded by many people all dressed for the heat, their boarding passes they use as fans. Their language like the Bushman tribes of South Africa is a small band of whistles, cymbals and bells, lilts and falls then suddenly rises. After waiting in the push for another hour we all find that our departure gate has been changed. Now the march is on. Up around and down again. To rest in a seat aboard a plane finally and learn that it has been delayed by the gentle mist, the soft rain. I am so near and yet so far away!

On the plane I am placed way at the back of the cabin. Two men talk as though they are one hundred meters apart. One shouts as he speaks the other laughs as he shouts, swallowing his tonsils, nearly drowns. Then a young child with a young mother across the aisle begins to cry and scream. I close my eyes and wait for the plane to clear but it is delayed by hot steamy weather and low cloud which, I am to learn later, is called pollution.

The orange lights of the runway send shafts of glow as if from space ships. The screaming child is laid down on the two vacant seats next to me. I supply my small bag for its tussled head to rest on. My bag has my computer in it. If only the child knew that it rests its head on such machinery and I wonder how he will dream? Maybe he will dream of flying to Australia and have visions of the forests and the rolling hills, the clear streams.

Suddenly fifty television screens drop down from the ceiling and a short film about a potter and his clay comes on. The spiritual nature and the naturalness of the clay and its vibrant colour are cherished. Then another film about porcelain and how it is an organic art form full of life and love. Chinese wisdom gained from the natural world immediately jumps out at me from the entrails of this flying beast. The contrast is profound.

Another long wait but soon we roar again into the skies. My stomach feels the coming of a new dawn. The labour pains of an expectant dream, pushing me on and out into another lifetime, on and out into another's arms. I am a hollow vessel waiting to be filled. A great arch of light fills my mind with all the wonder of a discoverer who seeks the treasure at the end of a rainbow. For as we are propelled into each other's lives we bring the wealth of all the world to share and a warmth to meld our two new hearts together.

Lilly awaits me at the airport. It is her birthday. There she is standing. In my mind I could see her ethereally, surrounded by a golden glow. Now, for real, she stands there aglow before me - the materialised dream as she would have looked on the day she was born. She has a beautiful smile. Her name means "possessing all wisdom" and "beauty in spring" And she is gorgeous. Her face is one I will delight to know. And she cannot speak a word of English!

In the long and distant future when she lays her head on my shoulder will she dream of Australia and see the tall trees, the forests and the rolling hills and call my place her home?

She has brought an interpreter. A young man called Wangli. He has lived in France for seven years. We all catch a taxi together. The streets are broad and winding with few cars. It is already 2:00 am. I have been travelling this day since 6:00 am. Lilly is yawning and holding my hand.

I am squeezing her finger tips, rubbing them softly. We feel like a couple of young children unable to talk and only look and feel.

My hotel room is twenty six stories high. I put my head to the pillow at 3:30 am and wake at seven. The view outside is of a city rusting, decaying, building, moving, loud horns from the streets below, cars and trucks and not many people. The pollution is so bad I cannot see a quarter of a kilometre away. Everywhere the hard edges of the buildings roar into the sky. They are painted with the soft colours of the flesh. A rusty crane above me spins slowly but surely. That is how Chinese people move, slowly but surely. Eventually, for instance, slowly but surely I have arrived.

Somewhere tolls the sound of a gong which has a shuddering echoing harmonic like a lady's singing. Their language is like sharp, singing insects or a nest of small chattering birds.

Who knows what the day will bring as I sit at the window peering out into another foreign world so different from the forests and the birds where I have come from.

In the morning I lie restlessly on the bed. Lilly is half an hour late. My mind is racing and I believe it is already over and she will not appear. Alas I have lost her before I even dared to try. But no, a gentle knock on the door and she is there as large as life in a beautiful green dress and charges in upon me with open arms and a strong loving hug.

She is a short woman with slightly rounded shoulders for a Chinese. Her face is not as flat in profile. Her nose not quite so squashed. She knows I love her because she is brazen, up-front and totally wild. Her eyes curl at the edges with laughter and her teeth are as pure white as snow.

How would she ever live in my home amongst the spiders and the snakes, the leeches and the ticks? How would she dig the garden with bare feet and eat simple meals prepared on the fire with an old smoky blackening stove? She is too good, too pure, too loving, how could I muddy her so?

Her jet black hair is all artificially curled and falls to her shoulders, one sprig of white rises above her forehead curling aloft like a small puff of smoke or tiny trained Australian Horse-tail worm.

She seems disinterested in the computer I bought for her birthday in Australia. Maybe she thinks I am wealthy. Little does she know it broke my bank. It turns out she has little time to use it and of course does not understand English. Outside the glare of the sun begins to wash the pavements.

The day is hot as we descend in the lift and I steal a kiss on the side of her head.

Somewhere we are going – she leads me by the nose, stopping often to ask directions. She is looking for some tourist information and a shop to buy a mobile card for my phone. She walks away from a shop which wants twenty yuan too much and then an endless dance ensues under a flimsy mauve umbrella in the wind and heat. I feel my face burning like a cabbage leaf from the pollution and the sun's rays which strangely penetrate the pall.

In the restaurant our breakfast arrives on a plate of cast iron. It is meat and eggs and noodles which I cannot eat. The plate spits boiling hot fat at me and Lilly risks being burnt as she reaches across to help hold the napkin up in front. To little avail as I am splattered in hot fat and she sacrificially burns her arms.

She devours with incredible gusto the giant slab of meat which lies almost alive and still hissing and squirming in front of her. She attacks it with her knife held like a dagger, miraculously it does not jump onto the floor! She helps herself to four servings of fruit and eats four times as much food as me. Her weight is increasing, her photographs on the web, which I fell in love with, look nothing like her now. For she is a glance short of being overweight and I notice she struggles up the stairs.

I explain to her the different foods and what they do to the body. I thought she was a doctor and would have known all that but she seems not to care, unless it is the language barrier. Every time she smiles I can see the same smile as in the photograph on the web. Then she is young again.

Constantly we are punching and poking a small electronic device with its small plastic picker which translates Chinese into English. She scrawls her picture language with incredible speed while I pounce out my English slowly. This machine keeps us greatly amused as I can barely see the small letters and keep making errors. At least we are beyond simple words like "yes" and "no."

The brave machine is capable of poetry and flourishes of the intellect, as well as cryptic love messages and out of key Chinese tunes. The machine is therefore open and constantly used. This procedure is tiresome for us both and try as we do our relationship struggles for understanding, lucid and free. It only after I realise that if I say my sentences backwards she is able to understand me better. From then on we do not allow the slightest misunderstanding to go without being deciphered.

The day is hot and after we return from the bus trip with our tickets for the following day and the endless slow-flat city walking, it begins to rain lightly. Hopefully it will bring some of the pollution to the ground. In the lift as we descend I steal an anti-gravity kiss on her head. She looks up at me as if to say,

"Oh Yeah!" so I steal another.

I have not seen a bird all day. I have seen some domestic dogs, very coy and well tethered, often held in the arms of very elegant ladies beautifully dressed, fluffed up in tee-shirts which read,

"I love my cat." Here, opposite to India where young boys hold hands, the young girls hold hands. They are not lesbian, they are feeling their way with friendship. In the lounge of the hotel a young frilly-clad woman has pale thin bare arms one shoulder is dark green and covered with the vine-like landscape of an imaginative tattoo.

I hold Lilly's hand to cross the road but it is a sausage hand that I grasp, lifeless and lost even forlorn. And I ask myself if she comes and goes with the wind? In my mail to her I asked whether the food was expensive and she said she would pay when I was over here. Now I find myself paying for her appetite for she eats to satisfy her timid lack of sureness about love.

Women over fifty decide that a man is a man and food is survival, the pain of loneliness then eats away.

In the restaurant she is loud and demanding, she knows what she wants, the faces on the waiters relay that. She often pushes my hand away abruptly if she wants to show me something quickly. She moves so fast, she has been alone for years.

She comes at me glinting and smiling with chop-sticks pecking at my inability to use them.

Aah China and your ways. She learns the English words fast and my Chinese will always be bad. Dare I fall into this trap which sucks my soul like one slurping noodles? As the lift ascends I carry its momentum and steal another kiss. She falls asleep on my bed and I put my arm around her.
She opens her eyes like a fluffy pet, smiles and pushes me aside.

I ask her to stay but she must go. Tomorrow we will go to the Botanical Gardens if it is not raining. She will be here judiciously at seven. If she is to come to Australia with me she will have to come down six notches and learn basic survival skills. She is gasping for air and very unfit.

She commands and demands. I will have to go. Half an hour of misery this morning, waiting, has become a feast for uncertainty. Goodness China if this is the Manchurian warrioress I would hate to find one in the kitchen. The meal, so full of exquisite delicate tit-bits is four times what I can eat and Lilly eats the lot!

Are all women like this, perhaps, or is it just me? Do they all substitute food for sex?

Which one makes a person happier, I know one kills you and can make you really ill.

Do all women after menopause eat themselves from the inside out and embellish their lonely sags with sexual abstinence?

I am in the hub of a giant electric wheel which is made of steel and cement. Everywhere its electric tentacles creep and illuminate the way.

On these flat plains of Shenyang many battles took place, many people died. Now the trees have gone and the desire to kill and slaughter is replaced by a desire to make money. Everything here is based on the expediency of service and the idea that cleanliness comes with everything new.

I use my tooth brush once and the brush and the opened tube are replaced as new. In the bathroom a sign reads,

"Help preserve the environment by not using a clean towel each time you shower."

The streets are clean they are swept by people with masks on. A diesel bus spews fumes and Lilly covers her face. Her hair catches the pollution, it is a filter, her lungs another filter.

We are the children of this ruthless demon, we are its meal. It will chew us mercilessly from the inside out like an unloved sacrifice and spit out the bones.

We will all be victims here, the battle field is on the streets. Our blood is those idealistic thoughts we spill for the environment. Our main concern is the battle of greed. This is a monster of darkness which each day receives electric shock treatment. It is blinded from pollution which gobbles us in large mouthfuls even at night when we sleep and dream.

The hopeless day dawns, the frivolous girls flaunt their legs and frilly frocks. They squeak plastic smiles and fear men. Lilly is late, her time delayed due to a traffic jam. In her mail she said I would be able to come to her family home three days after we meet. Now that three days has gone and I begin to doubt that I will see her family at all. She lives with her seventy six year old mother, her younger brother and her niece. I ask her delicately to stay the night but she delicately declines and speaks about Chinese tradition.

"Yes," I say, "I will sleep on the floor!"

She is not well. Through the day she breaks out in hot flushes and before and after a meal she feels so tired, she sleeps standing up. At fifty years old why do women feel they are more important than men's testicles? Oh they just roll along! Where is the thrill in refusing to enjoy oneself? We will find our way in the field of flowers - not daring to pick and sniff.

Today we have been to the Botanical Gardens. We walked miles through the manicured spaces filled with beautiful coloured flowers. Immediately I picked a little blue flower for her, Lilly's first flower and was told laughingly not to. At the end of the day she found it again all shrivelled like a foreskin in her bag. She threw it away. I watched it hit the ground with a certain ouch as if I had come twenty thousand kilometres to be thrown out of a bag!

The day is beautiful blue and the sun is out! Two young girls beg to be photographed with me. Lilly takes the photo. I know that is hard for her to do because she has suffered from the charms of love and the glint of another woman's eye which has been turned against her.

We meet a computer programmer, teacher, on the bus and he kindly helps us translate all day as we walk on his heels. His wife and young child are there and two other men who take it in turns to carry the child. The little girl's bottom sticks out of her pants so she can go to the toilet without taking her pants and shoes off. The husband is from Mongolia and his wife has a fine Tibetan smile.

Apricot lake comes into view and everywhere is the built environment with examples of traditional houses from all over the world set within corresponding gardens. In the centre of the park a huge one hundred and eighty meter tall tower shaped like a great Bromeliad flower rises in the glorious afternoon fog. It is a lookout from where people can view the gardens. Such colossal engineering makes all the signs about saving the environment seem futile. Governments around the world find it easy to say one thing and easier to do another. The environmental garden has solar and wind power and a pond of Phragmites vegetation for aeration. Our friend explains that everybody believes solar is the way to go but it is too costly, so everybody still uses coal.

"So why bother?" he says. Alas for us China, you, like most other governments are raping the planet. You say one thing and find it easier to do another.

Two elderly ladies walk by. Their dresses are long and frilly, their hair grey and coiffured, topped with highly textured broad hats. Their blouses are highly textured as well and blowing slightly as they walk. They are a couple of flowers.

Down a slight hill and under a long enclosure is a massive tree trunk some fifty feet long and a meter wide at its widest. It has been painted with varnish and the sign read:

"This is an example of what used to grow on the plains of Shenyang."

The city of Shenyang goes on and on. The massive buildings touch the bellies of the strange clouds. The smog runs brown streaks down their sides in the rain. They are tears of neglect, tears of industry. The streets are clean but the smell of sewerage wafts about. The skyline disappears into the vapours of the many. A large brown statue of Chairman Mao stands with his army beneath him, resolute. All young men in the act of war, lunging forward or so we hope. Flower-beds of coloured lives surround the giant roundabout he commands, at times in the hot wind all nod their heads in servitude.

An elderly lady street sweeper approaches, her head like a flower is covered in coloured gauze to stop the pollution. How does she breathe in the heat? Often people are covered in gauze their heads flushing hot from the vapours in their lungs. The streets are wide in Shenyang, wide enough for four tanks and the army to walk side by side and quickly expel any anger. Again as in my country the people all exude an air of being brainwashed, dulled into apathy, all spitting and coughing with a shortened life expectancy. The woman bus driver wears white gloves, red good luck symbols hang from above the windscreen, the colour red which everybody adores. It is both a symbol of love and here strangely, as it spins and dangles, reminds me of some coagulated dried road-kill.

The taxi driver swears at the traffic, cutting other drivers into small pieces of discarded romance. Lilly asks him to calm down.

In the bank to change money not one but six people join in to assist. They create so much fuss I am embarrassed. The family in China, as in India, is large and all want to know if they can help. Consequently people are kept waiting and waiting for the simplest task to be performed. With so many hands a crowd-consciousness envelopes and the original inspiration becomes muted, numbed.

A crowd in such a state though slow, is responsive, programmable and infinitely malleable.

Eventually we find the restaurant. It is very high up in a tall building. Many young ladies dressed exquisitely serve us. And Lilly wastes no time ordering a vast amount of food. From lamb's brains to sheep's brains rolled onto sticks with congealed blood squared for space saving.

Chook's knuckles skewered and roasted. Gnawed by our rabbit-teeth running along the stick. A large hot copper bowl is brought to the centre of the table. Within it is another filled with hot coals. Water is poured in between the two and the food is thrown in there as we cook it ourselves. Mushrooms, noodles, other greens are plunged in and under. No sooner has it hit the water than it is hauled out onto my plate by Lilly who insists I eat the squirming flesh still pink and moving.

I cannot handle the chop-sticks and food sloshes and slips and goes everywhere all over the flat space in front of me where it begins to wash and pool.

Sesame seed oil is added to the food as it launches itself around the table. This small sauce dish is placed strategically beneath my dribbling head as my mouth is not large enough to fit much in. The sauce turns many colours over the course of the meal. The meal has cost twenty dollars, a fee I cannot afford all the time and Lilly orders a second round of dishes to feed her hunger. I am too wet to use the translating machine at the moment, to say "no more food" it would drown and I have to feed her, poor famished thing.

As I look across the battlefield and admire the view, she seems to be starving. Miraculously she has not spilled a drop however she sounds like a vacuum cleaner or sperm whale breaching as she sucks the noodles up into her beautiful lips. I think that one day I may be her noodle.

Back in the hotel we lie on the bed. She so close, always touching and write furiously into the translating machine. She burps and her breath smells of the rotting meat stall we passed on the road. It was full of offal, goats hooves, ox hearts and livers. The man selling these things looked like rotten flesh, yellowed and pale, hunched over as though fly-blown.

Lilly asks me how many rooms my house has and how large is the biggest room.

And what is the house made of. In her letters she has told me she does not care about my house for our love is more important. Alas I smell a rat. The cultural difference is huge. And these ladies are well trained at leading men, especially Western men on. This is a trap and I determine to give her one more day before I leave for Beijing alone. I cannot play these games not at sixty.

It is doubtful that she will like my house amongst the trees, unfinished of wood and mud and stone. Surrounded by snakes and rats, leeches and ticks. She would not like to be bitten once, let alone thousands of times. And then she would eat me out of house and home! And throw out all my rock, old wood and dried rat collections! And perhaps worse, I cannot think. Having to leave her now tears at my flesh but all women have done that to me. Same me to them I suppose.

Who will love me who that I am, who singing from the water came, as if my soul were washed with rain, those leaves who washed you through? I slip slightly at the top of an escalator, Lilly's arm is there quickly to save me, as strong as the root of a forest tree.

She lies sleeping on the bed like a Chinese porcelain, drifting through the other worlds of Kuan Yin, not of this earthly body, a celestial water body. She looks like my Silou, my Shitzu dog who died the day Lilly joined the agency network. For Silou drifted into her body to come back to me.

Lilly is tired and voluptuous, she sprawls on the bed and shows her frilly stocking tops to me. Her clothed bottom often in my view. We loll together after our midday meal, I kissing and stroking her arms often biting and nibbling like Silou in play. I bite her stocking top and flap it against her leg. She does not like that and often slaps my back. I know now she will not break even if I drop her.

As solid as a luminous pearl. As delicate as a tree in the wind and yet so strong.

We spend countless hours punching letters into the translating machine from Chinese to English and vice-versa. She learns words very quickly. I am writing down their sounds in English in a book, long strange sounding "phyzsses." She has trouble with her "ess-es" and her "shh-es." She speaks as though eating with chop-sticks with swishing, sucking sounds. We laugh as I watch her mouth curl and her lips pout, her snow white teeth alluringly kissable. She is altogether edible and I tell her so. Expressionless she moves on to another subject and looks at me sideways like Silou. When I think she is not watching she is watching, she flicks her eyes my way all the time.

I think she is falling in love with me, she is happy in her eyes.

The lure of flesh is all around in China. They are as enticing as chicken's knuckles on a thin stick. The girls are watching me. I dress as a tramp with torn jeans, dark glasses and tee-shirt, shabby.

The men glance at me but Lilly grabs my hand and drags me through their interest and the traffic dodges us deftly. She is a queen among women. She does not dress in finery yet she has gouged their muscles, rendered their flesh and moxi-combusted them like potatoes in a fire.

She knows she will go to heaven, albeit quickly as she eats bad food. Often the food is old and expensive, the salads though few, are beautifully presented fresh and green most other greens always cooked or lightly steamed. I begin to eat everything raw, Lilly watches a little astonished.

Then I eat a quail's egg, shell and all and she says "no" and shakes her head. Usually restaurants give the customer a plastic glove if they are going to touch food with their hands. A meal can take an hour to eat with many small side dishes all ladled and mixed together. Then devoured with the sucking relish of an octopus.

This morning I went down to have breakfast with the other people in the hotel. They asked my room number and I could not remember. They must have thought I was an idiot! There were many young people at the tables. Their chop-sticks were rattling like swords. With great finesse I gallantly picked up my utensils like two long javelins and tapped them dexterously together, the conductor and his orchestra. Some twenty minutes later I was still balancing single grains of rice at their ends. A feat rarely seen, ever! The small girls with clothes of fine lace looked deep into my eyes.

They did not smile, not like the beautiful Indian ladies free and wild.

Everything is tight, sex is the great unlit candle and the women, I fear, are very up-tight.

The men reserved their wicks unlit. Dare I say frigidity is the norm? I suppose that is why some of them seek Western husbands. Do the Western men know that Chinese women are good at teasing and playing games? Do they know how their hearts can change from love to hate? Be prepared for the silent silver waterfall approaches and over the side you may spill in an effervescent drowning of diamonds and sparkling foam.

We come down from our love nest in the polluted skies. The sun has barely had time to shine through. The day is hot and the photochemical fog dense. As we walk the street in the late evening way down the end of the long straight road, the great red ball of the sun like a large red bubble about to burst is sinking directly in the middle of the tall dark silhouetted buildings which frame it on either side - a perfect fit. Sinking like an ardent man into the bosom of the earth. As it descends clouds of pollution billow up and boil and froth on each side. The sight is truly breathtaking. Perhaps that is the way all men will die, buried deep within her concrete thighs.

I decide to let the cat out of the bag. Or one could say throw the pussy out of the bed. Who will bake the bread and who will eat it? Whose seed have I come to China to sow? Every small item is packaged clean in plastic. Everything has two labels not one.

We may appear lazy in our country; here their time is wasted in the red-tape of uniform.

There are no dancing girls. Puritanical and small of breast their joy is in the toil of work, so strung up by the system are they. Their childhood passes like a breath of wind. So soon are the young girls buttoned up in uniforms and running the restaurant, hotel or shop. Trussed and stitched, cleaned and boiled beyond life into some artificial robot, not a young woman at all - whose fertility is slowly reduced until nearly neutered and too afraid to have a child.

The children we have seen are not allowed to cry, they cannot express their pain.

They hardly know pain. Here there is no suffering, it is all hard work. The pain is taken away by another who soon rises to fill the space. The pain is work and work is all they know and all they need to know.

I see a man on the footpath, his legs outstretched, his head down. Money is around him, he is too confused to know. A woman close by is still in her pyjamas, she stares out into the fog of her past lives.

My clothes I cannot wash. So I give them as laundry to the woman who cleans the bathroom. During the day three people knock on the door. The bathroom lady, the floor cleaner and again the bathroom lady with the washing which has safety pinned all over it little messages in Chinese, they may be messages of a different kind! The clothes are wrapped in plastic which is heat sealed.

Each person, a smile of brilliant teeth, each tooth like the light of their spirit flashing on and off with the rush of China time. In the city street, fumes exhume upwards to my room. A thousand eyes flash at me from outside. I lie down to sleep with the memory of her frilly stockings, flashing - China has it all.

Morning awakes with the wash of reflected sun from the concrete facades opposite which is my view. Splashing and dancing deep into the streets it penetrates the steps of lovers who walk some distance apart, resigned to so little foreplay. The snaking tails of the air-conditioning units crawl across the vertical landscape their shadows cast like darkened question marks on the hard pink flesh of lurid cement. Attached like kidneys or animals with tails; small brains, big fart. Like vines twisting and sucking, void of leaf and sap. The windows like brazen eyes looking into the abyss, the dismal abyss with its pulsing flow of raucous life all square and lacking in the freedom of sensuous abandonment.

Cities are pinnacles of intellect, straight and tall. Their shadows cast in melting curves flow into deep grottoes where grow static festering pools of lonely unhappiness.

The traffic lights set the pace, control the freedom, control the mind. Flashing, flashing everything pulsing like the waves on the sand. My eyes blood-red from the fungus in the food can barely open and observe any joy. There is no laughter here only worry. Even time shakes the rat by the tail.

The women's arms pale and wan, like thin mushroom stems, dangle and sway, grown from the shadowy grottoes their roots beneath the pavements, deep in the pockets of men. I am too cruel amongst these upright fortresses, these illuminati of the mind. There is no natural element to talk to, to feel with. This is a place of cosmic isolation. There are no ants, there are no birds, no lizards, no rats or cockroaches only one or two wily mosquitoes which float into my room more like friends, to suck my blood. I am told to attack them by putting a little package of something in an electronic device which flashes to kill them. At least the mosquitoes are friendly and love me and wish to talk, they give a pretty intimate kind of cuddle too, even if they do have suspicious flight patterns and thrust something into you to suck one's blood. But here they are terrorists with a weapon mean and nasty. Perhaps they carry malaria or are radioactive? I cannot poison myself to kill them. I am here to love and suck from China too. That is if it doesn't kill me first.

She has gone again, we spend all day oozing on the bed together. Looking at films and photographs of where I live. Her dress is beautiful and I tell her so through the machine.

Like a butterfly she flits in and flops on the bed. She hugs me like a friendly gorilla with a beautiful smile. She is a fine Chinese meal spiced with intelligence; she is an ancient Manchurian warrioress with sword, cooking fork and knife. I advise her about eating too much protein. The meal is thick with it. Meat, fish, squid, prawns with sesame seed sauce. The air is thick like sauce, her health is the meat in the sandwich. In a roundabout way I tell her not to eat too much. And she asks if I am so poor that I can paint and own such a large property. I reply that she is my bank!

After lunch we wander the streets looking for some blank DVD's. Lilly asks many people and they kindly assist us. She is bold and up front with many yet leaves them smiling or laughing.

Eventually we find the shop past the new underground railway stairs with the rats running across the stairs just on time. Past the nonchalant policeman who answers our questions amiably.

And the two men who follow us like shadows to show us the way. Then up six escalators through a huge array of shops. With girls, girls everywhere. Surely there are more women in China than men? Each like a butterfly, most arm in arm with another woman.

The shopping complex is vast with a huge fountain in the centre which alluringly spurts a jet of water intermittently twenty meters into the air, three floors up, into this vast womb of activity. Everywhere are glass cases which exude jewellery and watches. And everything for the expensive taste except blank DVDs. I want to buy Lilly a cake of soap for her mother and she says no.

I ask her how much and they do not say. Some distance away through the translating machine she says one hundred and fifty yuan which is at least ten times too much! Soon we are lost again in the huge shop and have to ask the way out. The amount of wealth here far exceeds anything I have ever seen in any other country. Rolls Royce, Mercedes and BMW traffic jams!

People are cleaning constantly. The woman who comes in to clean my room does it so quickly and efficiently I am ashamed of my laziness.

Huge bill-boards line the roadways one reads, "Learn English and have a better life." The girls look at us and wonder. Another bill-board shows a line of policemen on motorbikes, angels from hell. Another shows a green tree, people sell corn in front of it, it keeps them feeling fresh. And yet another shows the expensive glint of plastic architecture, shapes stretched and cantilevered to the stars even further than the gloss of order can reach.

The poor are everywhere trying to hide behind ironed creases for their clothing is so important to them. The rich in their expensive black cars move through at respectable bicycle speed. Most of the traffic is slow. People would be killed otherwise as they are in India where a frenetic speed mentality rules. Here everything is meticulous and slow. Yet it is high fashion to own a watch and the larger it is the better as time is swayed by work and the yuan. Lifestyle and love are far away from the middle of a large city. Underneath the clean gleam is a wasteland of fear, slavery and control where quick-of hand throws the dice.

No wonder Lilly wants to fly home with me. I am the wild man come from the bush to kidnap her. And kidnap her I may.

At the end of the long polluted street Chairman Mao sends his arm up. And those below him, the peasants and the workers, all fight for what...this? Why this is an illusion. With all the flowers and forests gone, as though the body has been stripped of its heart by some rapacious time piece. The single second-hand has scythed many as it travels the minutes across the face.

Is happiness having one child, one child who will mourn for its brother and sister, long dead? Surely two must make two or the population will go backwards. Then who would fill these streets and fight the wars? Who will build the buildings and live in them? No wonder the women want to leave, there are more fertile pastures elsewhere.

The government pays a parenting allowance for four months only and many couples cannot afford to send their child to a proper school. Consequently there are few young children in China.

Now however the one child policy has been waivered and some in government are asking that the parenting allowance be extended to three years.

For a woman to be forced to have only one child is an indication that the government is failing in its duty of care. Has thrown the baby out with the bath water, has opened the plug too soon and through that large hole the women of China are escaping. There are many other ways to reduce the population such as family planning - contraception and more recently in the West "trans-humanism" which is the rendering down, the de-construction of the human DNA through the various insidious engineering methods mentioned herein until hormonally disrupted "human machines" are produced which struggle at the helm of Reason like refugees aboard a sinking raft of memories!

Another day lights the streets with hope. In the night some giant animal roared as it stalked the pavements, blistering them and scraping the fallen rubbish from between the cracks.

Few cars were there to mount the traffic lights like dinosaurs dreaming. Their hot breath left to steam and smoulder in the dark gutters.

The pink blood of the concrete rises in the early dawn belching into large columns of cloud far above the melting time. Still Mao's arm is aloft untiringly. Still the people frown from their universal brown attire. No, frogs, no ants, no birds, no love only time etched into clean this and that. I have visions of trees swaying in a fresh breeze, fruit bouncing happily on the branches. Small breasts of fruit with nipples ready. Time will swing around and make it fall and hit the ground nipple up. The rest will rot into her womb to grow another fruit tree, not one but a multitude.

On the tall landscape of the flat-topped buildings cranes swing their arms around like the second-hands of watches. Dropping fruits and rising debt, these temples of the brain are made from the bones of men. Their forms dead, enjoy an everlasting peace beneath these rusting, spinning, helicopters of hope.

And she is there rapt within his arms. White, of pretty face and slender mushroom arms. Swaying in the smog they ride their round wheeled horses, their ashen armour of bright gauze tied in a knot about their necks and round their heads like bags. The silent dead before the gap, before the thin dark crack from which we all expect to rise again. March forward, floating on the concrete battle field, holding hands with other female forms, united in the battle for the one great child.

China your warrior arms are weak and lovely, you disseminate your ladies love far abroad to buy the good lands of the world and mother his testicles in the great wrapping game. Then with your peoples heart you turn the lock of gold and silver, yet nature is not slain. Little wonder the mosquitoes attack me, little wonder I let them feed. Poor lost souls from the battles of the ancient stream, still rolling-red on the rich shores of love.

Words like painted flowers, petaliferous traces from the transparent mind, filter through the dying smog to splatter on the ground. Large pools float feet as rivers begin to roll about the gutters from the sudden shower. The fruit stalls hastily pack, the vendors under flimsy umbrellas hide. Mother Nature's words are wet full-stops on the varnished street. We seek out a publisher for my mother's books.

"It is not dragon." I am told, "It is dinosaur!" They like the stories very much and we are hopeful that they will print the book and sell it as a language tool for children. So much to learn. The aching mind stripped of DNA spirals into seasons void of fresh air. How will spring shine through?

We are ancient beings, what more must we know that we do not know already? Outside in the bleeding air men drop up and down buildings on ropes across her dark hard grey surface. They climb trees for nuts with their tools of electrified teeth. Below their wandering spider legs, the cars beetle and shuffle and fart their scraps of food back up into our sky. The great hands of the cranes mark time. We are all angels, we all feast upon this ooze like ants and in the evenings carry each burden back to the nest of our love.

The colours of this concrete forest are pale and diffused like the voices of the soft clouds, polished by the grime of a hidden secretive lust, afraid to splash out beyond the grey and pink. Here from this twenty sixth floor, I look out into the hungry field to spy a dainty lady in the vast distance moving and fluttering, frilled like a jellyfish, pulsating like a tide. Amongst the fray the angry blast of horn and silent motor-scooter topples through time as women clasp the handle-bars in a massive effort to steer and or hog-tie the blasted beast.

The city is a giant fungus, alive with pathogens mutating into clones, sterile, subservient, all rejoicing in the wash. The race to clean and scrub is the foreplay of this gargantuan love of order, of logic and Reason. Washed-green and hopeful, yet entangled in the ropes and falling.

She lies on the bed outstretched. Her stockinged knees splattered from the large drops of rain. Her eyelids flickering, the dark cherry pupils half exposed and watching. Her round breasts like small cakes fluff beneath her rising chest. She moans as I kiss her. Her arms loose fly over and clasp my back unmoving. We are close, she is watching now, wide awake. Her small bottom tucks under like a tortoise as I grasp and pinch the softness. My fingers are the words and letters of my speech, they seek the ear, the smog filtering hair, the neck so warrior strong. Her back, the castle of her soul and deep within her folds a soft flash of delicate skin. My hand is torn away. She rolls moaning and squashes the other arm so it cannot move. I am trapped like a man on a string, pendulum swaying in the hot breath, rising and falling, swaying. I will not let her go.

The meal is a feast. They set a fire on the table burning, hissing and spitting. We spike it and play like children with pointed sticks. Our mouths like sucking machines slurp and punctured with these long wooden needles. Beyond fork and spoon they are grossly inefficient. My food is flicked and thrashed upon the floor. My face is a battle field of javelin misses, of needles aimed at mouth and eye, those other orifices of the mind. My "old man beard" as she calls it, is bleaching white as the food dribbles from its wrung out mop. The water-fall is aimed at the tiny singing over-flowing plate below which groans from pleasure a large pile of white paper towels as it rises virtuous like a tall building next to me.

How frail these dainty feet upon the pavements tread, all shod with imitation flowers and high heels. The modern woman of China walks on sky-scraper shoes designed with lifts and fire-escapes, with long laddered stockings for emergencies. They are pointed and sharp, chop-stick shoes, would penetrate a bull's hide, or pick a cherry from the sea.

The policemen at the crossings are all deaf from their own whistles which are stuck in their mouths all day where the chrome dissolves. They sound like a colony of crickets as they voice their control, rising to crescendos then fading. The only mate who answers their distressed call comes in the form of a horde of people from across the road. And if anyone drops a cigarette butt or a piece of paper, with great joy the whistle is pumped up and the noise blasted forth. This brings more people from across the road. The policemen are the first to be run over. They can't hear anything.

I feel her near again, as her heart beats like a distant drum and pounds the streets for me.

What will the day bring? Another adventure? Her lips further apart. Her breasts like cakes smeared with icing, rising once again. Yesterday I brushed a woman's breast quite by accident in the street, such ungainly things to point the way. Blind they are, yet all seeing, so close to the heart. While men like bleating sheep, follow with round things of their own - balancing precariously. Some to make and others to break.

Must we age? How many scars can we bare? I walk with my head on backwards after a transplant. The world is suddenly cruel.

The fish we are eating is very dead and dried, stuffed into yet another plastic bag, inside out, probably died of plastic poisoning. The Chinese will say "yes" and then say "no." One has to flow with them or be cast eternally aside. Like two fish in a happy plastic bag we walk the streets hiding from the rain under the pale purple plastic umbrella, which keeps pulsing in and out like a marine creature feeding.

The fruit shops are a glorious site like a green landscape in a desert of stone. Sprinkled with the colours of the stars, they shine forth glistening with good health. We are alive between the matrix and the sea, swimming through the spiced bliss of love. Our visions scrape the heavy ground at night, scratching morsels from her Earthly skin. Perhaps she is the devil within for her lips are green, her hair a purple sky full of the grey clouds of trouble. One day we too will rise and fall with her as rain.

We travel to the publishing house, past the fruit stalls, past the road-works, through the traffic where the cars are on the wrong side of the road. We are on the wrong side of the road.

At a steady pace the cars slow to let us pass. Now running and laughing like the sun, she under her small umbrella which at times amongst the crowd is all I see bobbing up in front which I follow like a paper aeroplane on a string. Her smile curls up at the edges of her mouth like my wings they give our spirit lift. Her eyes pinch at the edges with delight, her face is alive and happy. She has so much love to give.

As we eat and spear the floating squashed prawn meat from the hot water which boils in front of us, her eyes quickly glance at me and I feel her love. It spears into my heart, pokes me boiling down again to feel the lack of oxygen, breathless. She is happy when she eats. A stomach full of love rises like a moon.

Her childhood was poor. She lived in a mud hut with a straw roof. One day she was roasting potatoes in a fire for friends, the fire got away and nearly burnt the house down. Luckily her father came home just in time and put out the blaze. She said he scolded her for the accident.

I said it was not right for him to punish her for an accident. I added that I hoped she did not treat her patients like potatoes – a little burnt around the edges.

She can be downcast, especially if I don't teach her English. We communicate with drawings, hand movements, smiles and eyes. My fingers long to touch her softly all the time. To rub my nose between her breasts. And listen to her heart throb far above her breathing soul. She watches me like a bird, I am her fledgling. The food is pecked up and dropped in my plate. I try to clasp her legs under the table in my own. I can make her laugh like a child who burns potatoes. She has charcoal eyes like deep black pools.

She has twisted her hair into curls for me and produces some scissors and a razor from her illustrious bag. Ah the beard, worn as protection from the cold and used as a shield along with what other armour men may have. But not in defence of a woman with a pair of scissors, a razor and a smile.

After forty five years to be shaved twice in the one year is a record, having never shaved before. Soon she is entangled about me, cutting and twisting. I get the camera out and photograph her face of extreme concentration, the devoted housewife, as she suffers my silliness, my flinching and all else I use to distract her. The razor is blunt so for a long time she directs my head one way and then the other moving the scissors so quickly and slicing through my ear lobe - only slightly. One sharp move and she would slit my throat. Now she is in focus up close - very interesting.

Mouse and Dragon Join the Fire Brigade

Mouse and Dragon were getting on in years, long in the tooth as they say, so they thought they should help their fellow human being and contribute in some way to the world. They joined the Fire Brigade and Mouse was immediately given the job of driving the fire truck which she loved to do for she had a way with cars even though she had to sit on several cushions to see where they were going.

They made many "fiery" friends and they all rode on the big fire truck. Mouse and Dragon made two special friends, Frank and Bill and since Christmas was coming up they decided to invite them over with their wives for Christmas dinner. Bill was a builder and he was very happy to show Dragon how to fix his loose floor boards. He was going to come early with his wife Nancy, who was a good cook, she was going to put a Christmas pudding in Mouse's oven. Frank who was a plumber was going to come early too and was happy to help Dragon with his leaky taps and underground water pipe which Dragon was in the process of burying in the backyard to run water up to the house from the river. Frank's wife, Gloria who was from another country, made beautiful jewellery.

Christmas day arrived and it was very hot. Dragon was in the middle of fixing his floor when all the phones rang in all the rooms of the house at once, for they had phones in every room. Things were so well organised in Mouse and Dragon's house! It was Bill to say that they would be a little late. Mouse was stoking the oven with wood and Dragon was sweeping the floor which had floor boards loose and was not quite finished.

Unfortunately it had rained slightly the night before and Dragon's trench out the back was very muddy so he and Frank could not work on that. It was just growing dark outside when Frank knocked on the door. He had come to fix the taps and his wife, Gloria wore some large diamond earrings which flashed as she entered the room. She also wore a long bright green skin tight dress. Dragon got a bit of a shock and looked her up and down, she could hardly walk. She immediately went into the kitchen with Mouse and Dragon could hear them chattering away. Frank turned the water off and was banging the taps in the bathroom. Dragon decided to see if he could finish fitting the last few floor boards into the floor before Bill arrived.

Just as he was lifting the hammer there was another knock on the door. It was Bill with his wife Nancy. She had done her blond hair up like a funny cloud which didn't seem to be attached to her head. She had brought a large Christmas pudding for the oven and went straight into the kitchen to help Mouse. Meanwhile Gloria had gone out the back to pick some fresh parsley.

Bill came in and accidentally walked on a loose floor board and all the nails went flying in the air! Luckily he did not fall straight through the hole! As he and Dragon were both kneeling picking up nails there was a loud scream from the backyard and a deep "urrgh" sound. Dragon quickly stood up, unfortunately his foot landed on a nail which went into his heel so he quickly walked and half hopped to the back door to have a look. He knew what had happened though and sure enough Gloria had fallen into the muddy trench!

She was stuck in the mud with her green dress and struggling to get out. She was not happy and was saying things in her own language.

Dragon hopped outside and was pulling her up when there was a loud yell from inside the house.

Dragon dropt Gloria back in the trench turned around and hopped back inside to help Bill who had fallen in the hole in the floor and his hand wacked a loose floorboard which flew up and hit him in the face! His leg was stuck in the hole. Just at that moment Mouse was rushing out the back door from the kitchen with the pepper jar in her hand to help Gloria at the same time Dragon was rushing in through the door. She and Dragon collided in the doorway and Dragon got a face full of pepper!

He stood up and sneezed and a big orange flame came rushing out of his mouth and singed poor Mouse's beautiful whiskers! He sneezed again and Mouse's ears were singed! Nancy quickly covered Mouse's head with a tea towel. But Dragon sneezed again and Nancy's hair caught on fire, it was flammable and it exploded in a big flash!

She cried out and quickly pulled a curtain from the wall and wrapped her head in it. Being a fireman's wife she knew exactly what to do! By this time Frank had come out of the bathroom and was trying to help Bill out of the floor but a nail became stuck in his foot as well!

Gloria was calling from the trench out the back and Dragon sneezed again. Well this time Bill's eye brows were singed right off and he very quickly leapt up out of the floor. Dragon said,

"So s..s..sorry..." and sneezed again! This time Bill's clothes caught on fire. Mouse was still trying to get the tea towel off her head and then Dragon stood on another nail which went into his other heal so he had to walk on his tip toes! Bill ran outside with his clothes on fire and fell in the trench and rolled in the mud with Gloria but at least his clothes were out!

Then dragon sneezed again and the house exploded into flames. Mouse was running round looking for the phone to ring the fire brigade when she found one they asked her if she could drive the truck?! Meanwhile Dragon was dancing on his tip-toes banging the taps with the hammer. Frank was also in the bathroom standing on one leg, banging the taps as quickly as he could. He came hopping out with his head low to the ground to avoid the smoke like firemen do. He was on one leg and hopped straight for the back door as quickly as he could but hit his head on the table as he couldn't see properly and was knocked unconscious. Mouse was on her tip toes looking out for nails and Dragon was holding his nose very tightly.

Dragon lifted poor Frank's legs up off the ground with one hand and charged out the door with him backwards on his tip toes! Nancy had fled the scene but had managed to save her uncooked pudding. She made a spectacular leap across the trench on her way to the river but lost the pudding in mid-air! Dragon dropped Frank in the trench with Gloria and Bill, then grabbed Mouse in his arms and sprinted towards the river on his tip-toes. Gloria had rolled her dress up and was wiping her eyes of pudding and positioning the shovel so she and Bill could get out. They left Frank in the trench and climbed out. Bill ran for the river but Gloria went back for Frank saying words in her own language again as she jumped back in! Dragon went back to find Frank and Gloria. Frank was at the bottom of the trench moaning and Gloria was patting his face with mud-pudding. Dragon, shielding his own face from the burning house jumped in the trench and threw them both out at once. Dragon leapt out still holding his nose and picked Frank up with one arm around his waste and threw him in the river. Gloria fell over a few times but she managed to get to the water. Now everybody was in the river except Dragon.

Soon the fire truck arrived and they all waved to each other from the water and looked at Dragon who was prancing around on his tip toes. Poor Mouse began to cry and Dragon muttered something under his hot breath. They all watched as the house was completely destroyed. What a terrible Christmas it was!

The fire truck had gone. The night was dark and cold, the last few embers of the house were all they had to dry themselves and keep warm. Bill had half a burnt shirt on and a big lump on his head. Frank had a huge lump on his forehead where he had hit the table and still had mud and Christmas pudding all over his face and a hole in his foot where the nail had been! Nancy had no hair, and Mouse had short whiskers and singed ears. Gloria had lost an earring and torn her dress. Dragon had nail holes in both heels. He was so sorry and apologised very much but everybody said it was an accident.

They were all hungry. Mouse threw a few potatoes from the garden into the coals of their burning house to cook for Christmas dinner.

Then it began to rain. Lightly at first but then it poured. Bill invited Mouse and Dragon back to their place for the night and that is what they did.

In the next few weeks Mouse and Dragon cleaned up the big pile of ash which was once their home and Dragon found Gloria's earring at the bottom of the trench.

Dragon looked at Mouse and said they needed a holiday. So they went far away to the sea to try and forget about Christmas day.

While they were away Bill and Nancy, Frank and Gloria secretly organised the whole town to help rebuild Mouse and Dragon home. All the fire brigade people and more came over with building materials and all sorts of things. There were tables and chairs, curtains, ovens, taps, beds and even lots of telephones. In three days many people came and helped rebuilt their house. And it was a beautiful house in which all the floor boards were strong and all the taps worked.

Meanwhile Mouse and Dragon were by the sea thinking of finding work and buying a tent to live in while they slowly rebuilt their home. Dragon looked at Mouse, her whiskers had grown a little and he said he would buy a really good tent! Mouse said she would be happy in a tent so long as Dragon was by her side. But they did not have a very happy holiday.

When they arrived home and drove down their driveway and saw their new house they could not believe their eyes. They could not speak! Mouse went into the kitchen. There were saucepans and plates, cups and saucers, everything; it was so well organised. She was overjoyed. Dragon was jumping up and down on the floor and turning the taps on and off. There was a big bunch of flowers on the table. Mouse and Dragon gave each other a big hug. They were home!

Morale of the story:
Home is where the heart is.

Lilly has been here each day at 10:00 am and leaves in the night at 9:00. She must go back home and not sleep with me. But I will sleep on the floor I say again. She smiles and pouts her bottom lip.

She is alive like a sea shell, filtering the news, she spits out the grains of pollution like a man in the street. Her massage and acupressure business gives her hands of steel. I massage her back, legs and arms. The top of her spine is sore. She wants hard pressure there and everywhere else. She is a warrior princess devoted now to me; I can see it in her eyes.

We walk kilometres looking for the publisher. The air is hot and I dance about her on the pavement avoiding the metal prongs of the umbrella and the oncoming traffic. Her face is proud and I know for once in her life she is so pleased to have a friend.

She often stops to ask directions and most people when they see me smile, nod and assist us beyond their time. Lilly often makes them laugh; she is a doctor and knows people well.

Into another huge building we go. The Art Publisher is helpful and the young girl with the turned out ears, so polite as she smiles her ignorance of English. Bowing and ducking like a crane, her long straight hair held back by the ears. Now laughing at my ignorance of the Chinese language. Lilly helps and they seem to speak a thousand words to explain a simple thing.

In the foyer of the building sits an old man with a stick. He is upset about something and speaks loudly to some people who have gathered. The building is noisy enough with an echo from the cavernous foyer and peoples' coming and going. As we discuss publishing this man raises his voice until he is shouting to the walls. I cannot hear what people are saying and wonder if he will settle down. Soon there is an unusual silence and I see he is still there behind the girl. He is sitting quietly, with his eyes staring to the front. Often Chinese voices are raised with great force, their unusual syllables piercing in new ways unheard. Perhaps he has read something they published in a book he did not like? Why must people shout? Can he not stand back and let the other fish swim peacefully? Are his bones so fragile or sick that his temper turns everything to hot ash? Why does he hurl himself into the sea of fury and drag others with him?

The publisher wants to do something with my mother's books but I find out that they don't distribute or sell them, only print them! After the endless explanations, translations and words innumerable they recommend another place which publishes children's books.

With many thank yous and bows we back out of the massive concrete foyer, past the quiet man who does not move and are soon in a taxi off to another publisher.

The streets of Shenyang are long and straight. Some with trees and others with old houses whose bricks are a muddy grey. Through these alleyways girls with mobile phones clasped to their ears remind me of pretty fish who swim between dead corals. Their spindly unclad elbows swinging like the pale stems of sea-weeds in the swell.

Into another tall building through light security and into the neon light. Lilly eyes me sideways; she has cut my beard off and sees perhaps another man? She smiles from the tip of her toes to the top of her head. Once we arrive at our floor level after another kiss in the lift, she smiles from her heart.

There is nobody around. She walks about knocking on every door and then quickly disappears from view; lost in a maze of concrete. Presently we find a woman who directs us to a room where two other ladies are busy in front of computer screens. Lilly beckons me to follow but I am slow with my English manners and feel I need to knock. Soon we are sitting discussing paper size and quality and the translation of the text. Both women are so dainty like flowers they rise even taller on their high heeled shoes. One speaks good English and after my words says often,
"I get it." And I feel quite sure that she does. She is using words like "gorgeous" and "exciting" to describe the books and our spirits rise. Lilly rolls back on the couch and talks effortlessly, she makes them smile and laugh, they relax with her much as I do. She is a Manchurian warrioress with hands of soft steel. A masseuses and acupressurist of some twenty five years experience. Who would not be butter in her hands?

We walk home past the brightly coloured fruit stalls with black grapes the size of golf balls, mangoes, lychees, apples, green grapes, bananas, all of the highest quality and so cheap.

I am fed grapes by the shop assistant. Lilly eats away and drops the skins on the floor.

She asks me to decide which to buy.

From the walk I take a shower and then offer her a new towel. She has a shower and comes and lies on the bed. I rub her back and cup her breast, she is demanding and wants more massage.

After sometime her body relaxes, her legs are smooth, her skin is silk. I take my shirt off and she sees my body. I am sure she sees many men topless and she looks at me unafraid.

We sit on the bed together punching out words for translation on the machine. We watch a film and I show her exercises for her neck which she can do. She rolls over and I am tempted to kiss her again. She feeds me grapes one at a time and then two and I the same for her. Then I feed her ten all at once and she smiles. The very last grape I try to drop down her cleavage but she is too quick and laughs. She does not hug me when she leaves for she fears I might kiss her. She wants me to so much but her tradition, her mother and family, would wonder where she was.

Each day I wonder what she will do, how far she will let me go. I say to her that I am sixty with not long to live and why hold back the river of life? But then before the flood the river must run dry.

Not since I was a young man have I felt such strong affection for a woman and I tell her so.

Then I ask,

"Is this Chinese torture?"

Few pregnant women parade the streets, their bellies pushed out by divine wisdom.

And I ponder why I peer inside their tiny shrunken wombs. Their female to female holding of hands, their small tight pants and frilly dresses, their long mushroom-stemmed legs all point not only to a desire for the opposite sex but equally to a desire for closeness and understanding between women about the trauma of loss. Their desire has been revealed by the stripping away of their birth right. They have been neutered.

The one child policy in one way may save the world but in another brings many tortured tears and sore testicles. The young men hardly flaunt their masculinity. They do not grow a beard or show their feet or hairy armpits. They do not show their desire so much as in the West for there are few pastures where that desire may flower and shed its seed.

There is no time. Their watch-hand, the minute-hand is their penis. Round and flat with a second-hand which is viewed behind glass, rotating, ticking, unable to get out and express itself as it faces the trauma of old age. With a mind of its own is trapped and stifled by the smog which floats ethereal into every smiling eye and into every open pore to discourage conception.

It infiltrates the body to its very core and mixes and morphoses our desire for the healthy happy family of one thousand children all born from shear lust, gorgeously spilled in the soft grassy field, now a rock hard pavement.

Hence the women, dainty, move amongst the dying coral clumps, terrified of sharks and men. And if they did have sex before marriage they would have to pay a lot of money to have an abortion which is sometimes forced. Such fear would put you off men for life, would see a civilisation drown in a red menstrual sea where the great poets and cultural highs would be replaced by the machinery of the system and the gloating ambitions of the voyeurs and competitors, who only seek power and try with blind wisdom to sweep love under the carpet.

Lilly is here, she throws her strong arms around me like weighted chains, they flop about my body, their fingers numb from the fear of letting go or shear exhaustion. My fingers are alive upon her like ants. They dance and tease, seeking small areas of raw flesh. I am a dancing spider looking for the softest place to sink my fangs. Occasionally her arm comes close and I bite and suck it and watch her face which does not change. Instead inside I feel her rising like a whale from under water.

One day her face will gleam like a diamond, her onyx eyes burning from heat. And we will be young again. Those ripples that we make will float out into another dimension where the spirit children play.

As the elevator falls I steal a kiss. Buoyed by the loss of gravity, my weights are wrapped around my failing knees. How long must I wait before the whale breaches? Her sideways glance reveals her puckered lips and her wanting.

The inclinator with its load of building materials is still going up and down each day across the grey faces, tracing a story of China which is at its height of industry like a man who has inhaled a gas and can go no further. Only from the heat of perfect love can love descend. It is the rise and fall of a great civilisation which the West has always feared. Now as she throws her welcoming chains about the world, deep within her heart are joyous seeds of change. The river cannot flood without the measure of a drought.

A flock of pigeons flies through the dense smog breathing deeply. They only speak Chinese. With no outlet for sex and love where will your human birds of humble breast fly? Their wisdom links them in flight but the smog will unravel all that. Their feathers floating down like leaves.

We go to the Imperial Palace of the Emperors to view the adoration of red and green, opposite colours. In India it is easily seen, it is perhaps their favourite combination. I noticed it in the leaf veins of some of their plants.

Here in China the green is a pale blue-green but the red which floods, anoxic, is deep dark and strong like blood.

The Palace was built in the sixteenth and seventeenth centuries from the tunes of war, the spoils of the heart. Now electricity burns the internal images to life. Beautiful Qing vases of porcelain and ornaments revealed.

The layout of the Palace is quite similar to the great Chalukyan temples of Southern India with their squared courtyards. Yet the aim of this Palace was commerce and war which produced an ambience conducive to art whereas Hindu temples revelled in comparatively peaceful surroundings and were able to foster their art parallel to ideology.

Hordes of armourments were kept here in the Palace. The first cannon was made here, the glories of war espoused and revered as the glorious avenue of progress. Each building is supported by tall strong trees rendered and painted venous red like arteries. Trees from the ancient rainforest which covered the coastal plain.

The buildings' interiors smell of the old fires which lit them. This is where visiting Emperors stayed and were entertained by rooms of concubines who stoked the flames. Sex and war go together they are the husband and wife striving hand in hand for a better life for their child. Flying together into battle, floating on the wings of love.

"Why must men fight wars to catch ladies?" I ask Lilly and I answer my own question and say, "She must tell him to stop." She burns her eyes into mine, I have touched her deeply.

With these few words she is mine forever and the great folly of this place is crumbled in a single breath. Oh great woman take your man and tell him to stop with war. Take your shoes off and show him your divine soft feet. Now walk in the dirt of his love and throw his seeds in that richness also. For the world must listen to your feminine heart-beat. And do not worry if the seeds do not grow and feed the happy child. Without worry you will be rich. This is just to show you that you have everything you need in the handful of soil right in front of you!

We do not need to beat down the door to find what we need!

There is great fear of bad luck in China, as there is all over the world. If a person should die mysteriously the place is left alone for a long long time and stories, legends will arise. The crow is a spiritual bird in Asia. If one dies on a threshold the house is abandoned. The Aborigines who came down through Asia and have been in Australia for many thousands of years, have a similar story about the crow. In the Palace sacrifices and offerings are made to the crows on special poles. Offerings of offal are placed ceremoniously to appease the ill fates of war and love.

The roof corners of their buildings are turned upwards to prevent bad spirits landing and resting. They mimic the make-up of women who enhance the upturned corners of their eyes with dark lines like the wings of coloured birds.

The buildings of the Palace are made from small grey bricks, the walls thick and strong. Only on the eves of the roofs and some internal ceilings is any decoration jammed. Their intricate calligraphic style flourishes more under the eaves, tucked away like a frilly dress. Hidden and afraid to stand and reveal the individual whose flesh has already been stripped before the crows can think.

Back home in the afterglow of her warmth I write to the children of the world a small story about a mouse and a dragon.

Mouse and Dragon Go To War

One bright sunny day Mouse and Dragon were out in the garden when a fighter jet went over their heads too close. Mouse got such a fright she leapt into Dragon's arms.

That night on the news it said that their country was going to war with another country.

"I'm going!" said Dragon jumping up and Mouse squealed with excitement,

"I'm coming with you." Mouse and Dragon found a lot of potatoes and set off for the big city the very next day to go to war. Mouse became a nurse in a hospital and Dragon became a fighter pilot and fired rockets from his plane.

One day he was looking for a target and saw two people in a field digging potatoes. He flew so close he frightened them so much one of them jumped into the other ones arms. All of a sudden Dragon felt very sad and lost control of his aeroplane and crashed into a tree. He was stuck in the tree and his leg and wing were very sore. Luckily the two people came and spoke to him in a strange language and helped him down out of the tree. Dragon thanked them as best he could but he could not walk or fly. The two people carried him to their house and fed him potatoes for three weeks. After that time Dragon began to miss Mouse very much so he decided to leave the very next day. He thanked the two people for looking after him and being so kind.

He asked what their names were and they said Mouse and Dragon.

Dragon was overcome with sorrow. He spread his wings and flew into the sky. He circled them once then went back to the city to look for Mouse. She was in a hospital mending people's injuries from the war. She was so happy to see Dragon! He picked her up and put her on his back and flew out the window. They went home to their vegetable patch beside the river and never said a word about the war.

Morale of the story:
It is not them it is us; love will find a way.

Deep in the chasm of the street, in the early morning when I look down, a water truck is spraying the road. As it travels along it plays the Western tune of Happy Birthday. It is strange that today is my birthday and water is the great symbol of love. Apparently I was born on a city street early in the morning outside the Sydney Lottery Office. My mother struggled to keep me warm. The ambulance driver told her to buy a lottery ticket which she did. The ticket won the lottery.

Now twenty six floors up I have been reborn in China. No crows around here!

Today we visit the DVD computer shop to have Lilly's computer changed to Chinese so she can read it. The day is a Sunday and we take a crowded bus. On the bus she chats to people and soon the whole bus is talking amongst themselves. What did she say? I think she asked directions.

Back on the hard pavement walking. The grey of the street-scape exploding into huge buildings either side which a mere glance cannot encompass without severely twisting one's neck back.

In the deep hazy distance spire upon spire pierces the sky, looking dim and grey in the universal cloud. Suddenly loud pounding doof music threatens to bring them all crashing down and twenty delicate thin ladies in tight short pants and little tee-shirts with flowers at the back of their tied up hair, line up and strut briskly about the cold sharp cat-walk steps. Their young ankles balance precariously on high-rise shoes like tall grey buildings while their pointed tops puncture the air for beauty.

Wives to be, they must catch their men somehow – strange that only women seem to watch.

In all the passing parade of the day I see only six young children. No pregnant women dare go out in the street. Those children that I see are always holding hands with family, they are not allowed to cry or whinge, to express their utmost dissatisfaction. When they are young, so the parents believe, they are as free as a bird. Most will live within a city and never see an ant.

Their individualities are trained at an early age not to seek passions beyond normal prudence and security, for fear comes out of a dark box and must be trained. Hence they are over-protected. But I say that children must cry as men must love. Love is a cessation of all those conditions of servitude. It is a blind faith the young ones instinctively feel and the older ones try to control. Love is a naked foot which enjoys walking on the ground. Love and crying are opposite however one cannot have one without the other. And the higher one is off the ground the harder one falls. Pain and ill health teach us to be happy and grateful.

Even in the day the electric universe comes down to remind us that we are not alone.

The lights flash constantly and like galaxies clothe the streets. We try to create the stars here on Earth but pollution, from our trying, obscures those colourful ideals.

Air-conditioning systems cling like parasites to the sides of grey buildings, they are growths upon a tree. Lenticels, all sucking in air and spitting it out again as hot fumes. Who on this planet is responsible for the pollution? Not us! It is all our air, it is not fair. Will it become so bad that we die in blackness? Suffocated by our own ineptitude and inability to stand up and say "No" to their archaic inventions which plague us. For they give us tools from a poisoned mind which scourge and suck from love. Those folk who make money from oil will have us all stuck on their backs like air-conditioning units. They will belch their own bad air into the childless homes of their next of kin.

It is their filth we have to clean and what inventions do we have to clean it with, from *our* electric universe? None!

We wake with a start, the electric universe is sleeping at last in our room, for the lights are out and it is dark. The night has crept up on us like a small child. I swam about forgetful in a timeless deep dark pool, a dark and wondrous dream as I drowned in her black eyes.

After a day of plenty our bodies have felt the pain of love. For Lilly has her period and I very sore testicles. I can hardly walk. She looks at me sideways again with a half-smile.

I look at her as I walk sideways and feel my new face, the beard she cut so close so well.

Ahh, she said it made me look younger! I said I was an old man with a young girl. My chin wobbles, my mouth unsure, my teeth afraid to shine. I frown with pain and she laughs.

Quickly now she rises from our glorious bed and with small cat-like sniffles and whispers expresses her dissatisfaction at being late for she has to catch a bus at 9:20. I feel her anxiety and the half-smile flickers once again. She throws her strong arms around me, their fingers loose and still. I lift her from the ground she is my little mouse, so strong of virtue and in love.

She will not take the money for the taxi, I thrust it on her and she smiles and takes.

Suddenly she is gone.

I follow her mind to the lift, out of the building and all the way home. When she sleeps I am there caressing her dreams. Running my fingers about her ears and through her hair, nibbling her on the chin and anywhere there is soft smooth flesh. She wants me to dig my fingers into her neck where her spine meets the skull. What I do is not hard enough so I use all my strength till my thumbs and hands are sore. Realising that I am able to give her a massage she rolls over hissing like a snake.

So I rub her all over for hours. It is not hard enough and she complains. I rub her hard and long.

Many years ago she fell asleep in a bus and her leg was frozen against the metal side. She has suffered nerve damage there ever since. I show her how to rest and meditate on the sore spot. I measure her hips at her feet and pull her legs until the bed moves. I show her how to sleep with her hips and legs arranged, to help her joints lengthen and relax for her leg muscle is tight and will affect the knee. Now she is moaning with the pain and rolling over with sexual excitement.

Her bottom is small, her hips broader than the average Chinese. I know her well. I sit her up and roll her over, I lift her legs, she is butter in my hands. I rub her tummy, shoulders and feet pressing on the shiatsu pressure points till she whimpers. She writes,

"I come you place, you give massage?"

"Yes, all day" I reply. She laughs and asks, "What will you accomplish?"

"I will heal you" I say. She rolls sideways, her arms outstretched across the bed. I sit her up and come behind so that she sits on me backwards at the edge of the bed. She squashes my soreness but I do not move. I run my hands across her belly and the tops of her legs and clasp her hands together. Her eyes are closed her mouth open, her head flops back to mine. I kiss her neck and growl like a dragon. I pull her back on the bed and my hands feel her tight breasts, they are well hidden behind rough cloth. I rub them so softly cupping them in both my hands. She taps my hands gently but obviously loves my touch. I rub them harder and feel the soft skin between them. She shows me how to rub her sternum hard. She guides my hands which keep returning to her breasts, I sweep my arm across them gently. She is half smiling her lips slightly open. I kiss her face and hold it between my hands. I kiss her mouth at the edges, her full mouth she does not give. She rests, her legs wide, her arms apart, her eyes watching mine. How could God create such a beautiful thing and then freeze her leg? I have an injury too, it is in my hand, I broke it and it never mended properly.

The large finger will not close and I cannot make a fist, it only makes a rude sign. But I do not show her now. She knows immediately what I say about my body. Then I mention my shoulders which were injured about twelve years ago in the same accident. They both click when I move my arms. In my letters to her from Australia once I said I was in good shape considering two kidney transplants, a new heart or somebody else's heart, a head transplant – what a vision and she was worried. I had to explain that it was humour. Then all was well.

She reaches up and squeezes one shoulder.

"That hurt?" she asks, as I recoil with pain. "Hurt?"

Again and again. As she rolls me over on the bed. I feel her thumb is like my penis it knows exactly where to go. It seeks the great relief of pain, those adventurous fingers of steel. I am twisting now in a ball of pain, her knowledge of my body is awesome. In thirty seconds to a minute she has healed me. The pain she gave was intense. But now my pain is all gone.

She is a new woman to me. She has given me a great gift. She has pressed my buttons and programmed me like a robot of computerised love. Now, floating in her many scents, I fly through the window like a mosquito from the streets, my proboscis at the ready. She has a high intelligence gleaned from the ancient battlefields. Her high wisdom is simple and direct and infinitely pure. What secrets will she reveal when she opens her spirit to me, unfolding like the petals of a rose?

She is gone and the black night descends. In my dreams I am on a beach. There is a carnival going on but it is a half moon and mysteriously dark. Many people sit on the beach as though the sun was shining. I am there with the feeling that I am not alone. I am with some woman whether Lilly or somebody else I cannot tell. Then we move off a little distance into an oval tunnel. A hazy darkness ponders the other end of it, far away. Then suddenly I am surprised and attacked by the female entity which follows me. It is Lilly! I recognise the grip, the arms and the feeling of love.

I am forced to the ground and kept still. But is it an attacker or she? As I wake I am alone. She has gone but there in her arms in the darkness I lay pinned to the ground perhaps by all the women of China, in a moment of fear.

Mouse Has a Birthday

Mouse and Dragon lived in the country far away from the shops and the restaurants. However it was Mouse's birthday and Dragon being very fond of Mouse wanted to take her out for dinner.

He dusted and stretched his wings, put her on his back and took off for the big city some distance away. After flying for a while he felt tired so they flew down to a green field and rested.

Dragon felt thirsty and drank from a small stream, then he felt hungry and found a patch of ripe watermelons which they both began to eat. They took to the sky again but Dragon had eaten so much watermelon his tummy was sore and he had to fly down and have another rest. On the ground close by Mouse found a peach tree full of ripe peaches, she loved peaches and ate lots and lots, even Dragon had a few. Dragon noticed Mouse had a big tummy and was quite heavy.

By the time they reached the city they were not very hungry at all and had a small meal of bananas and ice cream.

After a little while Mouse licked her lips and ordered lots of chickens feet so Dragon ordered three chickens. Dragon then ate one donkey and sixteen fish! Mouse was not hungry at all and only ate nine pigs and twenty more chicken's feet! Dragon stood up he was too full, he had eaten too much. Mouse could hardly move she was twice as big as she normally was! It was dark but dragons can see in the dark.

He put Mouse on his back, she was very heavy but dragons are strong. After flying for sometime he began to realise they were lost. So he flew back the way they had come. But no, he was very lost and after a while he was exhausted, Mouse was too heavy. He flew down to a field and had a bit of a bumpy landing. Mouse was very cold and had to shelter under his wings. Dragon did not sleep very much because Mouse snored loudly.

In the morning they took to the skies again but they were so far away it took them ages to arrive home and when they did Dragon's wings were really sore and he could hardly walk! He was very tired and hungry, Mouse had to feed him and put him to bed.

Mouse kissed Dragon on the nose and he opened one eye and said,

"Happy birthday, my darling" and was soon fast asleep.

Dragons never snore.

Morale of the story:
Life is as light as a feather when we are in love.

A new day begins with the rumble and honk of the traffic below. It is the language of the dinosaur for their air is grey, their lungs full of chemical dust and the pitch of their song though insect like is a dying beep. For all their triumphs of rationale sarcoidosis has beset them. A futile asphyxiation from oil. Where do they go, the long lines of traffic? Far off into the grey distance into a great Black Hole.

I burn DVDs for China. Films on Weather Engineering, Crop Circles, Coal Seam Gas Mining, and The New World Order. No, China must not look up to the West for technology. China must return to the soil as we all should. Low polluting energy devices are being withheld from us. It is vain to assume that we can change the system which after all has given us a pen to write with. However it is not unreasonable to surmise that although we scribble a common language we are not able to perceive other languages beyond the pen and the audible whisper. After all how is a culture, a civilisation judged? Good art comes from long traditions and a love of nature. Without art our spirit dies. The naked foot finds the most artful place to walk and it is not alone.

Art is the expression of the inventive universe. Those ideas are transcribed into the cells and teaches them about new ideas and new indescribable, unpronounceable languages. Perhaps art and war are similar in that one seeks to explain this inter-dimensional dialogue and the other seeks to act out the technical dynamics of those ideas.

These high words come from the roots of trees and the soil. They did not spring from an idealistic sense of philosophy. Study life and eat good food, walk on the bare soil and love your higher self.

Money is an illusion, a symptom of worry and illness. Nations follow other nations, their people numbed into enslavement. Those who seek the power and follow the money have always had problems of health. Longevity is paramount in everybody's mind for we are taught to fear evil synonymous with death.

Why must evil rule us with its superstitious sword? If we are kind to ourselves and to others there will be no fear. But governments and others make money from fear. Take off your shoes and clothes and walk in the streets naked. Do no harm to others and they will not look at you. Fear them and they will attack like angry dogs or cats, that is the law of nature. A cornered brown rat will jump at its aggressor. Watch a policeman and he will chase you. Nations who fear their own people go out and fight wars in order to equalise the energy on the Earth. Where is the love in that?

Where is the happy child? I have answered my own questions. The happy child is at home playing in the garden. Playing creatively without fear while seeking the love of art.

Lilly is here. She sleeps already. Her womanliness has overcome her. She joins now with herself, the great moving Earth. The cleaning lady calls my name from outside and I meet her at the threshold and say "tomorrow" as I do not want her to disturb the beauty on the bed.

She does not understand so I let her in. On entering Lilly does not stir, she is tired from all the excitement. Like a small child she sleeps in her garden and plays and massages her dreams.

We visit an antique shop across the road. It is jammed with very expensive china-ware, jade bracelets, strings of beads and other cultural wonders. In this shop my father's artworks would dwarf the abilities displayed. He tangled with the human form outlining pathos not obsessive decoration.

Lilly settles into a highly polished tree trunk which has a seat carved into it. She beams at me for she is a woman of hard beautiful ornate and highly polished wood with a spirit of the forest inside.

She rubs the wood as though it is a human body and half smiles at me from the corners of her eyes. In one shop are small figurines carved from ivory. The poses are of sexual intimacy. Unknowingly I go straight to the cabinet and peer in. I am suddenly a voyeur and Lilly laughs. Quickly I move on and leave her knowing I am not a rabid sex maniac and perhaps a little embarrassed. Those images I see may come to pass with time between she and I.

The dentist drills of the city have come alive as they spear into concrete and morphed into monsters to stalk the early morning sounds, the bleating of sheep and the clashing of horns. Speckled buildings rise from the moulding gums of the gutters and on the pavements the splinters of rationale, the people, sift and crawl between the cracks on their way to work. The square buildings, clothed in grey-wash bluntly poke the sphere and from each window furtive glances like tooth-picks pry and pluck the lust for life from the smallest fractured cavities and cracks, trying, chasing, winning, losing.

The thick black smoke from an electrical fire rises from the dungeons of the alleys across the road. Like a dense flock of crows it muscles up and tickles the sides of a new building. Earthquake prone and rigid, these buildings seem almost sexless. They faintly discuss the dark smoke amongst themselves. Only their cement bones will escape the blaze. How would we escape the heat if it spread and came through the lift-wells like an out of control electric-dragon spewing flame? We would fall as if for love, would hit the solid ground like a tiny drop of red rain. No helicopters would come for us, no men with long ladders. The fire though is soon put out.

The parade of wealth continues. The fancy shoes, the frilly skirts, the shirts and tee-shirts with the happy slogans. Later the rain comes down and washes the streets creating pools of black pollution, cloud and froth which fall before the hungry underground drains. Rolling and tumbling the whole crust of China like char from burnt toast, disappears from the bonnets of cars, from the windscreens, from the umbrellas and leaves of the few trees and plants which hug and stretch their gritty fingers into any soft crevasse they can find. Washes the earth but not our lungs.

Now the colours come out glistening dark and clear, varnishing the waste and smoothing the rough. People still ride their bicycles in the rain, clad in plastic sheets, hovering above the ground like ghosts.

The restaurant is full. The sound of feeding chop-sticks like the many beaks of birds.

A huge pile of fungus mounts the table complete with a fiery sauce which vaporises up one's nose. Long dead fish, dried then cooked in a faint batter are pecked and eaten, bones, head, fins and all. Their sharp rows of little teeth no match for Lilly as she throws them down her throat and spits all the little white teeth out on the table one by one like shrapnel. The English lesson continues at the meal.

Her tongue is broad like mine. Even from far away she looks delicious, up close she averts my kiss. She wears luminous green gumboots beneath tight black pants and a red tee-shirt. She smiles and shows her beautiful white teeth. She flicks her eyes at me sideways and follows my every move.

She waits on me, washes my clothes in the small hand basin, makes sure I know where I am going and protects me from speeding cars. She pays the bills with my money and checks the change twice. She lies on the bed now sleeping, snoring in faint whispers.

The whole of China is within her womb alive and well. When she wakes I will cover her with the sheet to keep her warm and offer her some drink. She has been alone for fifteen years. Divorced all those years ago. In need of love her heart is sore. The petals of the rose have closed, with love will slowly open. Now stirring she watches me from a half-dream and moans.

We visit another book publisher with my mother's books. But they are too full of pictures for that particular publisher. They only publish books with words and small pictures not pictures and small words. Fortunately they give me an address of a picture publisher in Beijing who they say will publish them.

It is interesting to note how the long traditions of these people are enhanced through the generations. Any change must happen slowly and carefully. Even to step outside in the wet of the raining imagination is to risk the cold of rejection and being washed away. Competition is so fierce. Their security is their dollar not their soil and any connection to it. For they thirst for oil and other qualities of the Earth to justify and quantify their consumption of electricity. The status quo which on one hand lunges out to grasp the new on the other withdraws from the fear of breaking the repetition and exploring the unknown. Their society therefore is based on good and bad with shear good luck to open or close the great book of lore. In China how many non-polluting energy saving inventions have been saved and sent underground?

The wheel of life, bogged in bureaucracy's mud, will not move on except through an abstraction of fear which necessarily incorporates its opposite. As the wheel turns it knows an uncertain danger waits especially if it moves fast. Fear only gives birth to more fear. The word gives our dictionaries the flavour of an ill tide which knows that without the pain of uncertainty there can be no love to appreciate the wash of truth. Hence our greed is ruled by fear.

The rain continues. Varnishing the streets with pure honesty. The wheels of the vehicles shred the paper endlessly. The blast of horn less severe, the anger quelled, the traffic slower.

Yesterday as the wet day closed, the horns were agitated, quick and strong. This morning the people are more kind, the beeps shorter and more at ease.

In Australia, I say to Lilly, the cars only beep when danger threatens. They rarely beep to let another driver know they are there, it is illegal. We are taught with driving to be mindful only of ourselves and to literally forget about the other drivers as we hope they will watch their own driving with similar concentration.

My masculinity aches. She came and as soon as she arrived went to sleep in my arms.

Such is the trust she has placed in me, like an injured animal she knows she will be cured.

I put her to sleep and her tiny brown face illuminates as she drifts over the ocean waves.

Her soil is full and fertile, her water clear and deep. I am the whale which tows her boat to Australia while she sleeps. This is the real spoil that I bring home, a treasure from a distant land.

She has the wisdom of her age and of all China and the youth of a young girl. One day we will sleep in each other's arms at the bottom of the sea.

She wakes and stretches and I am next to her. Her half-awake eyes enticing me to increase my mindless ache for her. Her arms are smooth with no hair at all. She is born from the cocoon of a silk worm, a white moth delicate and strong. I am beside her stroking everything I can find.

Her feet are flaccid, her body uncorked, flowing. She lifts her leg over my body and throws her arm in the air which washes my chest. Now her fingers are light upon me. With my hand on hers I move my fingers between hers. I touch the tips with mine and compare the pleasure. My fingers trace the circle of her palm which is open, the fingers soft and bent, tower above her pleasure. I press gently some nerve depressions, going in deeper and deeper. She is languid, relaxed in the extreme. I kiss her neck and bite the back of it hard, grasping it with my teeth, thrashing and growling like a dog.

She does not stir she is my cloth toy, my rag-doll. I blow in her ear and trace its outline with my tongue, ever inward. Her neck is soft and I pucker it below her delicate chin, sucking in the flesh and blowing small raspberries up and down its delicious length. She does not move her face as I move towards the side of her slippery full mouth; I steal a soft kiss, another and another. I wet my mouth and kiss the side of hers. She does not mind she knows me now. We have laughed in the high clouds and smelt the green woodlands, climbed the tallest mountains and swam in the smallest streams. On our way down to the sea we have bumped into each other's souls like a couple of old floating tree trunks meandering down the river of life.

Her lips are wet and I am too close, the excitement too much so I move away. But her arms draw me back into the deep of her black eyes. I am at a loss, my mind has gone away. I rub her naked stomach and under her blouse feel her youthful breasts already risen, desperate to break out.

I trace round and round the mountains of their desire. Pulling slightly up then delicately pinching. Like tall strong peaks standing beneath the cloud. She is unmoving. Her half smile wafts its electricity from head to toe, her tingling sensuality lies dormant like a huge army or cat about to spring. We are fused together even before we begin.

A plate of black fungus arrives on the table. It is for her womanliness, her fertility, her bleeding. As she spears and spikes and pinches it the hot spice of love evaporates up her nose sending shivers up her spine, she is suddenly awake, smiling and sneezing. Her thunderous sneezes drench me and the food. Two long dead dried fish arrive and she munches their heads first to make sure they are dead. The bones of the skull are spat out on the wet table and after that sixteen little spits of serrated teeth dance like hail stones on the bones, a veritable battle field grows of strewn lives and the spoils of all men which she has controlled. She will not age; she will live on, trickling from the mountains to her own fermenting sea.

Somewhere to mark time and the essence of being, a gong chimes and tapers off slowly into the oily pitch of the traffic.

Across the road from this tall building stands an older square construction with white pillars on top. Above the pillars sits a large round clock which chimes and imitates the tune of the Big Ben clock in London. But at twelve midday it sings a Chinese song, sweet and melodious, the harmonies of which are extravagant in detail, florid and yet essential. As vast as their decorations on the eaves of every roof - as time taps out their favours, their whims and their fears.

All alone on the planet our only friend is time and the soothing role of the Earth.

For she is our friend, her shadow the moon, the round face of love. Man states his rationale in square forms while woman her curves seduce. She is the water while he the sharp stones.

All the way to dust, over and over, we will be wrapped in each other's arms. Men fall for her looks, women fall for his time.

Lilly is late. She said she would be. The heart pumps when she is here and even when she is not here. I can feel her footsteps drawing near; her heart sends messages fine and clear from twenty thousand kilometres away. Our hearts will rest when she is close, wrapped in petals and smelling like a flower.

Large red letters dance across the tops of the buildings opposite. The designs of which go back thousands of years. Each stroke the breath of a butterfly, entrained in a solid air yet gifted with the flight of intuitive design.

Suddenly we are blasted by noise as Lilly's phone rings. It sounds like the Chinese National Anthem. We quickly stand to attention and search her bag for remnants of the disease.

We are on the bed again feasting on each other's flesh. Then out to feast again at a table full of fine cuisine. She passes me the food until I am nearly breaking. She eats with the slip and slurp of the noodle-suck. There is so much to a mouth, I ponder. But much more to a stomach newly born. As we leave the restaurant she says to the owner that the dumplings had little taste and the meat was covered in red sauce whereas it should have been cooked *in* the red sauce. The owner looks grim and bows her head. A lady standing nearby looks dark and forlorn. Lilly speaks her mind. She is red herself cooked inside with love as strong and sweet smelling as a red red rose.

The rain has gone, the streets comparatively clean. Her eyes are fiery and full of life, she plays on the bed and laughs like a thousand trains. Her sneezes echo throughout the thirty story building, my ears are ringing like gongs within a huge bell.

We spend hours punching out words into the translating machine. She knows more English than she thinks she does. And now she feels worried about me going to Beijing on my own as I still cannot speak a word of Chinese. Will she come and hold my hand? Will she tear herself away from her traditions for several moments?

"I like your body and I need your love" is what she writes. I look at her amazed. She is the butterfly of my dreams, as heavy as a lead balloon, her weight upon my flower. Beijing is a long way and I have much to do there, I say. Beyond that too many words surround my mind and I am stuck, unable to escape and simply look at her dreamily.

It takes me a long time to describe to her how when I took my father's drawings and paintings to England - his series on the Convicts, the Australians in the Embassy thought the work sublime and wanted to exhibit them at the Embassy. But the English did not like the subject and the idea went no further.

Chinese people have not been taught that Australia is little more than two hundred years old, that we are the descendants of convicts. Lilly writes to me,

"England sent criminals as immigrants to Australia?"

"Yes" I reply "and America too. They sent the women out in the hulls of ships, in cages and washed them down with buckets of sea water, many died. In America they massacred many of the American Indians and in Australia the Aborigines suffered in the same way."

How can we still love the English flag? She, England, will never apologise for the brutal way she has treated some countries and still continues to dominate her own people, though England is perhaps more democratic than America.

The Queen pays no taxes and most authorities answer to the King. The Queen has abused her power and still maintains her rule. After all the people have voted for the parliament to rule them, not the Queen. The Queen is nothing more than a private entrepreneur with her fingers stuck in her own pie.

Wealth rules, it is the same all over the world. I write an email to a rich Chinese man. I crawl to his door and ask that he view my father's work. How else can my father's work be recognised?

To begin from the bottom here would be to throw all his work in the sea. Though now with another connection, at least a small step up for him would be better than none at all and in Beijing we will try.

Lilly is looking after me. She is my Queen. Slowly, slowly she is melting from the inside.

Her talk is rich and fluid and several words begin to make sense to me. Perhaps there is hope for my learning Chinese after all. I am a small step up for her. Reaching up she hugs me tightly when she leaves, her smile lingering on the walls of the room like the echoes of her sneeze.

At night I watch her in her sleep and view the patterns of her thoughts on the walls. She comes and goes flitting through the coloured shapes to see that I am here. In the half-sleep, feel her warmth and touch her body as I descend. Falling into my darkness she does not follow, I am alone.

In the early morning avenues of stillness it is raining once again. The wheels sound like tearing paper as they cut the skin of water along the road. The wheel of life moving the bosom of the businessmen whose spirits wish to escape with the freedom of the water cutting and shredding bureaucracy to pieces. They throw the threads out the window of this twenty six story building, flushing into cracks.

The squeak of brake, the bark of horn. China is a mountain that I climb with new addresses of people to see about my parents work. Their lifetimes' work and I wonder what the day will bring. The air is half fresh as its coolness comes through the window, still mixed with the acrid fumes of pollution and metallic dusts; so I dare not breathe too deeply.

Lilly's hair is on the shower floor. It is falling out! Nuclear fall-out or simply hair fall out?

She worries about her health and at the tip of her nose a small dark dot may be cancer or a beauty spot. What is this substance she puts in her hair to stop it blowing in the wind? Her body knows to get out of its skin as its hair is being released.

She is on her way now, to my country. Her spirit has had enough, her body needs to do what her spirit wants. The wheel of life is tearing paper so I write here but not to her,

"How can we let go when life's pleasures are before us? How many lifetimes have we waited to be joined and now slips away, that moment of truth?" Perhaps if I return to Australia and she grows ill here, I may never see her again! No, that thought I must never entertain. I tell her I can cure cancer and I will.

Her hips are broad, her tiny body alive and well - is relaxing now before the foam at the bottom of the waterfall. She will come to Australia with me and we will always be young. Her smile fills the room before she enters. Her heart pulses along the corridor pushing the electricity before it. She charges at me with a full hug and I nearly fall off the chair!

In the street she is silent, walking before me, leading the way. I can tell she is happy and proud to have me by her side. She looks at me sideways always in the lift, her smile echoes from the walls. And when in the room she is so excited she speaks her own language non-stop before realising I don't understand a word. I am the same, curiously we understand each other as though we have met many years ago or as I told her, in another lifetime.

Next day she marches boldly in. She is like a little girl all smiles. Her morning hug is for her deceased daddy, her still alive mummy, her grandparents, her great aunt, her step-sisters and brothers and her twenty six year old son. The whole of China is welcoming me. She sits on the bed and talks smilingly in her language, waving her arms around with great excitement. She soon calms down and takes the translating machine from her bag and rapidly with great alacrity is drawing Chinese words on its face, her smooth face unwrinkled, except for her mouth which is turned down as she doesn't like using the machine to talk. After considerable time she writes,

"My great pornographic aunt has elephant in her shower." I do not laugh. Sometimes the Chinese phraseology is backwards and after trying to read it many ways I frown and read it back to her. Once I offered to buy her a new bag as the one she has is looking well used. She wrote back to me then,

"Get your own life out of your own bag." I winced and coyly said okay.

She diddled with the controls and laughs with a frown. She continues her excitement and writes again to me saying that I have five different animals in my star sign. She seems pleased. Our birthdays match. I am a dragon and she a mouse. At the moment I only feel like a man with little room for anything else. She only has one animal and that is a mouse. Dragons are good friends with mice because mice are so small and dragons know mice are caring and strong and though capable of delivering a nasty bite are soft inside.

She produces a piece of paper which has some dates on it. Then she gives me a small rectangular box with a small, pale green dragon carved in high relief from jade in it.

On the paper I had written and mixed up my birth date, day and month as China writes the day where we write the month. She thought it was my birthday on the wrong month. She is delighted with the new knowledge. I then tell her again how I was born in the gutter and lived in a cave for eight years forty feet above the sea just to have this stone image of myself around my neck. Thanking the world for us both I kissed it and her and dropped it down my shirt.

The day rolls over like a belly to a back and the wheel does not move. She is in the clean bed again under the covers. Her smile is beckoning and her arm flops on my side of the bed as if to say hop in and hurry up. I am there amongst the curls of her stiff polluted hair. She smells of dead seaweed and all the spice of India and China combined. Soon her eyes are closed as I rub her naked stomach and plunge my fingers in her navel round and round. Unlike Western women she has no body hair. She is fascinated with mine and rubs my hairy arms till the hairs stand on end like a forest in a great wind, tussled and disturbed. I kiss her neck and with my newly shaved chin rub her chin and she smiles. I blow raspberries under her ears and softly pucker her cheeks.

She does not moan or call out only the half smile. I run my fingers up her blouse following and teasing the softness. She is half asleep, her body wide awake. Her breasts are average size and full. They do not resist my hands or my arm as I brush across their landscape. Her legs are half open and I rub her inner thighs, scratching through to her skin below the heavy denim cloth. I cannot undo her bra, my fingers fumble for ages. An eternity of time etched within her electric universe, competing with the speed of light to enter her celestial sphere. These Chinese knots, these China days!

Her bra is loose and soon I cup one breast, its nipple rising with expectation like the mountains of the moon or an uncontrollable forest fire. Then the other unleashed to rise volcanic from her gently heaving chest. But her stomach is soft cream and I kiss it all over tracing in little round pools the words of my desire. Dancing back and forth to circumnavigate those voluptuous mounds. Dark are they like the burls upon a tree rising and falling, swaying in a wind. They are my feast and my famine. From head to toe I feel her. My hand too fast for me, but then it is between her legs, her softness still protected by her pants, the Great Wall of China. Here I scratch and rub and push and dance. I am the mouse in her pyjamas which gnaws through the door. With rhythmic pressure I feel her grow within her dark enclosure. Her nipples once again rising in their youth. Through the soft quick-sands of her belly I negotiate desire. From groin to fingertips, treading deftly from the pocket of her navel. Her pants I undo and run my hand down to her legs but soon she calls out "no" and I retreat. She is alive after all, mummified in her traditions yet flying through the air.

Resting now my excitement plateaued, unquenchable.

I move and her leg is launched across my body. Her storm of love receding, growing into the light from the deep of her eyes. Her hair again, her neck, her wondrous soft stomach with the empty amphitheatre full of echoes. She groans and I roll her back to where she was. Unmoving, her legs apart, her breasts neatly tucked back under their umbrellas. My hands beneath her neck with one upon her left breast, round and round explores from her stomach to her breast. And then the lesson.

The English learning, yearning for a better lifestyle, to escape the smog and the heavy chemical plod across the earth.

"Breast" I say, rubbing it gently round and round and flicking lightly, pulling and squeezing. "Stomach" I say, round and round and as my hand descends towards her groin,

"Pussy" I say, rubbing between her legs as deep as the shield allows.

"Pushy" she repeats very slowly, then "stumik" then "bwest." This goes on until my left arm beneath her is quite dead. And after I extract it still we sing the song. Will she ever forget those words?

The vocabulary of her body grows as does her wakefulness, till far away from the sweetness of her being we talk about elbows, hands and fingers. Now I am bold with her and grasp her where I want. Her barriers all smooth. She holds me close and watches my every move.

Sitting up she realises her pants are undone and bangs me on the bottom, not once but twice pretending to be the naughty child. I poke her stomach saying with a smile,

"You did that." Now fully awake she goes to the bathroom to dress herself. When she comes back she lies across me with a great moan like two trees rubbing in a wind. I caress her back as smooth as glass. Then quickly rising she feels my groin by trick of gesture. I cry out from her suddenness and direct pressure.

I am the boy in pain, scared of the animal upon me. We are happy in our play though I am sore as though expecting a child or an avalanche of snow.

She makes tea and we sit so close together. She will be my wife one day, together through the snow and ice, will seek that target of warmth and understanding.

Thus we play about the day and watch it pass around us. Tomorrow is important for we have to organise paperwork for her immigration visa. These difficult sleeves of dust have to be read and stamped. The tiger in me snarls, why would man stop love? How could he not feel the warmth from his own groin spreading throughout the universe? When man goes to war he rapes women.

Women must tell him to stop going to war! To throw all paperwork into the cauldron of anarchy where it will come out rich with the fruits of invention and a sustainable lifestyle.

We are not alone in the universe, our brothers and sisters were implanted in our DNA long ago. Their love is of the boundless stars. Just as my kiss to Lilly goes on and on. There is no fear in the universe only an electric space; space connected by love like all the raindrops in the sea.

Each morning a small green woman comes in to clean my room. She carries a mop as tall as herself. She skittles around with an efficient gait polishing the toilet and observing my drying underwear.

She speaks to me as though I know her language which I do. The colour she wears is reminiscent of a jungle leaf. These dying symbols clash with the huge red letters which flower on the roof-top opposite. Try as they might to hold hands across the growling abyss of the road a hundred meters below, they never will. The red is the heart of a nation spurred on by an excessively fertile being of greed, sprinkled like lust in the dust. This little green woman sweeps it up each day.

Lilly and I venture forth into the hot metamorphosed streets of the rising Shenyang. With huge movie screens displaying parting lips and farting cars, brightly lit Christmas tree buildings spear into the sky, on the wet road they look like bush-fires in grottoes. We are off to find out about the pros and cons of obtaining her marriage visa.

We walk a short distance, stopping many along the street to ask directions. They all point the same way, waving their fingers over the sprawling bicycles, cars and carts. Down another street and round another traffic corner. The parade of people is fascinating. All the girls seem to be wearing high-heels and strutting, their backs thrusting their turtle-bottoms to the West as high in the air as possible while mangling their delicate toes. The gaunt men liquidate and barely look. Couples wrapped arm in arm deliciously drool towards one another.

The caress on the bus, the tap on the cheek, the happy youthful smiles of people in love.

Young girls sigh at the boys who wish to sire children as couples shyly show the world their affection.

The old stooped woman who creeps on the back door of the bus is barely noticed. She is just the right size to stay hidden on the first step, bending low.

The beggar with his music and his megaphone, bent-armed from time and the weight of life, squashed and twisted, crawls and falls from his limousine to call to the universe and the angels of mercy. The old man on his bicycle laden with long metal spikes charges across the pedestrian crossing like a bull with chrome horns, takes on the buses and the cops. The dainty police like de-sexed male ballerinas, their ping-pong-ball bats for stop and go, their white gloves for surgery in the gutter. Oh the victim has been gored with chrome.

We pass again the crimson and yellow flowers we passed an hour ago. In thousands of pots, flowering on the brittle pavement. Quite a beautiful sight. The beggar sniffs down-wind of them, some sprawled flat just like he. Again we pass him and the flowers while peering at the squared sky its round and menacing grey cloud boiling up and over behind the glass and steel.

We are lost. As we walk across the field of led fumes, now grey and frothing like the dank and humid sky, we stop to casually chat as a barrage of buses hurtles toward us beeping their stallions with their single giant windscreen eyes. Only slightly do we move as they dare to undress us with their feelers out front to view behind. Our naked ears cannot hear the directions anyway. And more arm waving seems to indicate we are all as mad as the buses. I come from the silent hills and the restful forests, I am not equipped with inner city nerves, these giant sharks of the city swallow me alive. Their brakes shudder through the soup, loud thundering the earth.

Finally we arrive. But alas the door is closed and Lilly asks the people outside how to get in.

"Just push the door harder," they say in Chinese, so we do. It is a huge revolving door which sweeps one in like the feathery tongue of a marine filter-feeder complete with little whiskers at its edges. We press the buttons on the lifts and wait and wait and wait. We are one hour late already and still struggling as though in a strait-jacket or an aeroplane without a seat. The lift arrives and twenty people are behind us waiting.

When the door finally opens Lilly rushes in only to rush out again as there are many tables and scaffolding equipment to be offloaded inside. The people behind us grow restless and wander off to find the stairs or use their friends as battering-rams to open the revolving door. At last we are in the vacant lift and look at each other with a sigh. The lift moves slowly for a lift and then stops, we are only going to the fourth floor. I am about to kiss Lilly again but several people get in and press buttons and slowly we rise past the fourth floor on our climb to the twenty eighth floor! On the way it stops again and again as more people jam in.

In no time the lift is full and still slowly rising. Ah but now it begins to descend with similar grace. Stopping at every second floor and filling and emptying. Eventually we arrive exasperated and are given a cup of hot water.

I am to return to China in three months time, that way her Marriage visa application for migration will be processed with even more certainty. After the application is lodged we will have to wait another six to nine months for it to be finalised. Such is the price of love when the governments of the world treasure their own uniqueness and are required to plum individual's depths of desire.

The pendulum must be swung with us dangling, the depth measured as though in a lift of cherubs whose arrows pierce the echoing walls, whose bow-strings snap and make us free fall to the centre of her Earth, passing time.

Mouse and Dragon Buy a Car

Mouse and Dragon bought a car. Neither of them could drive. Dragon got in and tried to start it but the engine would not go. He got out and lifted up the boot but Mouse said the engine was in the front of the car! Mouse got in and turned the key and the car began to jump down the road with Dragon still looking for the engine in the boot. Mouse could not stop the car and Dragon ran after her.

He quickly jumped on the roof and climbed down onto the bonnet and signalled Mouse through the windscreen to use the brake. Mouse found the accelerator by mistake and the car leapt forward, Dragon disappeared.

Suddenly it stopped and Mouse got out. Dragon was nowhere to be seen. Then Mouse saw his tail under the car. She squealed thinking she had run over him.

"Are you alright!? What are you doing under there?" she squealed.

"I found the brake" said Dragon.

Dragon tried to understand the motor but whenever it broke down Mouse would hit the engine with a hammer and it would go. Mouse kept the hammer under the front seat of the car.

She liked driving and she drove everywhere. Dragon would look at her and think she was so clever. One day they were out driving when they passed a school bus which had broken down.

"I can fix that," said Mouse and she drove back and hit the engine of the bus with her hammer. The engine roared to life and the children were very happy. Dragon looked at Mouse who was smiling. She was thinking what Dragon was thinking.

Dragon wrote a sign, "Car Repairs" and put it outside their house.

Mouse fixed many cars with her hammer and Dragon cleaned the engines. They had lots of business and were always very busy.

One day Dragon was not well and lay in bed with a sore head. Mouse said, "I can fix that!" and went to fetch her hammer.

"No!" cried Dragon but it was too late. Mouse hit Dragon on the head with the hammer.

Dragon suddenly sat up and began to make noises like a starting car. He jumped out of bed and ran around the room, quickly opened the door and ran down the street making funny noises like he was changing gears. Mouse ran after him with the hammer calling out,

"Brake, brake, use the brake!" But Dragon only ran faster. All of a sudden he stopped and looked around. Mouse had disappeared. Then Dragon saw her tail underneath him.

"What are you doing under there?" he asked.

"I found the brake!" said Mouse.

Morale of the story:
Life without love is life without a break.

With small money in reserve we looked for an automatic teller machine. We intend to go to the station to buy tickets for our travel to Beijing by train. Right there before us, as is the way with China, is a collection of ATM machines which have submerged themselves into the deep flesh of a building, their sombre countenances peer out silent and benign like crabs in a crevasse.

The last thing I remember is seeing the end of my card come back out of its mouth and Lilly reach up to grab the card as it disappeared back into the nasty little greedy slot. To be devoured by the monster and possibly digested into a thousand tiny pieces!

Lilly panics, the card has gone. She is on the mobile phone calling loudly. Soon her brow thickens and I am told to stay on guard so others cannot use the machine or perhaps she believes the card will be miraculously regurgitated back out which it may. She quickly disappears around the corner and I am left alone to ponder and observe the sleeping machines, the long naked legs, the busy Asian eyes which never watch but always do.

Lilly soon appears with her two mobile phones clamped to both ears. Overhead a load speaker roars music into the crowd. We cannot hear each other speaking. She looks at me in distress, but I am outwardly calm. Surely with all these people there are those who will be able to help?

She has called her younger brother, Cholong, he will help, she says. My bag with books and camera and paperwork grows heavy on my shoulder. Lilly throws her bag around my neck as well.

I am a Christmas tree of sudden bankruptcy, sagging and wet, in a strange world, in a moneyless agony. She disappears talking loudly into the mobiles, unable to hear. Half an hour passes then her brother appears from the crowd with his mobile to his ear. He barely acknowledges me or her and comes up to the ATM to consider its mute and steely countenance then disappears around the corner. The ATM has numbers all over it and I write in the translating machine that the bank should be rung, they will fix it. I cannot see the letters on the translator and awkwardly reach between the bags for my glasses. After an hour of considerable distress on our part and much mobile ringing Cholong presses his mobile to my ear. At last an English voice, frail, faint and whispering.

"What has happened?" All else is inaudible, as the loud speaker above throbs and the traffic roars in the other ear. I too disappear with dangling bags and swinging, with his phone around the corner while Lilly fends off all who try to use the contented machine. Around the corner, as I discover are other ATMs and a security man who looks extremely startled. He looks me up and down with great interest. I presume Lilly has roasted him since he is so jittery. But I still cannot hear. The woman on the phone wants my every detail, birth-date, card number, address. She does not understand, so I have to repeat each letter and digit over and over again like going up and down in a very slow lift!

As I am thus engaged an armoured van pulls up and out of it spills seven men and a very small man, half the size of the others, who has a huge machine gun and an oversized helmet on. The helmet covers his eyes so much that he has to lean his head back to see. His boots seem to be intrepidly large so if he did fire the gun he would not fall over. He helps Lilly protect the ATM from users, swinging his gun around to scare any feverish attackers.

The other men in bullet-proof vests all stand with their legs spread wide to confront the imaginary army.

I repeat my words to the thin frail voice on the other end of the phone spelling out my name for the tenth time and beginning to feel intimate. The quiet wash of the glorious sun suddenly gleams through the small curious crowd which has slowed and shuffles past, now many sunny faces are watching us, centre stage. Lilly is talking to the men. She will not let them intimidate her with their manly stances and stern looks. Do all men who suddenly gain authority have swollen testicles so they have to part their legs when standing, I wonder, or is it because they are speaking to a woman? Do they know they are speaking to a female Manchurian warrior who could send them twittering with a single thrust of her thumb? I lift up my shirt to extract my passport, feeling somewhat exposed before the many eyes.

Then I see it, my card! Out it pops, blue and shining like a clear day, flashing in their hands. Its number is observed and I am asked to recite it. My passport is taken from me and they all have a look then it too disappears around the corner. Cholong takes off with it but soon returns with a photocopy.

Eventually my passport is handed back to me with my adventurous card and Lilly is laughing so much. Two friends of Cholong's were passing and stopped to help. They were most kind with their assistance. The young girl spoke three words of English, "What has happened?"

I thanked all the men who had done an efficient job, they were all heads nodding with stern aplomb and flickering smiles. They wanted me to try my card in another machine which I did but again it did not work. More hubbub and confusion between the men. The man with the machine gun immediately became agitated and began swaying again wobbling sideways, tilting back to see.

Then Cholong's friend pointed to a small sign which read "Visa" next to one of the machines. The sign has been torn off and only the "a" of "visa" remained.

Lilly is still laughing. We say goodbye to all those who have helped. I am humbled by their sincere energy of assistance. Lilly holds my hand so tightly as we mingle with the crowd.

Out in the colourful procession again and Lilly's shoe breaks as her foot twists into a small crevasse in the pavement. Fortunately she did not fall to the centre of the Earth. Our hunger strikes, another hungry hole and we look for food. As we sit at a table, by the large window peering out, I expect the people to peer in but nobody seems to look at us. Quickly however I catch the ladies looks lingering on my chin which bares the scars of Lilly's razor.

Lilly has released her grip and holds my finger, it is hard. Perhaps one day it will change into something soft. As we are sitting in the restaurant a large cardboard placard unleashes itself from the window and crashes on our table.

Luckily there is no food to be splashed on the glass. Luckily there are no men with bullet-proof vests and large machine guns looking in and we are not the centre of attention. We are like goldfish looking out. Those outside are fish and we their unexpected food.

As I eat with long pronged feelers I decide that, yes, I am a fish in a bowl for most of the food dribbles down my naked chin and drips between my legs.

Off to buy our train ticket and look for shoes. She peers up at me from the nest of her tussled hair smiling and laughing. I see the youth in her as I first saw when I looked at her picture on the website.

We are lost again, the streets grow more crowded. There are groups of people sitting on the ground, a real melee. I can see the train station above all their heads and the ticket sign which Lilly cannot see. I grab her arm and pull her through the crowd. In the large room are two thousand people all standing waiting to buy tickets. The lines are deep and I am placed at one of their ends. I cannot read the signs. Again her Chinese saves me. After several short minutes we are served. She deals the money, I cannot even do that. With tickets in our hands we negotiate the crowd and after many questions find ourselves in an arcade surrounded by shoes.

The first shop is run by a man and Lilly tries on a number of his shoes. The next shop is run by a woman and Lilly tries on some more shoes. I am quiet and the lady speaks to me as though I understand the language. Lilly makes her laugh. She tries on six pairs, walking around chatting with the lady. Then she asks me, "Okay?" and I say,

"Yes, of course. Shu-dooer how" To several pairs I say okay, not knowing which look best. Lilly says to me two hundred each.

Finally she says, "Money" and I produce three hundred yuan. The money is quickly given to the lady who accepts. The shoes are already in the bag. Now the lady is laughing or crying I cannot tell and staring at the three hundred yuan. We walk off.

"She-a-see." I say to her which means "Thank you." Lilly has three pairs of shoes for the price of one! She is like that, she makes people laugh!

We decided to catch a bus home, though I wanted to catch a taxi as we were both tired. I am plonked at the end of a long line again while she punches "toilet" into the translating machine. She disappears through the crowd and I ponder how the call of nature can bring us together and separate us so.

The line is boarding the bus and just as I am stepping aside to wait for her she appears under my arm. The bus is crowded in the late afternoon and we stand again. As it grows even more crowded I press my body close to hers and blow upon her hair. She pushes back to touch me. My hand on the railing is touching hers so softly. The bus disappears beyond the direction I thought our hotel was in.

As I look out at the tall buildings on the horizon I can see the sky-scrapers of the central business district far off, kilometres away. We travel for half an hour our bodies moving closer together, sideways rocking.

All the cars below us are a uniform grey colour from the pollution. Across the street people hold papers above their heads as large drops of rain begin to splatter across the road. The once grey cars now reveal their true colours as the rain leaves leopard spots across their highly polished black surfaces.

Eventually Lilly realises we are travelling in the wrong direction. We squeeze ourselves out of the bus and dodge the leopard cars across the dangerous road. Other buses bilge their exhaust, their black clouds consume us. Lilly covers her soft nose with the little black dot on its tip. Now in another bus we travel the opposite way and after many peak hour traffic jams we eventually step down close to our hotel.

We are thirsty, as Lilly explains by pouring imaginary water into her mouth, so we find a fruit shop close by. Now laden with watermelon, apricots, apples, giant peaches and mangoes we aim directly for the hotel.

She takes my lower leg in her paws and feels the cold.

"Not good." She shakes her head and begins to rub my leg hard. She stops and plunges more words into the translating machine.

"Collateral channels stuffed." Then she begins to give acupressure to my foot. Great searing spasms of pain sizzle up my leg. I recoil in agony as she pushes her thumbs deep into the nerves of my numbing leg. I am dissolving in her strong hands. At the end of ten minutes my whole lower leg is tingling as though asleep. I plunge some words into the translator.

"It is not dead!" Then the other leg is similarly treated. Her thumbs are arrows piercing deep into my flesh. Her palms are battering-rams which threaten to tear the muscle from the bone.

"No, no," I cry but she continues. My legs are mincemeat. My angel a monster of torture.

Gasping I lie on the bed and open one eye at her. She plunges more words into the machine.

"This cold is disease," she says. "Hot bubble bath for one year, each day." I smile at her, she has grown lustrous wings. I am happy that I cannot feel my legs. How could I not be?

She does not hug me when she leaves, she is a little late this evening, though I catch her eye a thousand times as I hobble to the door.

Today the sun shines through a blue sky, transparent and deep. The first wondrous sky I have seen in two weeks. Yesterday the wind blew all the pollution away. Now the searing light splashes on the austere faces of the buildings, shaved and smoothed to the bone. In the early dawn few people enjoy the clarity of the streets which are empty. Soon however the noise rises, billowing up from a multitude of cars, the pollution freed finally from subterranean depths within the oily ground, painfully effusing into the blue again. And from those dark fissures the manufactured monster rolls forth.

The bell across the road sings its Chinese melody. The flocks of pigeons circle it, dancing to its tune, swirling in the fast disappearing blue. A cloud froths across the window, a real cloud.

I have brought to China many DVDs. One of them on Coal Seam Gas Mining in America where large companies are drilling up to three thousand meters below the soil and fracturing the shale rock. Drilling into our Earth, our bodies. Water is pumped down into the cracks and the gas extracted as it bubbles back up.

There are trillions of tonnes of gas underground. The water people are drinking is contaminated with the gas and the water which is used to make it belch out of the ground is laced with strange chemicals. A gas-well can be fractured up to eighteen times which leaves the ground susceptible to earthquakes, the equivalent of sharp pains, kidney disease and possible bowel cancer!

Some drinking water from taps close to the mine sites is catching on fire. Do not smoke and drink or you may explode! There are thousands of wells now in operation. The gas is being exported to China.

With my small stack of DVDs I intend to go to the newspapers in Beijing and I hope to bring to the mind of the media the fact that the rest of the world is being swept up by China's huge energy consumption. Power is the name of the game. It is either dealt as force or insidiously sequestered out with the aim of subtle ownership of the human being as controlled by a central bank. Every country which has a central banking system uses and enslaves the people to make money for itself as each person becomes a product on the stock exchange, de-humanised and void of compassion.

This day Lilly greets me with her happy smile and soon finds out that my feet are cold.

She empties the garbage bin and fills it with hot water and tells me to put my feet in it which I do. I am not allowed to move. The water is hot. She has spent the morning peeling the dead skin off her own feet. She has brought a small box of metal tools and uses them to scour. She says I have a disease. And I think the only disease I have at the moment is my cold testicles which suffer from Lillyitis and have descended to my feet! Cold and foreboding they roll along the pavement as I walk, occasionally flipping over each other, bouncing.

There I sit, in the garbage bin. Strange the places one finds oneself, while stabbing the electronic interpreting machine with phrases like,

"Boiled feet for lunch" and "cooked husband" and "I will spend my life in a garbage bin of hot water just for you!"

She laughs but I am not allowed to move until my feet are bright pink and *do* feel cooked.

Next my hands and arms are forced down into the small bucket with my feet. With barely room to move I feel like a stuffed elephant suspended in a glass. She is happy now, she is cooking her husband in a plastic garbage bin! I cannot move and just sit there, bum on bed, poised, my head between my cooking knees. I sniff the air as though I am burning. After an eternity I am allowed to extract my arms. My feet she cleans with her own hands, scraping the old dead skin away, peeling them like potatoes. Eventually I am allowed to withdraw them from the water.

They come out soft and pink, unlike anything I have ever seen before, definitely not like the feet I once knew. They are at last free. I dare not move them as I fear the flesh may fall off. But not for long, I am refilled and plunged in again!

I watch them disappearing, bubbling, steaming and feeling like some special Chinese side dish, "boiled foot on leg for lunch." After sometime the water cools and I am at last able to retrieve my strange feet. Walking will never be the same again!

Now before we hug she feels my feet. She knows in her wisdom and from our anatomy lessons that it is my heart.

"Yes" I say, "It beats slowly when you are not here." Feet first I am forced under the covers of the bed fully dressed. With more than her third eye open, she watches me as she climbs in.

My heart is racing now, my hot dragon-feet seek out her toes and she flings her steel paw in my direction. It has lost its metal and relaxes like my heart. Her face rests on the pillow as though a perfect being. Its Asian contours so different from my own. Her nose is not as broad as most, the eyes not as elliptical, their smiling edges curl up like waves about to break which happens when she laughs. Her lips are full and luscious, her cheek bones high and strong. Her forehead flat and tall, she has an intuition far more advanced than most I know. In ages past she would have healed Emperors. They would have squatted, poised in buckets of hot water and dared not plead for mercy, as mercy she would not give.

The cars have all gone home, the night is old. As I burn DVDs to the newspapers and other media outlets the excitement of the day catches up with me. Most of the time has been spent in bed, rolling and caressing and massaging each other. Her hands are like steel claws when they want to be, at other times like butterfly wings.

Her sexuality is far advanced and borders on the realm of infinite wisdom. For she knows the channels and meridians lines of the body like the bottom of the sea. I feel like a fly in her ointment.

Now she lies sleeping beside me, her ownership of me complete. Her face like a perfect rose, brown and rich like a shale deposit four hundred million years old, with the wisdom of those years. She is warm and kind to me, I feel she will always be that way.

Another day dawns with the smog somewhat lifted. The sky is sliced into squared sections by the sharp buildings as the light penetrates to the pavements. The sky above is windy and a scratchy, wispy, high cloud reminds me of her pubic hair, coarse, wiry and black, from the day before.

She rolls on top of me and we peer into each other's eyes for some time. The ancient of her days comes out and joins with mine. She is the ultimate in simplicity. Beautiful beyond compare. As a younger woman she must have been chased by men. She wore high heels like the young girls of today and now has a lump at the side of the knuckle of her big toe. She wants to cut it off and makes swishing sounds with her hand like a sword. Her spine where it meets her head is still sore and she wants me to rub it hard. The side of her thigh is very sore too and she wants me to rub that as well.

I spend ages breaking my fingers at these points. Her spine is slightly kyphotic and I spend a long time explaining the calcium, vitamin D, feedback excretion system with the interpreting machine. She is confused and my words I cannot simplify. Between her skin and the sun, the shield of the mauve umbrella liquefies her bones, hence the calcium deposits next to her large toes.

She lets me rub her stomach and her flanks, her neck I kiss and her cleavage. She asks what the English words are for her anatomy and we go for a little tactile journey.

"Foreleg, fore-arm, fore-head, nose, lips, eyes, stomach, breast, and…. vagina." I feel each as I say the words.

She looks at me questioningly,

"Pushy?" she questions.

"No, vagina." I say, extending the syllables as I caress between the folds for a second time.

Her eyes asleep, her mouth tightly closed. Still she will not let me kiss her. Her tangled hair is falling out, as evidenced by the amount she leaves in the shower. It is dense, dark coarse hair, as dense as a rainforest.

Her navel floats like a great hole, high in the soft pool of her belly. I trace her hips her hidden bones and other secrets.

Beneath her pants, black hairy clouds await my touch and deeper down the great abyss of life begins to breathe. Round and round, up and down, the wheel of life moves on. And there upon the soft, soft bed my fingers in between, feel away her fear. So sweet her form beneath the summer flowers. Rocking now her body on a river moving toward a sea. With many shudders her eyes never open, her mouth tightly closed, wrapped in a smile. Her flaccid body half exposed, her breasts released like great mountains rise. Their nipples hard and round from subterranean depths reach blindly up to sniff and check the air. Round and round, my fingers up and down until her breasts thrash from side to side.

My mouth exposes their wondrous mind, beyond the normal grasp of men. I am in wonder at her ease of play for she unmoving rests. Her chest is lifting slightly, her breasts like tall buildings after an earthquake topple. I kiss her stomach round and round. My tongue it dances on its jellied skin. Then with my hands on her hips I kiss her lower down. Still unmoving, through the darkness feel as the softness of her form lights my way. Then as the ancient of my days sways in a rhythmic sea, she expands and ever more rolls on. Now rocking from the pulse, her heart is in my mouth.

I try to be gentle but her desire leads me on. I buzz her with my lips, to pick those raspberries in the early fields of spring. She rocks and shudders, again and again. The great wound has caught us both and sheds its wetness vast and warm. This is a new life for us both. She the simple mouse while I the dragon feast.

I have not told her my testicles are sore. I am committed to walking across the pedestrian crossings sideways like a true cancer-crab. She does not laugh, she does not understand.

Do most men suffer this pain of love? We are not meant to show pain, how would she know?

She will not let me kiss her lips. I know there are other agonies to await them. She sits on me not knowing of my dilemma and squashes me. She wants to feel me through my clothes.

I toss her off and cry out in pain!

She has gone again and like the wind in spring leaves me tussled and frayed.

What life is there without the joys of love? Fragmented and disturbed I rest in an ocean of desire. The perfume of love lingers in my bed, anaesthetising me to sleep.

How many oceans must a man cross in order to sate his desire? These wretched balls which have been dropped on us from heaven enslave our beings, our very minds! What dilemmas have we wrought on the universe that we should be inflicted with such pain, such toil and misery?

Lilly is here early. I usually leave the door open but this time it is closed. A tiny tap on the door reveals her smiling eyes and welcoming arms.

Today I am not forced into a tiny plastic garbage bin, head first. Instead I fashion the first hour with a tight English lesson in front of the computer. She is all "aahhs" and sighs and finds it difficult to read even the simplest of

English words. I encourage her with a little practice, soon everything will fall into place for her.

"Like driving a car." I tell her and she looks at me downcast.

"I will never learn" she says. Then I say,

"You will have to!" and she looks at me knowingly and says

"Okay." It does not take her long to master eleven steps, in and out of the computer. She will learn fast! She wanders around talking in Chinese as though I am her Chinese husband. She soon realises that I am like a foreigner, dumb and stupid to her words. She does not look worried only smiles.

In the restaurant I punch out,

"You are love and light." She smiles - beams at me and says,

"Okay."

She orders the food once again. And in the time it takes a stomach to growl a huge bowel of delicacies is put before us on a small gas stove. A chimney above the table evacuates the gases and the steam. Soon it is bubbling away and she reaches like a native for the wooden spears. Eating food in China is like attacking a wild animal with a pair of chop-sticks. With great haste and gusto the food disappears, perhaps the fastest thing a visitor to this country will ever see, certainly the most enjoyed.

Lilly launches great dollops of food across the table accurately into my tiny bowel with the sticks. Her hands are so strong and dexterous. I cast my eyes about the room and elsewhere the sticks are snapping like long claws, thrusting food into loquacious gaping holes. White wriggling mop-tendrils or oodles-of-noodles like wreathes of cosmic string disappear into black-holes. I look back at Lilly, her head stretched out and down doing the noodle-stoop, her long black hair covers the table and her bowl. From underneath, the sounds of the sea. It is the feeding time of the high tide when waves gurgle up under stones squeezing air out and burping. I attempt my own rising tide and fish a long green forest tree from my bowl. But other things come attached, now swinging like a wet acrobat at the bottom of an impossibly long and slippery rope. As it pendulums above my waist it drops and lands again right between my legs. Another and another defies being picked up. The confounded sticks like a frigid woman keep crossing their legs and spitting at me. Beside the bowl an expectant spoon glistens mockingly, beautifully clean. And the table, all about begins to flood with hapless splatters of food. Still from under the black hair before me issues merciless sucking sounds. Aghast at last the food all gone, the dragon slain, killed and poked dead with sticks, rests up the weapons of the insects, the long pointed mouth-parts or apparati. My newly shaved chin drips and drips. It is the feast of the vultures dressed up as small birds.

Lilly takes me home, my legs apart. Will anybody notice my crippled state? Then from the corner of my eye an elegant woman sends her glance my way from across the road. I quickly stand up straight. And in the legless lift I bend and kiss the real one. Her bottom round and soft her lower back so strong. I follow like a three legged mouse as she champions the corridor. But the key-card does not work so in the legless lift going down, I steal yet another kiss and smile. Back up again and I swear my head was down. So often in this country small menial tasks take so long to do like walking sideways which does seem to help.

She lies upon the bed again. Will wonders never cease? Her belly rubbed, anatomy lesson over and over again! My feet and legs are still in the lift as I kiss her neck, her breast, her quick-sand stomach which I have kneaded like soft clouds or dough above an ocean of Chinese food.

She sits on top and squashes me. This woman knows all the tricks. Soon I am down again and tell her so. She is like a small girl at times laughing. I call it "pussy" and "penis" and she smiles. But she doesn't understand the word "pussy" as I have confused her with the Latin word "vagina." As we play she makes up two little stories about them. She says,

"Pushy and penis make little person."

"P-pussy and p-penis makes p-people" I add. Then after a short time she continues,

"One and one makes three." Her face burns like a sparkling fire-cracker, she is laughing, her white teeth glistening like the sun on snow. We rub and role and entangle ourselves in each other inextricably. Again she is my childhood sweet-heart, the one I played with all those lifetimes ago.

She climbs up on to me once again and lifts her skirt above her breasts. Her nipples hang down brown and ripe like the fruits of trees, dropping and swaying in a gentle breeze. Under the slavery of torture I reach up and put one in my mouth. So soft they roll from side to side round and round. What does she like? She will not say. Her mouth is closed, I cannot kiss. Perhaps her agony is the same as mine?

I fall asleep to help relieve the torture. A deep sleep like an ice-berg with three quarters of me below. Yet the sea is boiling, frothing and fuming, draped in a dark peace. My turmoil here is that life still rules me, I do not rule life. Risen from the ashes by an angel then cast down upon the vast rolling sea by the same angel. Who likes to tease and torture and play games. It is not fair a woman does this to a man. She knows of all men that they are weak between the knees from going up and down in lifts.

The sea rolls on. There is no shore for waves to break upon. To spill their bubbles and rush back, to shed their shells of flotsam, seaweeds and corals. Instead an endless recoil of starvation and salt air while the cruel sun bleaches and dehydrates the bones.

I rise at 5:00 am, the light is sprinkling from the east. The pollution exudes a pinkish glow over the whole sunrise spectacle. The traffic noise is shut out by the window and I wonder if today I will be shut out by love. Already the inclinators are working, going up and down the tall buildings under construction. Two cranes on top of a building one kilometre away are fixing eight meter high sheets of glass on the top two floors forty stories high. As they move the glass around it occasionally catches the emerging sun and reflects a massive flash of orange light.

On the side of the building hang many movable stages. On these men cling with welders already glowing like fire-flies. The sky is blue as it was the happy day before. However yesterday several white trails from the west snaked and sliced the blue, their contents spread out over the city until visibility was severely reduced.

The nano-particles of either silver iodide, or strontium, barium, magnesium or aluminium settled on the furniture inside and on the cars and lungs of innocent people outside. And all of us went to work as the sky misted over and we did not question or complain. Asthma, respiratory and neurological conditions are becoming a symptom of this sick cloud-seeding and Solar Radiation Management technology. To say nothing of the silver affecting the thyroid gland and creating thyroid-storms as they are clinically named. America for instance is going to spray twenty million tonnes of these concoctions world-wide! To make the weather change, to *own* the weather for monetary gain. The clouds are not real anymore! There will be no sun to power the solar electricity! How many clouds to fog the mind of man? Does anybody care?

Today we catch the first train to Beijing the capitol of China. There are twenty million people there, here in Shenyang there is only eight million which was the population of Australia in 1960 when Lilly was born and I was a boy. Now China's population is static, which means it is falling. Who will inhabit these proposed two hundred and twenty story buildings which will go up in a matter of months? Such a building would be in the clouds and the upper jet-stream airs.

The cloud-seeding will be just outside their windows. The people will grow wings or bungie-jump to lunch, their bodies will hang from the noodles of their minds. Where is the future in height when the simplest shift of the Earth will break it all to pieces? And countries with the ability to manipulate the weather and plate tectonics by sending pulsed radar beams to bounce off the ionised stratosphere will have an advantage if unsureness grips the world.

So life is all about being comfortable, of having enough money and toilet paper to survive.

Well I am poor and I am ugly and I turn my back on this tall building technology. I would prefer to live in a cave. These new constructs are clothed in green shade cloth like long green phyllodes or leaves, millions of square meters of plastic, all made from oil, to dress their nudity, their adolescence, like green pyjamas or nappies to remind us of trees. Every now and again these pubescent cold grey buildings put on their long green stockings.

It is the rest of the world which has created China. For China lusts after what the rest of the world has. But China is right when they paint their buildings gold. China has everything and gives little back.

So who is spraying these skies with pollution? Who is not letting us have the energy systems Nicola Tesla, Victor Schauberger and many others invented? Who is using the propulsion technologies from the nine back-engineered alien space craft which were shot down with over the horizon lock-on radar in 1947 over Roswell, in Mexico?

We will be left on a dying planet, our hormones picked clean by the tooth-picks of Reason, by the chop-sticks, knives and forks of greed. While those who have pillaged and destroyed journey off to find other planets to further chew and destroy. Such is the greed of man. Governments tucked into small men's pockets rake the small change and rule the world.

It is not by this pen alone that love will rout these dishonest crimes against humanity.

For by doing so we become one of them. Yet even here, with all the ladies tee-shirts emblazoned with love, there is not enough compassion to go around.

Here all men are slain and thrown into dismal depths of a feminised self-abuse, many smoke tobacco. And all hide from warm sunlight and vitamin D which would otherwise make their tall bones strong, their hormones ripe. Their bones are therefore week in contrast to their tall strong buildings, their ideals. This lifestyle, though the food is good, will chew up and inhibit their endocrine systems. For sunlight is the engine of love which is now frustrated by the clothes of seeded cloud. Soon the plants will hide their photosynthetic engines embarrassed to wave their flags, to flout their organs of procreation.

Back home in the bunker of my imagination I hold the flaming torch of Lilly and Ian, the Mouse and the Dragon and write a short story about how love is the technology of the universe, broad and sharp the words flow out beyond the measure of a smile.

For a Long Time

Mouse and Dragon were getting on in years and even though they had a micro-wave oven, a television set, nine radios, ten watches, a modern car and four mobile phones they always felt they needed something else to keep up with the rest of the world. So Dragon bought a computer. Mouse was the first to use it and she downloaded lots of recipes from the internet. Dragon began to make movies and talk to people in foreign countries using all the internet translating services.

With all this extra knowledge Dragon began to think he knew everything because he could find all the information he required on the computer.

Then one day he saw something which truly changed his life. He found a website which had lots of information about a special secret which has been kept from everybody for a long time. All the world governments know about it but they do not tell the people because the governments are owned by big businesses and they need to make money from us somehow. Mouse was very interested to hear about this secret too. So they began to tell their friends and send information all over the world.

Mouse would have tea parties and invite all the neighbours over. Soon everybody was talking about it and wondering why they were all still poor and had to pay lots of money to all sorts of businesses just to survive.

Mouse and Dragon thought of a plan. They would stand for government and see if they could change the world and let everybody benefit from this big secret. The secret was very easy to make and they began to gather information about how to make one and use it so they could help small farmers and simple people like themselves.

Every night they would go into their garage and tinker away. Mouse with her magic hammer and Dragon with his inventive mind. They did not tell anybody at all, it was their secret. Meanwhile they stood for parliament and went to talk to people all over the country. Mouse would drive and then at night they would come home and work on their special engine.

Oops, now you know what they were building. Yes it was a special anti-gravity time machine. One they hoped would take them to visit people in other galaxies for that is the big secret, that we are not alone and that we are a mixture of many different minds from all over the universe. Our ancestors came from the stars.

Dragon bought lots of wire and big lumps of metal which he breathed on and melted into fine shapes and Mouse would tap them with her hammer and the machine began to move.

One day Mouse and Dragon invited all the newspapers, television stations and film companies to see their machine. It was a grand affair and they both dressed up for the occasion.

Everybody came. There were bus-loads of reporters and camera men. Then Mouse and Dragon lifted up their garage door and revealed their flying-saucer. There was a gasp from the crowd and Dragon stepped forward in what looked like his pyjamas to give a speech.

"This is an anti-gravity time-machine" he said. "It is capable of sub-luminal speeds and this is the answer to our future here on planet earth. For with these devices we do not need to spend money on petrol cars and silly air polluting aeroplanes, or coal for electricity. All our energy will be free." The people stood absolutely still and quiet. Dragon continued, "Mouse and I are going to be away for three days and when we return we will bring you gifts from the stars."

The people cheered, the cameras rolled there was great excitement. Mouse and Dragon held hands and went inside their machine. Dragon sat in his special chair and began to think about where he wanted to go because that was how the craft was steered, with the mind.

"We will go to Mouse-land first" he said looking at Mouse.

"Oh no!" said Mouse, "Let's go to Dragon-land."

"No," said Dragon. "You know my favourite fruit is a mango, they don't make women-goes so mangoes where woman goes... to Mouse-land." And with that Mouse banged the table with her hammer and the flying-saucer disappeared!

The garage was instantly empty. All the people stood back speechless. Then one man stepped forward and said to the crowd.

"This is a terrible thing, we must not let the world know about this, only the rich will make these flying machines and all the poor people will be left on the Earth to perish!"

Mouse and Dragon flew through the stars until they reached Mouse-land. They stepped out and were greeted by a beautiful Mouse lady who shook Mouse's hand and said,

"Welcome, we knew you were coming, we have been watching you for thousands of years." Mouse and Dragon had a thoroughly good time in Mouse-land and were given lots of little hammers to take back to Earth.

After what seemed like an eternity they said farewell and took off for Dragon-land and exactly the same thing happened there. A friendly Dragon gave them lots of little hammers to take back to Earth.

In no time at all it seemed, they were back on Earth, back in their garage. Mouse stepped out first and was greeted by a military person who ordered her into a car. Dragon too was stopped and ordered into another car. They were both driven off into the night in different directions. Dragon was very worried about Mouse and Mouse was worried about Dragon.

The military people warned Dragon about making any more flying machines and the same was said to Mouse. The military people then took all their little hammers and said that if they made any more flying machines they would have to separate Mouse from Dragon and send Dragon away to live somewhere else. Dragon said he only wanted to live with Mouse as that was the most important thing in his life and he would ask Mouse not to build any more flying machines.

Mouse was asked exactly the same questions and gave exactly the same answers.

The military then drove them home again.

Several moments later a big truck came and took their flying machine away and they never saw it again. Dragon looked at Mouse and gave her a big hug.

"You are my flying machine!" he said.

Morale of the story:
We can go anywhere any time with love.

I have seen only three pregnant ladies. In all the thousands I have passed, only three.

A small wide eyed child in the restaurant chops into a huge steak with knife and fork.

Her mother chats with Lilly and I hear the word "Australia." Lilly orders meat, her eye-teeth are pointed like a tigers and she grips the knife like a dagger. Her mouth opens as she masticates, belches and farts and spits like any normal human being, though not in the restaurant.

At the end of the meal the young girl whose eyes I catch watching me, comes close and whispers in my ear in impeccable English.

"I hope you have a very happy time in China and a very nice day." Lilly nods and smiles at me. How much do these people know?

In the street far below a man is calling. Over and over again the same words. Is it a prayer or a song? Whatever it is contributes to the general roar of noise.

Why is it that pollution of the environment goes with noise pollution and perhaps even pollution of the mind?

The world spins and my own mind looks out on the Weather Engineering of yesterday which has today come down low as thick as mud to haunt us, penetrate our skin, our lungs our eyes, silently. They make us subservient to the great wheel of life, to accept its juggernaut of Reason which this modern world espouses to the core.

"See this pollution?" I say to her punching out the words in the machine. "It will kill everybody in China."

She nods of course and nits her brow into little polluted runlets of erosion, erosive, ardent and mischievous, my demanding little mouse. And I muse about the purity of the water which has made those furrows so deep.

Lost in the Smog of Beijing

Lilly arrives with a wonderful smile and a great big hug. We exchange hand signals about time and booking out of the hotel. We work out that there is plenty of time so she jumps into bed.

She demands I get in with her. How can I refuse? I am soon breathing hot air between her breasts. Tossing her ear-lobes around and fondling her skin. She closes her eyes in ecstasy and a young delightful smile flickers across her face. We are united once again. Soon I cannot resist and am on top of her. She spreads her legs wide and says,

"Hard," to which I reply, "soft."

There are many things in the world but nothing can compare to the love of a woman.

There are four ways to reach enlightenment, through the three different types of meditation and through the love of a woman. There is a knock on the door and we are disturbed from our devotions by a little green lady.

We are ready to go. Her bag is twice her size. I bend low to kiss her in the lift as we descend for the last time and I notice her nipples are raised up like the beautiful buds of ripening fruit trees in spring. And I wonder where next my own body will lead me. Like a pet animal the Earth has tied me to a string or a long rope which one day may garot me. To rot in my own furrows and be covered - washed by her waters so pure.

We book out of the hotel and head for the restaurant.

Lilly orders duck or some sort of large bird and it arrives all cut up and arranged in the shape it once enjoyed as a living creature. We both devour some, dipping it in a rich hot sesame seed sauce. Outside in the street it is hot and men parade around with their tee-shirts rolled up above their bellies, some like fat geese. This exhibitionism may be an extension of the meal. For we "think with our stomachs" as the German philosopher Gurter observed. I think Gurter may have been a well fed person, who grew up with an aunt who baked giant loaves of hot bread. Or maybe he was a Chinese peasant reborn, who grew up on a wealth of rice, corn and duck? Certainly the stomach is an organ of pleasure much like the mind. It is the eye of a being which walks. In it is the mind and the fuel combined, below which sleeps the unborn and if all is well, above sprouts the imagination - more so if one is well fed.

Our meal finished, we negotiate the slow stream of traffic, the swarms at the traffic-lights, two armies approaching ducking and side stepping. Lilly says she wants to catch a lunging bus with the bags but I insist on a cab. The whistles of the policemen still shrill as we collect our giant bags and jam into a taxi like a couple of squashed ducks to resume our foetal positions in the back on our way to the railway station.

After staring at the notice board for some time, she disappears and leaves me to mind the mountains of bags. Out of the crowd she is running and laughing. She hastily grabs my huge bag and lifts me onto her shoulder with the other arm and begins charging through the crowd, throwing glances my way to assure herself I am her kite in tow following in a wind.

She commandeers a cab, even though it has somebody else in it and we are off on an adventure. Yes we were at the wrong station! The young driver chats with her and soon begins to laugh. She is infectious; she makes everybody laugh, her smile is a million years old. I don't know what she says but I smile her smile from ear to ear.

The railway station is immense and thousands of people beneath its huge roof await the arrival of their mechanical chargers. Lilly again asks directions and is soon at the front of a three hundred person queue. She talks to all the people around her even a little boy who has a rag-monkey in his hands. He looks up for she and I are having an English lesson about monkeys. As I look around nobody looks at me but when I turn away all eyes are on us. Lilly is free at last and expressing her love.

As we travel we ask people to photograph us for immigration purposes, so the government can see how well we belong together. Now in front of the queue we stand to be judged and shot before the crowd.

She is so happy and holds my hand so tightly.

The train is long and white and shaped like a large worm. It travels at a terrible velocity I am told. Now as I write I am within its stomach with one hundred other people per carriage.

Flying through the flat green fields of Northern China.

Rice paddies, all squared and beautifully groomed, flick by. Acres and acres of deep green corn raise their ragged heads to cleaner air. For it is a great relief to escape the pollution of Shenyang. Yet we will never escape the contrived order of China, or the weather changing aspirations of the government which aggressively binds agriculture and the people to the economic environment.

In this broad and sweeping country every small particle of lint has been reared from the ash of a once great forest. Now with so many people to feed they have to cultivate every square centimetre. And on each millimetre grows something of use which is nurtured and spoilt like a small child.

The larger the stomach the bigger the pocket and supposedly prettier the view.

Lakes, dams and pools of water have pumps operating in them to aerate their brown and grey interiors. These aquaculture farms are run on electricity all year round.

Unlike India with ox carts and the occasional tractor, all I see is bitumen roads and expensive cars. Most of the buildings are precise and dusted. Even the ticket collector is so well dressed with not a stitch of clothing loose or worn. A hole in a sock can bring on a heart attack and is a big worry. Lilly inspects some blood stains on my pants from Australia, friendly mosquitoes I say and she pouts her bottom lip.

Sometimes I am dressed in torn jeans and thongs, my crinkly old shirt, hand-washed to save money. My beard now gone must have shocked them. It is none of their business what I wear. Everybody here is united and clean whereas in the West the individual is lauded though the authorities are clamping down on free speech while preaching democracy. Here in China I will call out loud. It is not my wish to be a stomach-bug which makes them ill. That is not my agenda. Though I do feel at home here in their alimentary canal. Wandering their intestines and trying to access their blood like a friendly bacterium. We can help each other on this planet. Why must we all compete?

Lilly rests her head on my shoulder and sleeps. She holds my hand and I punch into the translator,

"I am thinking of you every minute," and she writes back,

"You are in my dreams." She asks what I am writing and I say,

"I am writing about our dream, you and me."

The Yellow Room

Beijing railway station and long lines of people. Traffic police direct the masses, ordering them into their little protected mind spaces. Coloured lights bring one back to the electric universe so far away. Yet this is real. We are bundled into a waiting cab the driver of which is shielded on four sides by transparent screens. Trapped is he, coughing or dying slowly with nowhere to spit. The Western music he listens to is reminiscent of the English Death March.

Coloured lights fly through the air up and down, reflecting off the huge glass facades of tall buildings. They fizz and disappear amongst the flitting crowd. Some of the people brightly dressed like coloured butterflies fly by on dangerously silent electric motor-scooters.

The hotel we are in has a Spitz dog in the foyer. It comes to me and rubs its nose on my pants. Our room is yellow the colour of daffodils and so full of furniture we can hardly move.

The double bed is the largest flat space.

Outside in the lane-way the smell of stale urine assails us, reminding me of India.

That smell was not just here and there it was everywhere. Further down the road people are roasting meat on barbecues in the street. Clouds of smoke fill the alley-way and smell like urine-basted bodies. I feel at home amongst the movement and the dross, it seems to me more real than spectacles, shoes and clothes. Perhaps I am a primitive and still in my cave, never to mature into a greedy self-seeking megalomaniac, determined to extract one's wealth from the bosom of the Earth.

Lilly is tired, the wine of the day gone to her head. The English lesson on the train was a trial for her and she is relieved to escape her chores in Shenyang. This is the first holiday for her in twenty five years! She has worked so hard. Her sweet nature deserves a free world where love flows unencumbered and no family looks over her shoulder and ties her to the grind-stone.

In the restaurant a small turtle is kept in a square glass container hardly larger than itself.

It struggles to get out. I feel for it so much. I have not fed it, I do not know it, yet its poor frail existence is of great concern to me. I want to rescue it, take it to a pool and let it go. It is dying, I can feel it. At the moment it carries the weight of all China.

After the train trip we are both tired and over excited about being away from Shenyang and finally on our own. Her family not expecting her at 9:30 pm to arrive safe and sound and not spend the night with me. In the train she looks tired and wan. Her age bearing down upon her old frozen leg. She looks at me sideways and her face illuminates with a childlike joy.

We shower separately and she emerges fully clad with a pink top on and pyjama pants.

My hands upon her are fast and too keen and soon, after some furtive grasps, we both let sleep wend its way to our dream-time.

Lilly sleeps with her open palms next to her ears, grunting and whimpering like a little pig.

She rests unmoving, dead to the world. While I am tormented by my aim, spurred on by the unrelenting passion of needing to give, to express, such as a woman may feel with a feeding child.

She wakes me on sunrise, so romantically with a loud bang nearly blasting me out of bed and jostles my body to attention. She is up and in the bathroom. She has a shower and comes to the bed with a towel wrapped around her. She is a small woman now. In her photographs she wore high healed shoes, a black and white striped dress and a beautiful smile. Now she can be downcast and thoughtful, her eyes penetrating a distance.

She was married thirteen years ago to a man who left her for a newer younger woman. She remembers her pain. Sometimes for many years people turn it over and over again and again until the field is flat and green, the distance less far.

I pull her down into the bed and under the covers. The towel falls away and reveals her little brown body. Her face drifts back to the dream-time as I kiss her hands, her arms and her cheeks. Her nipples have risen again like mushrooms springing from the ground.

Her stomach moves and ripples outwards from her navel at the centre of its pool. I stroke this female form born and gifted to Earth from the stars. There she lies warm and inviting, how can I refuse? The hair of her love is coarse and wiry but soon relents and gives way to my softness. Her vagina or pussy as we call it with some humour, is folding back and puffing out like some creature in a sea pool.

She smells like a Chinese restaurant, every dish on the menu rolled into one. The river of life has slowed, the surface draws itself on and down. I feel the waterfall approaching and hear its roar. I grip her tight to save her heart and roll her top-side up so she may breathe as over the waterfall we tumble and fall. Gently as I raise her hips and slowly merge, a cry of pain spills from her lips!

Her head thrown back and whispering. She is small and tight. I will not hurt her in our moment of intimacy. She reaches for the translator and quickly writes,

"Pain!" I rest my frown on her forehead, our troubles glued, for a little while then throw myself off her. She types again, "Sex - pain!" We rest in each other's arms silent and hardly breathing. My mind between her legs like a crumpled flower or letter on the floor, dry, shrivelled and unread.

The day throws itself at us like a mad raging bull. Beijing is a massive city. With sky scrapers twisted into profound fungal shapes. The glass facades defying shadow and three-dimensional space. Their long necks peering down from impossible heights, watching cautiously as the cranes on the smaller buildings below threaten to gain a better view.

We visit a book publisher and he sits in his smoky room and calls to his minions. I read the story of the "picture" books I have brought of my mother's. They are not interested. The room is full of pollution. In a low and cancerous throat he says the stories have nothing to teach. That they do not say anything and that his publishing company prints cartoon books for adults only.

The traditions are strong, with not much imagination for the new. To expect a child to learn all the time takes away half their freedom of thought, their inventiveness and enterprise, their intrinsic love of life corralled into submission.

"A child's delight is worth a thousand words. Take a chance." I said, and add, "A child must love to learn, must be happy to remember." It is not for me to say however, how can we expect to touch the imagination of a child when we as adults hide behind smoke-screens of conformity?

We are entertained to lunch, to feast on the salty food of Southern China. The manageress, Eve, is a gracious soul who can speak reasonable English. She liked me reading the stories.

I give her two DVDs and she is overjoyed. One on the Crop Circles which are unexplained phenomena occurring world-wide with very little media attention. The other is on the secrets of the United States military and reveals some of the propulsion systems used by the alien craft and opens a window on the electrical nature of the universe. It includes the dynamics of time travel which is a reality and simply another dimension of electricity. This information has been around since the 1950's. And I ask where do we go to now? Which planets are we on and why do they treat us and the Earth with such banal hatred? The placid, humble Eve with the DVDs is in for a surprise! Perhaps she will make a comic book from all the information - for adults only.

I will always feel as though this new information is being suppressed by the many governments of the world. Not specifically China but all the world, especially in the West where the people are kept under close scrutiny by the authorities as though we are their children who have discovered matches and may learn about the fires of the imagination and possibly burn the house down.

We must be closely observed, controlled and monitored for our own good. Our new ideas are snatched from us, used for their schemes and often turned against us. Governments dumb us into sheep which they do not fear for they are dinosaurs themselves. We believe they hoist us up on poles to appease the fates but I believe we climb up there unwittingly ourselves.

We wander home, side stepping the hot gutters. The world has too much learning and not enough feeling. We discuss the best things to teach a child and beyond sharing and love what else is there to know? Back home in the bunker of my thoughts I thread a small story of our growing love.

It is meant for children young and adventurous who are half Chinese, half Australian.

Who are born half dragon and half mouse with tails which intertwine. Stamped on his/her forehead where the third eye is, are the words, "Love not Teach" or "Teach not Love" something like that!

Mouse and Dragon

Mouse lived in a little house next to a river and grew potatoes for a living. Dragon moved in next door and began fishing in the river. Mouse thought Dragon was destructive because he caught all the big fish in the river, even though Mouse thought he was handsome. Dragon thought Mouse was destructive because she dug up the river bank and disturbed the soil too much, even though she had a lovely long tail and nice long whiskers.

Then came a big drought and no potatoes grew and fish were scarce. After the drought it rained very hard and both their houses were washed downstream and Dragon's fire was put out.

There were no potatoes and no fish! Mouse and Dragon were lost in the forest and they were very hungry. They both wandered about looking for food. Then by chance they suddenly met and began to talk. Mouse thought Dragon was very nice because he wanted to share the only fish he caught with her. Dragon thought Mouse was very kind because she found one wild potato and wanted to share it with him. But they could not cook the food so Mouse lit Dragon's fire.

From then on they became very friendly neighbours and Dragon only caught medium sized fish because he had so many potatoes to eat and Mouse did not dig up the ground so much as she had so many fish to eat.

Eventually they built a large house together and were married and lived happily ever after.

Moral of the story:
When we share our treasures we become rich.

We travel to the Australian Embassy by air-conditioned taxi. The cool of the car is a welcome relief. Beijing is hot and has a stagnant air. After passing a strict security check, we are met by an endearing cultural exchange attaché who was born on the Central Coast of Australia, who speaks fluent English. The building is austere in the square-grey tradition of the Chinese brick and cold from all the air-conditioning. She explains to me the budget in relation to Cultural Affairs and the imagination. Again art is the opposite of guns and money. Without art we will lose the power of love. What is the use of fighting, or spending money if we cannot protect art? Lilly falls asleep while we are talking, she does not understand English and begins to float out the window on a cloud.

With various addresses in our pockets we venture out again into the world of Beijing.

Tall buildings rise above the smog like mountains which capture brown cloud. As we drive the taxi freeway I feel like an ant reborn from thousands and millions of years ago who now walks and dresses like a human being or like a dinosaur now clothed in another new skin.

After a long day of lifts and stairs, taxis and being lost, we climb the last few floors to our yellow room. Surrounded by the noise of building and air-conditioners, horns in the distance and the flutter of electric birds with eyes of flashing lights, staring and watching. There is no peace in Beijing only the quiet space between her legs and nobody has invaded that space for fifteen years.

Lilly is small her pain intense. There is a life in there tucked away in the dark.

A life so desperate to escape, to find expression. Like an artist who has no paint, who draws with clay on the walls of caves. We exchange words on the electric machine about what we do and how to do it.

"Gentle," and "soft," and "no, I am not too big," and "no, you are not too small, just right,"

and "with love the door will open." Desperately I seek to alleviate my frustration and my pain which I now share with her.

We spend hours in the night finding the youth we lost long ago and in the morning she forces me in deep and cries out in pain. She sits up to see how much of me is inside!

It is hard to explain to a woman who has been so hurt in love that to over-eat is to substitute ones sexuality for food. That the pressure of the food forces itself down upon ones sexual freedom until the door closes entirely, the cervix is pushed down and can open the wrong way like a train in a tunnel running backwards.

She lies sleeping, no secrets do we withhold, no tied up anxieties about secret lovers lurking in the concrete jungle. Suddenly the Chinese National Anthem makes us stand rigid to attention as Lilly's phone rings shattering the silence into small regimented frozen squares.

It is a male's voice at the other end. My toes begin to curl and I have visions of Chinese men lurking in the lifts. It turns out to be her mother who feels concern for her daughter's well-being. Underneath, Lilly is similarly concerned about me for she catches my furtive glances at the young girls who stand on high-rise shoes far above the smog to view the forbidden fruits of life or gape at the giant testicles of God.

Mouse and Dragon Go Fishing

Early one morning Mouse and Dragon were sitting on the river bank fishing and watching the water slowly swirling by. All of a sudden a huge fish jumped out of the water and gobbled up Mouse!

Dragon dived into the water and chased fish into the depths of the deepest pool. He caught fish and punched him in the nose and out popped Mouse into Dragon's arms. Dragon quickly took Mouse to the river bank and told her to light a big fire. Mouse ran to find some wood. Dragon dived down again to find fish. Fish was angry with Dragon and tried to bite his tail. Dragon kept punching fish in the nose till fishes nose became so swollen he could not see where he was going. Then with a big push Dragon threw fish out of the water and into the fire.

Later that day Mouse and Dragon had full tummies and sat on the river bank hand in hand and watched the water slowly swirling by.

Moral of the story:
When you have something you love hold on to it tightly.

Beijing roars like a dragon on heat. The noise issues from everywhere as if some slippery stream of poison has been broken and released from the people's innocence. From youth to age the mill of time takes in the pain until the door is tightly closed. Through innocents we all wander like lambs with our eyes closed. The government will keep Lilly and me from each other for nine months maybe longer!

That will be an eternity! Perhaps there can be no pleasure without pain like the cover of an exciting book which, once closed and read, brings us to tears.

A wispy insect chirrups in the afternoon. Only the one who calls in vain. Its mate was buried seven years ago in the small park across the busy road opposite. There she wept and withered away for the road was suddenly too dangerous to cross. The pedestrian over-pass was not built then.

Now this city strives for world recognition though it is the world which must recognise China, whose young women hold the balance of a pregnant power. Pendulous their hips sway beneath their fulcrum chests, their delicate arms balancing like the measurer's scales of fortune.

Lilly sleeps, her snoring is breakfast-wrapping her stomach in fields of soliloquy.

This morning, as always, she woke me with a loud fart and a chuckle in bed. I have never been woken like that before! She complains of pain in her uterus and asks me if I have an infection. I reply that I would not do that to her. She lies on the bed in pain.

"To hard sex?" I ask and add, "Sex is the language of love." She says she wants to have a girl baby with me after we are married. She is fifty two years old, she will be fifty three when she does.

I look at her for a long time and she looks at me with a half-smile. We make love endlessly, the young curious child in us. We shower together where she squats to pee.

During breakfast I spill my rice bowl, it floods across the table like a thousand pulled teeth. Everybody laughs hysterically, white teeth are everywhere, it is not funny, the dog comes in and wipes its nose again on my pants. After more rice, salted cabbage leaves and a boiled egg we go back to the room to wash our mundane clothes by hand.

Today we are off to the largest newspaper in Beijing. I want to show the editor the Crop Circles and Coal Seam Gas Mining DVDs. As well as another on Weather Engineering which is interlinked with the ambitions of the New World Order and another DVDs on Orbs which are a newly found electrical phenomena involving what people believe are living entities. There is so much information and dare I invade the protocol of another government? Well, yes, I believe I have every right to bring new knowledge about our world in a small effort to unlock the gates of peace and bring us all closer together. Everybody wants us to share the same Earth and respect each person's right to enjoy love and peace without interference from a higher authority which locks up secrets, important knowledge which could benefit humanity and directly affect the well-being of the planet.

Lilly and I can communicate beyond the mechanics of simple language using electronic devices. It sounds cold protocol but it is distinctly the opposite. If the entire world communicated about their secret power systems and utilities, like Lilly and I, we would all come down to Earth and share the same exciting future.

The newspaper precinct has security cameras at every point; it is the same all over China.

The government is afraid of its people just like any other country and believes the population reacts like juveniles and must be told what to do. I am not allowed to see the editor without prior arrangement however the DVDs are placed in a sealed bag with assurances from the girls at reception that they will be delivered. Little do they realise it may be their own baby in the bag which they possibly intend to disregard and throw away. The crime is in not wanting to learn.

Far beyond the security of the cloistered flame, the controlled order, I stare into the distance down the many arms of those who would block this information from the world. And now the flame is bright and lustrous, my itching palm does not seek reward, I have no sword, I do not threaten. See this hand is empty the other holds Lilly innocent and almost free.

The electric rumble of the air-conditioning machines pervades the smallest space. Only the loud blast of horn and squeaky insect can mount any kind of acoustic challenge. The cicadas mimic the noise of the day for it is hot and a few more have climbed the welcoming trees.

The background roar of the city gives way to the passionate scream of a child which issues from some modern children's toy as it is pushed along the pavement. A piercing scream foetal and primeval. My heart also screams as the toy is allowed more humanity than the child.

People's thumbs gyrate around mobile phones, their ringing brings the insects to their ears.

The blood red sun again sinks into the Beijing sunset spilling over like red wine at a feast of plenty, its face has been hidden, a translucent silver ball behind curtains of smog all day.

This is the concrete jungle, the land of the rising dream.

We walk and we walk, then we walk back the same way we came, lost again. At night we see a film, past the tall treed streets of Beijing and into an open square. Our way is followed by inelegant sculptures, round fat figures either looking up, delving the distance or expressing actions reminiscent of some martial art - red faced and happy. They comment more on social structure rather than any expression from the individual artist.

The film is about China and the difference between a demon and a human being.

The only difference is that one has a heart and the other eats hearts to survive. China has a heart, it is on the street crawling and earning money. From the bicycle-stall full of fruit to the large shop-front windows and revolving doors which flap like butterflies wings, rotating to try and squash the buyers hearts before they enter and squeeze them of their cash like an unweary cockroach, jammed.

Lilly wraps her early morning legs around me. She wants me to rub her stomach and as I do she relaxes on her back and bites her bottom lip. There is still pain but I am forced in deep again. She will not let me go. There is no end of her love for me, I can see it in her eyes and feel it in the language of her sex. She is like a young girl who learns for the first time about herself and her man, eager to explore. What would the Chinese say if they ever read this? Her family would ostracise her, she says she would lose face. As we walk the streets she is somewhat aloof from me, her hand often just a flap of skin. But when at home she is a laughing child, a revolving door which snaps and grabs, with very lively hands.

I blow raspberries in her navel and turn her over again and again. But she is strong and I obey. I place her in front of me between my legs with her facing the other way, biting her ear and kissing her neck. I bring my fingers down upon her, within her softness up and down. She is smiling now and pushes me backwards, her mouth wide with glistening teeth.

She is as happy as a woman can be and wants me more and more. A woman's passion is more than a man's. Once aroused they can explore and climb great heights. A man must withhold himself sometimes for days so she can enjoy the ride. The great climax or the orgasm of the West is nothing more than a revolving door for once it is fully open it can only close again. It is far better for the man to only half open the door and wait patiently for the rising storm and rain before opening it fully for the flood of happiness to enter.

The woman can learn how to help the man with this, so long as there is dialogue, the great wheel will turn. With every good marriage comes a length of foreplay. The longer the better for love is the crown of concern and marriage the easing of the worry. Before us is the wonder of the opening door and within are many flowers. The scent brings the insects which act as marriage celebrants to join male and female beneath a dome of petalled light.

As masseuses by trade there is great force in her play and I have to explain that I will go away by degrees of pressure. In the night her eyes are suddenly alive. She will always be young to me. She sleeps as I write and stares with her dreams wrapped in my thoughts, far out into my space.

She is my servant and my pet, my princess and my demanding queen. Her snoring stops and she watches me sideways. Her young body is small, hairless, with skin as soft as early morning sunlight. Now sitting up in bed, her fallen nipples no longer ramparts to castles, droop and sway like pieces of pendulous bark.

We spend the night in coiled bliss and in the morning discuss the nights' pleasures and new experiences. The English anatomy lesson is aimed at exploring love and marriage.

The contract and relax, a prelude to love. The ancient electrical ties we have, give us the power to control, to jettison us into the many galaxies beyond.

We are already married, we have been married Lilly and I for thousands of years.

I can see in her eyes that we have known each other from the earliest beginnings of time.

Her leg is sore. I am engaged in therapeutic massage twenty four seven. She is demanding and I plunge into the translator.

"You are a demanding patient, you tell the doctor what to do all the time." She takes a while to decipher it then smiles and laughs like a little girl. "Not funny" I am thinking and write,

"Doctors arms fall off." Well the smile and the laughter. She is a happy person.

I say we have to cut her leg off and she thinks that is so funny.

Mouse and Dragon Bake a Cake

One rainy day Mouse and Dragon decided to bake a cake in their wood oven. Dragon went outside in the cold and collected some wood and Mouse explored some recipe books to make a special cake.

She found a lemon cake recipe for she knew Dragon liked lemon cakes.

Dragon found lots of wood and they decided to make two cakes instead of one. Then Mouse found she had lots of flour so they decided to make three cakes instead of two. Dragon said four was an even number for two people so they decided to make four cakes instead of one.

Dragon started the fire and Mouse began the mixing. She added butter, eggs and honey and so many other things she lost count and forgot what she had put in which cake and was very confused.

She asked Dragon to taste the mix and he nearly ate it all! So she thought it was alright but then she added a little bit of this and that just to make sure! Dragon lit a big fire for four big cakes and Mouse had to get him to mix the ingredients because there was so much of it.

They were having such a good time and they kept thinking about how each of the four cakes would taste! When the fire was just right Mouse put the cakes in the oven.

Then it started raining very hard. It was so loud on the roof. Dragon looked outside and saw a lot of water everywhere. He decided to go outside to check the drains around the house. Mouse stayed inside to watch the fire.

It wasn't long before Dragon came rushing back saying there was so much water he was going to have to dig an extra drain. He disappeared and Mouse watched the fire. Dragon came back again and said that the rain was going to wash the vegetable garden away and could Mouse come and help? Mouse put on her raincoat and rain hat and went outside. Dragon was in the garden digging furiously but then he stopped and was looking at something on the ground. He had found an absolutely huge worm.

"Look at this!" he called to Mouse who sloshed over to him. Mouse was used to Dragon finding things in the garden. Dragon put the worm up out of the water so it would not drown.

They both began to dig and dig, the water was strong and was washing their soil away. Soon their drain had collected all the water and their garden was safe. When they went back inside the smell of the cakes cooking was beautiful and they dried themselves and sat down by the fire to get warm. Presently there was a knock at the front door so Dragon went and opened it.

All at once four big watermelons and a great wall of water raced into the room! The watermelons bobbed and rolled across the floor and nearly washed Mouse away. The water quickly filled the house and Dragon grabbed Mouse and put her up on the table.

Next all their vegetable plants came flooding in through the door! First came eight more big watermelons then all Mouse's cabbages, then two more watermelons, lots of corn and all their carrots. The room began to look like their vegetable patch and Dragon's entire watermelon patch was floating in their living room!

He waded to the back door, opened it and a lot of the water escaped and left all the vegetables on the floor.

"Oh!" said Mouse remembering the cakes so Dragon sloshed over to the oven through their vegetable patch. He opened the oven door and there they were, all beautifully cooked and smelling delicious. He reached in and burnt his fingers but eventually managed to carry them over to Mouse one by one.

While the water was still flowing strongly through the house they stood on the table and ate all the cakes one, two, three and four. Dragon looked at Mouse who was now two times larger than she normally was and rubbed his own tummy.

"You are such a good cook!" he said.

He jumped down into the water again and disappeared outside. Mouse could see him digging a drain in the rain. A few capsicums bobbed in and floated by and then lots of potatoes and mud.

Soon the river stopped and Dragon came back with more fire wood.

It took them a long time to clean all the dirt out of the house and they made a large pile of their vegetables which they would replant when the rain stopped.

They both sat down in front of the fire to get warm and dry. Dragon looked at Mouse who was half asleep. He put his hand in his pocket and was surprised to find something cold and wet inside. He put his hand in again and pulled out the great big long worm.

Mouse thought that was very funny!

Morale of the story:
For the warmth of love to endure never put your hands in your pockets.

Lilly sits on the edge of the bed half naked. Her brown wooden nipples popping out from their wonderfully fleshy little hills. She looks down at them and says in perfect English

"Bigger" then points to me.

"Yes." I say, knowing that I have made them so. Perhaps she is feeling fulfilled at last as a woman, this young bodied Chinese lady of fifty two with a Western man. But as I keep telling her I know her face from thousands of years ago.

She takes my hand and squeezes it in several places then pokes my shoulder saying, "Hurt?" Then several other places around my shoulders. From the hard muscles in my hands she knows my shoulders are sore and presses in the exact place.

Her fingers begin to dig in deep and work down my arm. She shows me how to massage with all her force. Pushing her thumbs into my flesh as though my muscles were a custard tart. From my shoulders to my hands, then suddenly to my toes where she hits painful pressure points immediately sending spears of pain into my spine. She stops only after I grasp her claws from me and hold them tightly. She bites her bottom lip and glares at me sideways. Next she stamps in the translating machine.

"Lungs stuffed, generally body in bad shape."

Still reeling with pain, cramped up like a ball, I uncover my face. Has she discovered my agony? Will she consider me an old defunct body ready for the trash heap? I am silent as I lick my old surfing wounds.

The day is hot, the roar of the air-conditioning machines blocks the sound of the chickens in the small garden below our window. They freely roam the back streets of the inner city and lay their eggs in motor-cycle side-bags and under taxis. In front of our hotel are huge buildings, sky-scrapers which reach way up into the muddy sky. Our small hotel is dwarfed by their shadow of wealth and pride.

We eat the food of the people, the eggs, the rice, the salted cabbage, the fruit and noodles. Lilly's breasts are like noodles which have to be sucked up, my fingers like chop-sticks, crossing. As we walk the streets, under the mauve umbrella, I can see and feel in her the pride of being a woman once again.

Beijing barely sees the sun because of the pollution and when it does come out it is a vast raw silver ball so far away yet seems only just above the smog. Many of the older people are bent over from too much calcium in their diet and not enough sunlight. Twenty minutes a day is all one needs, on breast or bottom, arm or leg.

In the brittle heat the sky is blue but soon the gashes and scars of white chemtrails appear from the civilian aircraft which try to make rain. Lilly disappears into a small shop and buys sweets, plastic wrapped. She shows them to me and I say okay. Every small amount of money she can save she does. She bargains with everybody and is horrified when the hotel attendant tries to charge us twenty yuan for dirtying a small towel which he has to wash. Lilly washes it defiantly by hand.

We catch a crowded bus and halfway down the street she opens her sweet packages and draws out something white, takes a bite and hands it to me. I take a bite and with my eyes, not so good, there comes into focus a raw seasoned chook's foot with one claw bitten off and a straggling piece of tendon hanging from it. I hand it back and continue on the ride, chewing slowly. After a while she passes it over again and I wave my hand to say no. She looks at me and offers again. But no and I point to my own dirty feet. Lilly thinks that is so funny and breaks out laughing. Half the bus turns around to look. She laughs, she is alive, no old chooks around here!

Something must surely happen in this country to allow me to exhibit my father's work.

Some gallery or other venue, or has the Great Wall of China come down between his work and Beijing?

The sky grows dark as rain threatens. Lilly's leg is sore, a good barometer for the approaching storm. Her stomach also, unsettled like a restless sea torrid by the flood of blood - the rush of love. And then it rains or they say it does. Soon the gutters are full of water and overflowing. The people seem afraid of the rain. But it is not raining I say. What will she think when the rainforest storms hit the mountains in Australia and the rivers swell to raging brown serpents? What will she say when the leeches and the bugs attack her so far away from the gentle easy streets of Beijing and Shenyang? The rain turns out to be a flood, the worst in fifty years! The sky is like a cobweb or the surface of a pool, pull it in one place and it all moves!

Our foreplay has become a way of life. To touch when near. To flop one's arm about her neck or rub her knee. To hold her close and kiss her head or blow sweet nothings in her ear.

She cannot go near me without touching. Like a fish in water she now swims in a vast sexual sea. Whereas before we met her life was void of love and plagued by an uncertainty of self. Such concerns have led to her peeping in the mirror whenever she can. The mirror, the windows, the shadows of our lives. Once she was a beautiful young girl who rode the white horse of high fashion and kicked-up heels. With large earrings and pierced ears, sitting on the bus to work as she gnawed a pigs ear delicacy. Dancing on those long dressed legs. Whose mind was breaking out of the tradition of sexual slavery as imposed on all young ladies who desire the broader world as a consequence of the media splash which extolls the virtues of good health. The magazines and the television which cocoon people in a transfixed state of illusion, vanity and servitude where women are corralled, their imaginations aligned to men's wishes, unable to break out because of being Earth bound. At night the shooting stars point the way to romp within the celestial sphere.

After hours on the sexual stage, the largest flat area in the yellow room, the colour of which symbolises the dying of old sexual traditions, we sit up and watch the rain beat in on the window of our love. It trickles down the wall from our window-sill and wets some clothes. It runs across the floor and drips further through two rejuvenated hearts. It washes all obstacles away and gives us a freshness Lilly has never known. Now, for her, is the time to fly like a great bird and explore her sexual freedom which has been taken away, suppressed by a system clothed by fear.

We sit and punch letters, words, short stories, into the translating machine. Her hand moves so fast to draw the figures of her language. Exploding lines to match the symbols of her thoughts, the flowers or water splashes of her being.

I ask her questions about when she first saw a vagina and if her mother told her what to expect from a penis. She was told nothing, she knew nothing. I asked if her four brothers teased her for being a girl. And she said nobody ever talked about their sexuality, it was taboo and never mentioned. I described my own sexuality, how my father drew anatomical figures and naked ladies from his mind and how my mother would visit my bed in the nude in the morning and let me see her but never touch. I had a burning curiosity and a peculiar fear of the great wad of hair between her legs and her upturned nipples which as a young child I would have suckled.

Such was my early curiosity that I began to study the anatomy of sex at an early age.

Then later when fifteen, people would ask me questions as young boys do, even then I knew too much. My appetite for books on the subject became voracious. I had three girlfriends at school and fell hopelessly in love with all the young female teachers. And for most of my life, always a special one whom I fell in love with and made me feel like a round red sinking sun thrown from a great height into a fathomless pool.

The mystery of woman unfolds like the petals of a rose, many times - the petals of their beings. They were such lovely things, there to be enjoyed, teased, seduced. Yet that fear of them never went away until now in this yellow room where I can see across the bridge of two cultures, lost in the smog of Beijing.

Now there is an ocean of desire sweeping before us, which we will ferry each other across.

The ocean is broad like my chest and has a pulsing beam of light within the darkness which she attracts and draws toward her.

These angels come from the stars. They are implanted under the eyelids of men from where, once our eyes are open, we can only see hips, wombs and breasts and be enticed to touch and revel in the divine space where we all came from.

With this knowledge of love and beauty there can be no fear. The lightening and the thunder flashes but it is love which is stronger than the world, stronger than the storm and was in the very beginning the beautiful spring from whence the lightning came. Love issues forth electrically from the musings of the receptor, the one who opens to the flow. For when the new enters us we feel the desire and the great rush of life.

In the restaurant in a picture on the walls is a crying woman with her head bound.

She prays to Allah, never ending. He has drawn a tear on her face which rolls down through her being to her fertile soil and implants itself there.

In the street, the cold and grey pavements, the dust of the new falls and is vacuumed back up into our water, our soil, our sleep and our beings. It lies embryonic in the pictured woman's womb where it will pupate and rise again as a butterfly full of song.

Wouldn't it be better to give our children the love which pure water can only give?

What use is a tradition when greater threats bear down upon our wombs such as the infertility caused by a chemical world?

Once we were all children and now our sexuality in adulthood is stamped with naivety for fear is the great obstacle of love. There is no fear in pure water and it reflects a bright eyed daughter and a sparkling sun.

The streets have been washed like a baby's bottom. The soup of spittle and urine which are stepped through, is far below and travelling now with half the once murky sky to the sea.

In a pouring gush it cascades through a million tree roots dancing in its rebirth, wrapping round and round her pulsing form in a last dance to be freed from the inorganic realms.

Now she sleeps, her legs entwined-vines from the medicine of need - snores loud and coughs in my face. Picks her tiny nose in public, carries her body like a forlorn sack of potatoes, dark and still covered in dirt. Her old self is dying in this yellow room. Washed clean and boiled. Its dark water will flow out from her navel until clear. Her footsteps will grow light and tall. With a determined glow, will mother her fertility and not waste nor shun its needs.

She will allow her body to show her the way, separate from traditions. What flower has not known the wind, the luscious wind which shreds its force within the body where the sleeping seeds lie and splashes them around? They sleep to be disturbed to scatter and spread, to roll and run their fingers through an entanglement of long pubic hair. Like an old Chinese beard hanging down, which I tied in a knot. She sat up to look. Such dreams are reality, as real as the tear, the drop of blood, the silver sun, the wailing moon. These are the truths of nature we all know yet few can dip their fingers in.

She smiles at me and a golden beam of light shoots forth and penetrates my being, I untie the knot.

In times of solitude which occasionally squeeze up from below, I remember
that we have to wait too long for the visa to be processed! Over and over it
sinks in. The sharks are upon us, they want our money. There are consultants
and lawyers who will say this and that over and over thousands of times. We
will go to Shanghai and put the application in. We will let our love guide us
through those folk who would leech upon our love.

If love has a light to shine the visa will be passed. For what other honesty
can a man show to another than his open heart pierced by an arrow which has
been fired from her bow?

The government has blocked my internet. It is my fault. Just a pompous
Westerner expecting to change a five thousand year tradition overnight.
Change though is not the right word, "inform" would be better. In a world
plagued by secrets the dialogue must be maintained for peace to be appreciated.
Peace does not come like a white angel in the night. It is uncovered from the
grave, from the very pit of hell. Peace is hell's partner, beautiful and serene. For
without hell how can a body know peace? And what is peace but knowledge
and freedom to express oneself?

Those grains of sand washed by love, rolled by her thighs to become an
air born grain of dust again, concomitant to a seed or a fragment of lint and
swept up into her pregnant universe.

China had few cars ten years ago. Now everybody wants a Lamborghini,
Mercedes or a Rolls. MacDonald's and Kentucky Fried Chicken are outside the
schools. With one hand on a chicken's thigh and one hand on the till. Waiting
like traps to snare the unwary child and the neglectful busy parent who cannot
afford to read the labels on the food packages, who cannot afford the time to
cook a good meal. The children can hardly fit through the doors of the buses.
The hospitals will be full. I call them "horse piddles." The authorities know
that the environment and good food makes us healthy and try as we may it is
difficult to obtain the rights to the air we breathe let alone control the food
additives and what we are fed. Do they want us to be sick, with side dishes of
expensive pills? Who pays the bills?

The day after, the rain melts with the white rays of the sun. We go to buy
some sunglasses from the ventilated shops below the ground. Fresh air at last
and clean air skies. The sunglasses are expensive and Lilly tackles the poor lady

selling them and beats her down into a merciful sludge so we pay only one sixth the price she is asking! I cannot understand a word they say and bring out a huge luminous wad of money. Lilly looks at me horrified and grabs some making me hastily put away the rest.

She is like that, born in the forest with survival skills like a little marsupial mouse. I shall shape her bust from porcelain and stick it on the prow of my ship, she will help forge an easy path for us through the storm.

A man stares straight up into the sky. Nobody notices. He is standing with two small baskets at his feet. Everybody else is moving along and looking down. He is a beggar with a rigid back who constantly watches the stars.

As I am engaged in looking, a certain umbrella jabs me in the eye. A mauve one, I often see it twirling and dancing in front of me. Lilly's flag, to protect us from the Beijing glare.

It bobs and moves and weaves between the crowds. Without it I would have lost her long ago.

It is a kind of battering ram or crowd dispenser. Where it goes I follow and dare not lose sight of it.

I have carved her from the stone pavements of Shenyang, sculpted her bust to plough through the seas. Fixed to the bow of our ship, she holds her dainty umbrella aloft to keep the salt spray from our eyes. Her breasts forged from the purest alabaster or porcelain, parted with sweet smelling flowers. The Earth is eternal, the sea is wrapping and lapping in her Earthly arms.

Lilly's leg is sore. She has made me rub it hard and I fear it may be bruised internally.

Her upper spine at the back of her head needs all the pressure I can exert on my thumbs.

Her stomach requires pummelling beyond the normal loaf of bread, rolled and twisted, pushed and squashed to the very limits of my strength. My arms are falling off again. The only exercise I get besides rubbing her gently. She is like a little brown witchetty grub or a gum-nut recently fallen from a tree and warming in the sun, slowly spilling its seed on the rich red earth around.

Now her little turtle bottom is the centre of play and I rub it hard with my elbows.

Eventually I cannot bare her aches any longer and I fall wasted by her side grasping her soft breasts on the way down till the nipples pop out like terrified sailors from a sinking submarine.

"Penis, no tired?" she says laughing and drawing an imaginary figure of its dimensions in the air. "You are?"

"Yes," I say, "Fall off." She laughs with the call of a jackass rolling on a branch and flapping its fleshy wings. She has a bottom like a little brown peach. Her body is made of India rubber at once malleable and strong and again soft like a summer gale. Her pussy, as she has learned its more affectionate name, is relaxed and enjoys the gleam of the golden rod as affectionately known by bankers. Together we lie in the deep of night oohing and aahing beyond the measure of mortal human beings.

This morning her leg seems better. She refuses now to eat so much since I observed her eat three bowls of rice for breakfast without stopping. And told her that it had little food value and would be stored as fat if she didn't burn it off. She believes rubbing her tummy will reduce her weight.

Now she is barely eating at all. She loves me I can tell. I knew when I first saw her that we would fall in love. Perhaps my study of faces and skulls taught me that. Such a wondrous soul to meet so far away.

Today we venture into the playground of the art world again, this time by bus. We have ridden a thousand escalators and lifts and walked up a million stairs. I have made dozens of phone calls to large companies and individuals. Time is running out for me to fulfil my business mission in this country. Maybe it will not eventuate.

We travel in the heat on a bus to the artist's precinct called 798 Art Space which is an old industrial area now converted to numerous galleries. Some of them modern. One has an exhibition of works from India by contemporary artists. The work is bland, static and gaudily Westernised.

It lacks the love of the Indian street, the passion of their vast religious spectre - man and woman, there is none of that. The show may as well have come from America or the distasteful wastes of a moribund England. For the hopelessness of our social dilemma pervades even the richest cultures. I suppose many contemporary artists find themselves as squeezed out drops from a worn out turps rag.

Other works hanging at 798 show the familiar dry assemblage of flippant mockery towards the trauma of life which awaits us. Why has modern art lost the beauty of the human form?

Again only the pickings from the artist's noses are displayed. Where is love? Why has art turned into "programs" and "agendas?" The high minded artistic appraisals coming from galleries both in the West and China underline a rational of contorted vernacular squeezed through imaginative fangs like toxic tooth paste riddled with too many chemicals. Critics huddle together in shadowy corners discussing words and meanings while showing off their tee-shirt credentials. The fibre of the brush, the texture of the paint, the connection to the worlds, forever lost for words.

China flies headlong into an orgy of ill health, of family breakdown and no dreams, barren and severe eclipsed by radiation poisoning. Even now the urine floods the streets like dementia, the excreta of wealth moves as slowly as the speeding bicycle. The tall buildings, a mere status symbol, built for the granddaughter to fill with her many imagined children.

Lilly is horrified by the ants on the table. At last these small vestiges of life come about me to talk, take notes, crumbs and play. At 798 they are probably the souls of dead artists judging by the way they dart about, all copying and exploring in circles. She is disturbed and moves inside away from their fierce interest. I punch some lines into the translation machine and describe some of the things which will bite and suck her blood in Australia. Among them large ants, one inch long, which can tear one's small toe off. Huge leeches which go for penises and vaginas, eyes, noses and bottoms. Snakes that wriggle in the bed at night and a dragon called me, which will devour her. She is wide eyed in the extreme but soon smiles when I mention the dragon. She asks if these things chase you inside and I reply,

"Yes when you are cooking the meal, they get hungry."

She is horrified by the price I pay for a cup of English tea, the first I have had in three weeks. The leaves in the bottom of the cup left by the plastic bag are speckled texturally with a flamboyant artistic chemical wisdom.

We ask the price of food at the 798 Art Precinct and find it to be four times the expense we normally pay. We consider an ice-cream but at that price we look at each other and say no.

"Time-Space" was the catch-cry of the Art space, all very neat, all very cosmic and thought provoking. They liked my father's work, I showed it to many. But none could see, their vision probably impaired amongst the many flashing lights. Yes that phrase "time-space" is there to help elaborate and explain the most wistful expressions whether from politics, the gutter or the heart. Modern art to many conveys meaning through the naming of the work. As those concepts of the mind with little heart need the enigma of "art" to qualify their meaning or rather their distraction and are often plastered with the gloss varnish of Reason.

Lilly disappears across the road into a shop which is as dark as a small dungeon.

She flusters about on a shelf flinging questions at the young girl about price. Then comes out with bags of plastic wrapped food. Chook's feet again and long tubes of dried goat or donkey meat which look like frozen worms and a long dried dead sausage in a plastic bag. Two containers of ice-cream for one sixth the price of the other at 798. She gleams at me and I say on the translator under the shade of the bus-stand.

"Will you marry me?" And she looks up straight into my face and says, "Okay."

Back home we trudge up the stairs to our hot yellow room. There are messages on the computer from the Australian Embassy. More contacts, my luck may have changed.

Inside our single heart the many flutters of a growing happiness seeps out into the cracks around the window. Desperate for the clean fresh air to sing like a free bird I write again of Mouse and Dragon.

Mouse and Dragon Go Shopping

Mouse and Dragon were out shopping, it was a very hot day. Dragon found some money on the ground and wanted to buy Mouse an ice-cream but Mouse said,

"No they are too expensive! Save it for a rainy day." Dragon's tongue hung out with the heat.

When they went to catch a bus home his tongue got jammed in the door as it closed! Poor Dragon had a sore tongue.

The only thing to reduce a swollen tongue is an ice cream. Fortunately the bus stopped to pick people up right in front of an ice-cream shop so Mouse hopped off quickly to buy an ice-cream but the bus drove off without her! Dragon was very distressed.

Mouse jumped in a taxi and Dragon looked out the window and saw Mouse in the taxi with a large ice-cream. Dragon opened the window of the bus and Mouse threw the ice cream into Dragon's mouth! Hehe! Mouse stoped the taxi in front of the bus however the door shut too quickly again and the bus left without her! Mouse jumped in another taxi all the way home.

Mouse had spent all their money on taxis! She was hot and tired after all the excitement.

Dragon found money in his pocket and wanted to buy Mouse an ice cream. Mouse said no and drank some water. Dragon was very fond of Mouse and cooked her a nice meal.

Suddenly there was a bright flash of lightning and it began to rain. Mouse looked at Dragon.

"Save it for a rainy day" said Dragon on his way out the door to buy Mouse an ice-cream.

When he got home it was a little wet. They sat together on the couch and shared it, one lick at a time.

Morale of story:
Never get your tongue caught in the door of a bus!

Now Lilly does not eat. She takes my heed that too much food will shorten her vagina, will give her a prolapse. I punch in that she should eat bananas for the potassium to help balance the high salt intake of Chinese food. One a day, I say and she smiles and takes out the chook's foot packages and the dried worms and the sausage wrapped in plastic which I refer to as a "jeeba" or erect penis. At that she absolutely cracks up. She laughs like no other; we have tears in our eyes.

She has clinching fingers of steel and to distract her squeezing obsession I give her a toe-wrestle on the bed, my toes ferocious on hers. She sits and looks incredibly disinterested.

She cannot come near me without clasping some morsel of flesh and wrenching it from my body. I call her a cancer-crab with nippers and bind her hands with my clothes.

Lilly has no shame when it comes to using the toilet. She is often on it exploding and blasting forth several meters away from me. It means no embarrassment for her, it is a kind of end-game to foreplay and companionship. She is worried about my stomach saying it is tight so I let forth some very minor anal utterings myself. She seems delighted and visibly relaxes more towards me. Obviously an important language, perhaps man's first words, ancient sounds to break the ice.

Chinese ladies are so reticent to have sex before marriage. Yet the ritual of defecation is observed in acute detail as is the belch and fart listened to with keen ears. It is part of her fondness for me. Part of the female/male bonding process. It has its roots well below the ground, coming from primordial antiquity, the first outward breath. She likes to feed me, to peel grapes for me, is ever watchful and listens to my body as if it was her own.

We spend our days either wandering the streets of Beijing, the dragon city which constantly roars, looking for fruit or eating in a restaurant. Or riding in a bus, taxi or train looking for business contacts. Getting lost and asking the way. Or making love or play in the yellow room.

I have contacted large steel and iron ore companies in Australia to see if they will help me exhibit my father's work. I have contacted publishers for my mother's books. I have delivered DVDs to artists, journalists, newspapers and individuals. We have walked a thousand kilometres, down roads I fear not tread on my own and each has ended in a great wall.

As I peer out to the other wall opposite, an image flashes past my mind. It is the logo of a gas company which I saw on a building close by, the same logo as a gas company we have in Australia. Perhaps if I asked them they may let me use their foyer to exhibit my father's work in that way I may be able to talk to the Manager and convince him that Coal Seam Gas Mining is ecologically insensitive and irresponsible and see what he says. Perhaps I could show him the DVD and garner some consideration for the environment. Next day Lilly and I set off in the direction where I last saw the building with the huge blue logo which depicts a happy face.

We are lost; my neck has been strained looking up so high. Lilly does not know where we are going. She looks amused as I cross the same street fifty times and walk in a large circle a kilometre across, miraculously ending up where we started.

Having totally given up we find a nice low wall to sit on and rest. On our way back to the hotel the blue logo suddenly appears only five hundred meters from our hotel! Determined I lead the way but Lilly has her head on the side and wonders what I do. In the huge polished foyer which covers a hectare with massive columns spearing down like a cement forest of mighty tree trunks, we find a large desk with some people hiding behind it. They live here, they are like insects under a rock. I talk in English and they stop me and guide me to another smaller room with another desk. Here a man attempts to understand that I want my father to exhibit some work in their foyer. He nods approvingly and gives me their email address. Lilly and he exchange words however not much seems to be getting through. We scurry home and I fashion an email with links to websites and other information.

There is no reply after four days. One afternoon I decide to pay them another visit. This time there is obvious disturbance at the second desk. And after dodging and ducking my impossibly bad Chinese the man says "electricity" Lilly says the word too. After more time my brain landslides to the fact that this is not a gas company at all! Indeed it is a Korean Electricity company! With that my own light goes out and I reverse backwards shuffling and bowing and feeling like an idiot. Though it was wonderful to see them smile when I said "Sorry!"

On the way home I muse that my father's work is better left in a dark room untouched. How can one put a price on art? Once something as pure as art is sold it becomes like a broken vase.

Lilly sleeps, her bottom and back revealed and all else covered. This is life wrapped in white, an offering from the Gods. She smells like seaweed cast up on wet sand, as slippery as slime on smooth stones. She is a priceless Chinese meal washed in for free. A white beached whale who wants my child. She wants all my love but her vagina is sore. Only once a day she says to me and not for very long. How can I refuse? Little does she know it is enough for me to simply hold her hand and roll along the ground behind. She will be better when the sea comes gently in with little waves like a full-moon tide and stays all day.

It is not the age of China it is the incredible indifference of the Chinese people to the rest of the world. They believe China is the centre of the Earth and everything outside must be viewed with caution. If a woman falls pregnant out of wedlock she is considered a joke and ridiculed. She is not even allowed

a residency permit! So she cannot rent a house. Lost in a becalming sea, her
identity stripped from her bones by the hungry sharks of wealth and power. I
cannot imagine a larger baton of fear a government could wield than to have
power over love, sex and marriage. Even though sex makes the world go around
it is seen here as a force to corrupt social cohesion to the point of de-stabilising
government.

In every country of the world they use fear to funnel and feed the central
banking system which runs the country. They do this by first owning you via
your birth certificate. You now believe you have to pay taxes because they have
told you that you *are* the birth certificate - that is your being which proves you
exist. But how can a birth certificate pay taxes? For instance, after I was born
out of the gutter I fluttered as a piece of paper which my mother unwittingly
signed and gave to the government and the bank. In their offices, to pass the
time away they fold us into paper aeroplanes and fling us at the walls.

We venture off to follow up another contact this time it has been
recommended to us by the Australian Embassy. It is a private entrepreneurial
group which has the endorsement of the Peoples Republic of China under
the portfolio of Cultural Exchange. They are organising a huge Art Fair or
International Expo.

We determine the best way to travel and Lilly decides to go by bus. We
are off in a flurry and a little late and hit the pavement in a spin. She does
not know the correct bus stop and walks one way and then the other asking
people directions. Eventually we find the right bus-stand and wait with the
agitated crowd.

Having first primed these people with some information about my father's
work, we are immediately whisked into a conference room and I take out some
images for them to view.

For an instant the woman is wide eyed then closes the book and talks to me
for a long while in Chinese. I cannot understand a word. The young woman
who is the International Organiser speaks good English, interprets and says.

"She says she is familiar with art and that she thinks the work is worthy
of a high profile position in the building."

We catch the bus home and it seems to float above the ground. My father's
work will be recognised in China where it belongs for he is a master of the brush.
The little jade dragon Lilly bought for my birthday is smiling around my neck.

We go back to our yellow room the happy dragon and the mouse. We buy some fruit on the way and I buy Lilly a dress or rather she buys one, then another and another. The last shop owner charges us half price and the other dresses are bargained down to one third the asking price. Luck is surely with us this day. My mission in China is over in one way and in another has just begun.

Lilly wants a child. She asks me constantly about a small person. She wants a girl. We make love for what seems an eternity. I throw her about the bed like a young woman. She has an impossible grin on her face occasionally writhing in agonised bliss.

The empty sea of Beijing roars like an angry surf. The thunder of the trains underground shakes the smog filled air. Some desperate mosquitoes filter through the blinds. And we sit in front of the noisy mindless television which sucks our thoughts to reminisce the month we have spent together.

At last my bowel has moved. After nearly four weeks the whole of China falls from my body. The pollution of Shenyang, the rich meals, the green tea, my hand medicine, the brightly coloured fruit, all there. My highs of love condensed in a brown script as rich as my blood and hers joined and issuing from the same hip. Our life, our love fused beneath the water.

The storm is here, flashing with the Beijing lights, rolling up the sides of impossible buildings, electrifying the very dead fish which is sprinkled with hot chillies and spiced with soy and other kitchen pharmaceuticals. Then drenched in the exhaled tobacco smoke from the table next to ours.

A woman holds a young child on a two wheeled wobbly skate-board and together they explore the cooking street where fires and large pots of boiling oil line the way. Over the mountains of spittle and discarded shrivelled grape skins, through the thick ancient food gutters and the sauce. Her thin chop-stick legs of rubber will teach her only son not to fear. One day she will ride the skate-board and he will work.

China thunders incessantly like a dragon. This is their year of the dragon, perhaps that is why I am here. The high pitched cicadas sleep now for winter is approaching. The single black and white bird picks kebab sticks for its nest. Unravelled, in a spindly existence of knotted words, spirals and cracked egg shells above which it has mounted a red flag of plastic underwear.

Lilly's little brown body is wrapped in the nylon from the infertile West. Those garments suck the magnesium from the soft skin of the groin like an old man who plays a single string fiddle at the railway station. His steely thoughts, rasping for harmonics, ripples about their frills as he romantically asks the ladies for more money.

The rich cars spill their brown waste in the restaurants, through the lungs and into the stomachs of the well-dressed children. The West has spawned a demon. Man is the servant of woe, who slashes Mother Nature's bosom and sucks there like a leech, her blood, her luscious blood.

How will his rubber body, his elasticised nylon body, bare these wounds? For even as his buildings rise to impossible heights his fertility sinks to the muddy depths of the bowl. After that the bowl is empty. And after that again, the wind and altered weather will fall like bricks squashing love and hormones in a mash of ill-health.

The dragon will devour us all, this being of geek who big-foot tramps through the windy guts of the underground, where trains race and shear, playing with fear. There perhaps the ghosts of men will only sing one note, a high pitched squeal of rusting lust which seeks to round each corner while dangling from a single string for her attention. Aah the innocence of the single string as luxurious as one love!

The flowers nod haphazardly in the park, their pretty dresses and long legs spiralling up and up to a lustrous light. As men we climb those ladders and bite through the cloth in small delicate holes. After money there is nothing else to find. All the art has gone. The petals with their music nod and sing, all the art has gone.

A single day remains for me in China.

She lies sleeping on the bed. Her blue nylon underwear pulled tight about the crutch.

I will not be similarly restrained. Any excess let out and over. Each flower the most it gives, all for the splendour of the Earth, its lingering perfume. Her small breasts heave slowly up and down while I a restless sea. Joined at the hip we dance and play, all notions meld the chorus. For all we know is flowing through the clouds, is vapour rising. For all we know we will never tame our greed.

Our tongues hang out and down after the party is over, we must move on to hang out and down in other realms.

There are more storms on the way, Lilly is in the bathroom making thunder.

Now she is on the bed with thunder between her legs. She is flashing her teeth like lightning, laughing like a little child blowing a funny trumpet.

In the afternoon we stamp out our hearts into the translating machine.

We spend hours deciphering the simplest thing, playing hop-scotch with words and understanding. Slipping and sliding, laughing all the way.

Earlier we visited a DVD/CD shop which sold DVDs. Lilly was cautious at first and asked my intentions. I said I am doing this for the people, their knowledge and to help honesty in the world. I wanted to give them my remaining copies which I could not give away. The shop assistant with pink curls in her hair took me to a hidden room behind a swivelling cupboard where there were thousands of DVDs. The room had television monitors all over it. Very soon the owner came into view through another secret door and said that Lilly had spoken to her and wanted to go.

She accepted the DVDs from me. We exited out another secret back door of another shop after dodging pipes and machinery in the bowels of the underground and went around to the front of the shop where Lilly was waiting. The owner showed me a DVD by Al Gore on global warming and nodded approvingly. And I wondered how much the Chinese youth really knew and felt.

I did not mention that Mr Gore is *not* expecting the sea level to rise as he has bought, from the proceeds of that film, an eighteen story apartment building right on the coast!

Lilly lies half naked on the bed, covered in a wet towel, her fluff peeping through like a little cloud of dark wisdom. She is positively explosive and keeps saying "watermelon."

She punches in that I must be careful as there is black-money in China. I say that I trust all people. She says they make money from "taking from me." I tell her I have eyes in my bottom. She laughs and farts again. Nobody trusts power and those who strive for it. There is no gain in competition only loss for the heart. For the heart is more powerful than the sword. Lilly goes on to say that they would have asked for my money and if I did not give it they would say I raped them.

"I do not fear" is what I said and she punches in,

"They is gang-land." And I say,

"That is why I went there." She punches in again,

"They say you rape, you come in cell!"

The cupboard had a secret door behind it and Lilly was restrained from entering. I had to be led out another way as we could not go out the way we came in. While I was in the secret room Lilly had become very agitated and worried about me and questioned the owner. Now she is saying they would have asked for my money and may have tried to take it by force. Maybe even lost a kidney or some other organ. And I muse that a few weeks ago I was so sore I would have gladly given a few other things away! I am lucky to have this little angel to keep me safely on the ground. Her wings are made of leather and her heart is made of gold!

The Balloon Ride

One day Mouse and Dragon were taking their watermelons to market to sell when they saw a big red hot air balloon in the sky. Mouse looked out the window and thought that would be fun. Fortunately they sold all their watermelons at the market so when they arrived home they made a booking to go for a ride the very next day.

They became so excited about going. Mouse thought she could take lots of flowers to throw over the side for all the people. Dragon said he would take some watermelons as well.

Next day they went to the launching place and saw the great big red balloon. It was ready and the ticket lady looked at all Mouse's mauve flowers and said that was a lovely idea and with any luck they would float over the town and the school where all the children were. Dragon went to the car and brought over a big box of watermelons but the lady did not see him put them in the balloon basket, she was talking to Mouse and looking the other way.

"If you lose altitude just give it more hot air" she said. Dragon smiled he knew he had plenty of hot air.

They were off. The lady waved goodbye but the balloon did not move.

"More air!" she called. So Dragon lifted his head up and with a great hot breath blew into the balloon. Slowly they began to rise and Mouse was wide-eyed and excited because they did not know where they would go.

Up and up they went far into the sky. Mouse could see their car as a tiny dot and then their house so far away. But they did not go over the town. Mouse was disappointed and was getting giddy so she sat down in the basket for a while. Then a cloud came about them and Mouse jumped up. She threw a flower into the cloud and watched it for a moment disappear below. Then a slight breeze rocked the basket and it became quite cold. Mouse was shivering. Dragon thought he should let some of the hot air out so they would go back down into warmer air. There was a great whooshing sound as the hot air escaped from the top of the balloon and they began to slowly go down. Soon they were below the clouds and in the warmer air. A bird flew by and they waved at it and said hello.

Then Mouse could see the town and what looked like the school. She started throwing flowers over the side and Dragon picked up a watermelon.

"No!" cried Mouse, "You will hurt the children with that." Dragon looked puzzled, he had not thought of that. Then he realised what a silly idea it was. So he leaned over the side and watched the flowers spinning below and threw them instead.

He was looking over the side when he saw a large flower float down and he turned around to ask Mouse what it was. Mouse was gone. Dragon got such a shock he looked over the side again and realised that the flower must have been Mouse! He quickly jumped over and spread his wings and dived. Faster and faster he flew. He turned his body into a speeding bullet and caught up with Mouse way way below. He caught her gently in his mouth and flew down to the ground as the ground was not far away.

"Are you alright?" he said. Mouse could not talk she was so upset. Dragon put her on his back and flew back to the car. He lay her down on the back seat. Dragon then took to the sky again to find the balloon. But it had climbed up very high. He had to go a long way into the cold air to reach it. Eventually he caught up with it and landed in the basket. Now he had to take it back down so he pulled a rope and released hot air from the top. Slowly he began to go down.

He looked over the side and could see their little house far below. He knew there would be nobody there so he dropped all the watermelons over. With the loss of weight he started to rise up again so he had to release more hot air. Down and down he went. By this time Mouse was in the car following the balloon. Dragon floated gently down until he landed on the ground. Mouse pulled up in the car.

They were both relieved to see each other and when they reached home much to their surprise there were squashed watermelons all over the front veranda and when they went inside there was a big hole in the roof where lots of watermelons had crashed through.

There was watermelon everywhere!

"Oh!" said Dragon with surprise. Mouse did not care Dragon had saved her life.

Morale of the story:
Life with love is a whole lot of fun, life without love is a hole in the roof and a whole lot of hot air.

I am assigned to massaging her buttocks again early in the morning - must be something about my touch. My reward is sex as she says. I am hardly awake, my hands like feathers on soft skin. Then the world rolled over, its softness swelling like mountains in the melting snow. My fingers slip and fall, a virgin angel who learns to fly. Falling into impossibly soft cracks, behind hidden doors. Unravelling the dreams, looking for water. I am upon her now, more awake, my elbows thrust and pound her bottom. She talks and moans. Her sore left leg by now nearly wrenched off. Her third eye winks at me and I am fast to my reward.

She is unflinching unmoving as resolute as a woman who enjoys. There is no pain or discomfort in her face, only light. And today the sun shines through a blue sky, one of only two that I have seen in four weeks! Splashing on the pavements, dancing on people's shoulders and down their spines, playing on their muscles and bones, making energy like leaves absorbing sunlight, absorbing and producing vitamin D-factor in their skin.

"I will not rub your stomach forever," are the words I plunge into the interpreting machine.

She wants so much to be a mother again and give me a pretty daughter. Her heart is filled with a desire to please. She is a woman enveloped by the beauty of spring to burst open as a new seed.

She sits astride me and clips my chin of tiny bristles one by one, she squeezes me all over extracting sebum from places I never thought I had, I begin to feel like a mining deposit.

She is in symbiosis with her woman-hood she wants to flower again.

Finger tips touching, rolling, squeezing. Was the universe created in a day, like this? Did the world rub noses with the electric universe and wash the salt into the stones?

All men alone without her are only a tormented sea.

Silent motor-bikes carry fruit and tonnes of water through the narrow streets. They have no horns or warning signals, suddenly they are behind you, commerce on the run. People gather at the scene of an accident, an expensive car has a dint in the rear bumper bar. Cameras are out, the police are called and voices raised. Their wit of uncertainty ascends in lifts and explodes through the roof tops in a flutter of anxious lights.

Outside the expensive hotel Westerners with large rimmed sun-glasses look out and observe the crowd. They chew their coffee pills and later fart profusely in ascending lifts. All eyes are on us, as we shuffle along, the mouse and the dragon with the mauve umbrella.

We go looking for clothes. I want to give her another new dress, she has helped me so much. There are people everywhere jammed into the great polished building. All sorts of garments are hanging from every conceivable hook. Delicately dressed ladies prance about on stilts and wobbly high-heels. Frilled at the elbows like the feeding membranes of shells, filtering the bags from the pockets, the coins from the notes. There is no time to bargain, voices raised are not welcome. Western people drop to their knees. The friendly dragon of commerce, stuffed and ill from over-eating, rests and fulminates in a corner of the room.

Here hair is coiffured like sonic antennae blowing in the air-conditioning. The smells of pure woman waft from the greasy mirrors as men like myself plod like draft-horses outside, pulling an impossible load. Young girls squint and wag their elbows, their swing-bridge hips reaching across any pit of scarcity, where the wealthy spawn. Here there are acres of femininity. Lilly is ready with her knitting-needles and her sharpened pig spear, ready to skewer those who would dare to argue or bargain with her warrioress heritage.

Then her first victim falls. Lilly coyly walks away after considerably screwing up the poor woman's face, mangling it first with her fingers of steel, her words of flame, then her sweetening voice which made the poor woman care and lower the price.

To my side I notice someone staring at the ceiling. Not doing anything, a woman, just staring at the ceiling. She is well dressed and I am sure smells like washing powder. She has unusual blue eyes and long lashes. Her covered bosoms are surrounded with frills like a shell, scalloped, to give the illusion of movement. She is not a beggar. She has a good complexion.

Lilly wants me to help her choose. She keeps looking at me sideways like a young girl waiting for my opinion. She chooses dark watery colours, mysterious blues and greens. She is a water sign, fresh, wondrous and clean, with a blue flame.

Another victim falls and I step in to choose a dress for her. She cannot choose for herself and rather enjoys the slaying. The dress is pale blues and whites. It is covered in white roses with a dark blue trim. She is so happy. The woman who sells the garment after the hard battle, smiles with her and holds the dress up to Lilly's chest admiring the choice. Lilly has beaten her down to half price. She is pleased and races off to the toilet past the lady who stares at the universe. She soon appears wearing the dress, all smiles again and I say,

"Yes, beautiful." She is alive as never before, a young girl of fifty two. Then all at once I catch the other woman's eyes - she still stares at the ceiling. But I am sure she glanced my way, her quick of eye moving, piercing into me like Lilly's sword. A cold and distant stare reminding me that soon I will be gone.

Westerners parade in the glossy corridors bludgeoning their cents from the underwear vendors who are cleverer than they. Unravelling their ravishes on the slim bodies of the ladies who dream. Lilly scores another victim. She goes down frowning profusely as Lilly walks off shrugging her shoulders.

Past the shops are more shops, decked with garments barely able to move. Then all at once outside another shop, another figure staring at the ceiling, exactly the same, or maybe it is the same woman? Different clothes. Peering into an endless distance, remembering her love.

We go to find a meal, peering into doors, sniffing the air. We only eat once a day. Lilly eats with slurps and sucks, she is my pet vacuum cleaner, her voice high pitched with inflections of "esses" and "cees." We watch a TV show of high pitched shrieking and squealing with special quivering vibrations made by inflaming the upper portion of the nasal cavity which seems to mimic the vibrations of a gong at the highest pitch. It is not easy to speak their language to make the "esses" and the "cees" which their glorious voices extol.

Lilly and I roll towards each other. Her strong arms wrap around me, her slim pointed, up-turned fingers do not speak, only sleep. Her breathing, fast in little gasps, her sore leg flopped across my naked body.

She is fully clothed and her slothfulness her game. I tease her endlessly like a cat with a mouse or a dragon with a spark. Each morsel of skin is touched, puckered and kissed, her flesh as smooth as talc bends and groans, her black tussled hair a dark forest of mystery wrapped about our faces.

Then huffing to rouse the sleep she swoons, her mouth curling at the edges as I blast air and grunts in her ear. Her chin like her nose is small and both neatly fit in my mouth as my tongue slaps across her tightly closed lips. Those doors are closed as tight as the secret self at her other end. Then the warrioress woman on guard opens a wary eye.

She lies naked on the bed with the figure of a small girl. Her long black wisp floats between her legs. Her eyes barely open to view the scene. Her senses raised to a gushing river. Swollen and engorged the force of love within her squirms as I touch for the last time the bottom of her deep and wondrous pool. What else can life give that is not more beautiful than a woman?

We pack our bags she to Shenyang and me to Australia. We pass time by lying on the bed punching our different languages into the translation machine. She says she rewards me by letting me rape her.

"Yes" I say, then add, "Sorry." and she laughs. She is worried I will find another woman in Australia and I say,

"I have no money, how could I find another woman?" and add, "You rob bank for money and I come and rape you." We laugh, she is happy in her new dress and shirt and shoes and large full stomach, what next I ask and answer, "You rape me, that is your reward!"

We charge down the stairs with our heavy bags, she lifts my bag with one arm as though it was a feather in her shoe. I follow her with her clobber and memories, shoes, food and other spoils from the journey.

We head below the road into the catacombs of Beijing where the giant roaring worms pulse and engorge and disgorge. The train is full. Lilly with relative ease charges in beneath the multitude of armpits to find her position behind the front line. The people close over and I am left outside the train with bags in both hands. The door closes on my body cutting my penis in two and I wonder for an instant if I will be severed in half but the doors jump back open. Thus I hold up the train and like a rapist force my way into find her. There is no room as I tread on peoples feet, unfortunately aiming the cumbersome bags below their belts to see them double over. She nods approvingly and we entertain the squash.

After not too long in the people-soup Lilly squeals that the train is going the wrong way.

She looks at me and I agree. Everybody looks at her and she says something which makes many people reply. The next station is an eternity away. And pushing and falling like dead fish from a net we sprawl back out on the platform sucking many out of the carriage as we fall. Eventually we manage to travel in the right direction.

My flight has been cancelled. I will have to catch another plane and a bus to get to Shanghai. In the train we sit opposite a Greek man. He is dark eyed and handsome. Lilly averts his looks. I watch his mind fluoresce as he brandishes many thoughts our way. Other countries invade our love why must we be on show?

I am late and must make haste. Lilly charges around the airport with my passport held out in front of her talking to everybody a thousand times. I follow like an octopus covered in seaweed, with all the bags hanging off me like extra legs.

Now that I know where to go I stop our rush and turn her to face me. She is there before me - now is the time of our parting.

We cannot speak to each other; we do not know what to say.
Those words neither of us can understand. I mumble,
"I must go." And she mumbles,

"Miss you." Her eyes flush red, her mouth begins to tremble. My eyes go red and my mouth begins to tremble. I hold her hand and she clasps my arm and I kiss her on the cheek.

I must go I say and she nods and comes with me like a kite on a string.

She is there beside me right to the last. And as I go in to customs she grips the glass wall flattening her wet cheek and wiping her eyes. I look at her and she nods and nods again.

I cannot turn away from her. She watches like a little girl, her red eyes looking far into the distance of our future. I turn away and wrench my body from China but leave my heart with her.

It is sometime before my eyes clear and I can see where I am going. The customs man is there but I am alone. I turn around again for a last look but she is gone, an empty glass waiting to be filled.

China silently passes below me like a jewelled bracelet. Everything is precise and square.

The curves of her flat body undulate around water courses and dark forests.

Then she disappears behind a dense fog or veil of bridal-ware.

Mouse and Dragon Find an Audience

One day Dragon was out fishing in his little boat when he heard a strange sound in the trees by the river bank. It was the sound of the changing season stirring in the leaves. Dragon began to whistle and hum and he thought he would like to play a flute like the wind.

Mouse was at home in the garden and she looked up at the new clouds and the gentle breeze and began to hum a tune as well. Mouse was very fond of music, she had always wanted to study the viola which is a big deep sounding violin. Dragon came home with a fish for dinner and turned to her and said he wanted to learn how to play the flute. Mouse looked over her glasses at Dragon and said,

"Viola" Dragon smiled. Mouse sometimes seemed to know what Dragon was thinking.

The next day they went into town and found a beautiful old flute and a beautiful old viola. Dragon picked up the flute and blew a perfect note. He had so much breath; the note went on for ages. Mouse drew the bow across the strings of the viola and a deep mellow note filled every space in the room and danced around Dragon's note.

"Oh Dragon, this is beautiful!" she said with a smile.

Mouse and Dragon practised a little every night, more and more. Their notes learnt how to follow each other as though talking like birds or leaves in a breeze. They would often play deep into the night and sometimes in the mornings they would practice.

One day they both looked at each other and said,

"Holiday."

They packed some clothes and their bathers for they were going to the beach. On the way they stopped at a big forest and had lunch beside a small stream. Dragon began to play his flute and immediately a bird came and sat on Mouse's head much to her surprise.

The more Dragon played his flute the more birds came to listen. Mouse played the viola and in no time they were surrounded by an audience of different sized birds sitting in the branches and hopping on the ground in front of them. Dragon smiled at Mouse her playing was so beautiful.

That night there was half a moon and the trees around were dark. Mouse and Dragon began to play again and soon a big owl came and sat on a branch nearby, bobbed its head and watched and listened. Then another and another and soon the sky filled with little bats all flying and listening and watching. All the animals in the forest came and sat in a big circle around them. They could all see each other with their night eyes. Mouse thought Dragon's playing was entrancing.

The following day was overcast and rainy but they decided to go to the beach and watch the waves and have a swim. Everything was wet as they sat and watched the sea. After their meal they went down onto the soft white sand of the beach and sat and watched the orange moon begin to rise out of the ocean. Then Dragon began to play his flute and Mouse played her viola and their sound curled around the small lapping waves on the shore. Their music blew away all the clouds and a deep starry night filled the sky.

Mouse and Dragon were so absorbed in their playing they did not notice the little beach crabs which came up out of their holes in the sand to watch and listen. They did not notice all the schools of small fish glistening and flashing in the moonlight as they came in close to catch waves and look and listen. Many of the creatures of the sea also gathered in the water near the shore. There were sting-rays and schools of prawns and bigger fish too which did not try to eat the smaller fish or scare them away. Some fish were swimming on their sides waving their fins out of the water. Everything was quietly listening.

Then Mouse noticed something dark moving up out of the water onto the sand, it was very large. Gradually they could see it was a great sea turtle coming onto the beach to lay her eggs.

Very slowly she came right up close and looked them in the eyes. She must have liked their music! Turtle began to dig a hole in the sand and for a long while Mouse and Dragon played and watched her.

Their notes flowed far out over the long dark sea until turtle had finished and went back and disappeared under the waves.

When Mouse and Dragon stood up to go, all the audience in the sea got such a fright there was a great splash in the water like a thousand people all clapping at once and the hundreds of tiny crabs waved their nippers and scurried back into their holes with a sandy gritty sliding sound.

Morale of the story:
When we are in love every note is perfect.

Guangzhou airport

At Guangzhou airport on my way home, three men kneel on prayer mats which are stiffened from dried spittle for they carry the mats everywhere and put them on the ground. These men have jammed themselves into a corner of the room and salute their bottoms to the crowd. The Chinese people are watching and then turn away quickly to not expose their natural timid curiosity. One of the three yawns, another has a bow and arrow in a box, it is a deadly weapon to appease fear. One is of African descent. They bring an air of peace and quiet to the busy departure lounge. One man now does his shoes up lackadaisically which he took off before kneeling. The other two men have departed.

The African man takes time and reverently roles up his mat. Underneath their quietness is a ferocious desire to pay homage to their God Mohamad. Their God, yes - is in all of us.

Thank goodness they pray for themselves unselfishly. Another man has joined the last man and has a compass in his hand.

"This way?" he asks,

"This way," the other man says. They join in a brotherhood of men - friends from the start.

A Western woman passes by and both men observe her bottom lasciviously without fear of exposing their rapacious curiosity to either the crowd or to her. Now they prostrate themselves the other way having changed position in the corner of the room like naughty children and the whole room full of people observes their rising and falling posteriors. Young women stop to photograph them.

More come, there is a group of them in the corner at the bottom of the escalator. Why there? Are they unaware of other people's right of way? People getting off the escalator have to dangerously negotiate to step around. They cannot be asked to move; such a request may be conceived as a threat to their freedom to pray or perhaps misconstrued as an attempt to stop them from believing.

Presently a man with three children and a hundred bags clots the bottom of the stairs and with an agonising crunch flattens one of the prostrate men. They all leap to their feet and dust themselves off. The Chinese man says sorry bowing profusely as the man stares down at him. One of the children throws her tiny arms around her daddy's legs and begins to cry.

These people who pray are an anachronism here. Chinese people have no time to pray, they have no time to do anything other than spend every second of the day making money. They used to pray and enjoy the time-wasting luxury of it, long ago when the mountains were green and the streams pure, the clouds all fluffy and white - not any more. Now in the airport lounge some young Chinese men are laughing silently, hand to mouth. We are all fools in God's paradise! Do not laugh at others for those who demean, demean themselves. Yes we only know how to think of ourselves with self-righteous pity which is a fire stoked by a troubled guilty soul, whose charred remains we gladly give away for salvation.

The great unspoken word here is that these people look silly within a five thousand year old culture. Why do they have to compete with their visual display of religious fervour amongst themselves - with their fellow man - a brother? Why can't they sit quietly and think of Him? Sorry I do not understand! I have never understood religious gatherings. Each person is God. Even the Pope rises and falls as that church's honesty fades. Why do we need plastic idols jammed into tight boxes? Religions bring wars - look at history. It is the small animals in our bodies which determines our fate, the soils of the blood, the stones of the bones.

In Moslem Kashmir in the 70's after travelling for seven months, I noticed much unhappiness amongst the women. Every night there was shouting and screaming wherever we went. I since learned from Moslem friends that the women get jealous of each other as there is only one man to go around. And he, poor fellow, has to prove his masculinity not only to his ladies but to appease the competitive natures of his masculine friends. I am surprised the Chinese government allows them into the country as one woman one man is sacrosanct here. Of course they can leave the country to marry others, then return.

In Australia I lived next to a New Zealand man who had nine wives and thirty children. He found that it was easy to make babies. He did not work only made cups of tea all day. The government paid him a huge benefit each week. And each week he would take the family shopping in a bus. After some time he ran away literally and became a Hare Krishna devotee. The Hare Krishna faith observes that one only has sex when one wants to procreate.

The night is falling. The luminous globes of the airport lights are the only stars we can see as the breath of China is so dense. A loud vacuum cleaner hisses in the background like an unseen serpent and all minds are transfixed on the destiny of our pure white aeroplanes each like the departing whites of God's great gleaming eye.

Australia

Misty smoke cloud as Australia winks her early morning brown eye.

Aeroplane floats above the sea, then drops its legs, roaring - flutters like a three legged dancing Brolga - to bring me home.

Old stone walls, convict made, cut lovingly from the beautiful yellow sandstone of Sydney, two hundred and twenty six years ago - is England's legacy to this city birthed by her so called criminals. And amongst these rocks hide tight little dark cold streets all trying to forget the pain and be quaint. The little shops with English doors all huddled together as if in fear of England's retribution - one hundred lashes with the cat-and-nine-tail whips – if one does not triumphantly sing the songs of the Queen. Those songs in the early days were accompanied by the chatter of little birds the bark of axe and the thunder of the falling trees.

Manly Ferry slow and sinking in the waters of Sydney Harbour - coarse and crude, a fossilised angel - rusting since the pre-Cambrian. Dolled up by dolphin wisdom and the prospect of sighting a whale. Foreigners everywhere. From the tug of the engines on the shore I can see an old Chinese man urinating behind a tree. I see the stream of his water, his penis, his age. China is blooming! China is here.

Harbour Bridge, coat hanger, slow and sinking in the water. Rust and foreigners, urine and dark, misty and humid. The breasts of tight ladies, inorganic now. The ferry's mind is old, I can hear its rattling thoughts, no longer secrets - her long legs revealed.

Take these dreams and wash them in the Pacific ocean-blue, clean and pure. Life no longer safe. Australia's sexuality, her fecundity ravaged by fire and unhappiness. Ravaged by the contraindicating inorganic clouds. A humid breeze of unsureness streaks the blue. The dry sky is weeping, the clouds have ragged edges like our disease, billowing up like grey-matter then dissipating like the memories of her frilly underwear. The little pounding waves, the splash-patter of the dimpled sea.

The mind crowds itself with scenes of yesterday - Graffiti like spiders webs on the walls, smeared Guangzhou toilet - the uncontrollable old man. The ladies - the women, all sometimes in a wretched heap - glamorous even in decay, often squealing with laughter, lying on their backs like beetles kicking their legs in the air.

As I breathe the clean fresh breeze, the fact that I am back again to fight the great Australian audit sinks in. Now again the letters, the bills, the receipts, the endless procession of the walking dead.

And it is good to be home amongst these sweet smelling eucalyptus flowers away from the ice and snow, the hot breathing monster - China. I have returned from the dead with one broken leg to live in two worlds - two very different worlds.

I wait on the cliff near my old home for my love. Time is wretched and gnaws again at my flesh. We have to wait three months possibly a year before I can return to exhibit my father's work. Each of us will long for each other. China is cruel to make us wait twelve months for the visa. But then how can a bureaucracy measure love? So I sit and wait patiently for the flowers to unfurl. For love only knows the longing much as immortality measures the ethereal, a bottomless drop. When together, we will play like young children again as though time will never end.

About my feet the Water Dragon lizards dance. A male and three young females. He is in control and comes across to nip my toes. But I do not move and he looks up at me sideways. I bob my head and he bobs his; we are friends, brothers. The sky is hot and full of smoke from bush fires. The blue sea whipped by a strong westerly wind dances with the racing smoke as it comes down and clips the foam.

Oh time let me hold you in my hand to view your many faces. Let me stand on my tip toes tall to watch your changing tides. My love come hold my hand and whisper that all is well. That love will be eternal beyond the sheets of time.

The splash of wave and slap of skin, washing clean the old old eyes, to sleep, to dream again of clearer skies. To roll voluptuously once more upon the swelling bosom of antiquity and drink refreshingly from the waters of her skin.

Tyalgum, New South Wales

This rock beside the mountain stream will be my pedestal. From here I can look across the water's flat form into a never ending bright green vista. The sodden ground after rain, the warm illusive breeze the bobbing heads of flowers and again the spit of rain.

I have to go. The rain will wet my page and my memory will dribble away.

I have to go. I am a small drop of water rolling down the hard surface of the mossy stone, turning over with rainbows on my brow. There the universe greets me with electric time as I drop into her soil and fade into her welcoming arms. What more to life than love, to write about her wonders and be absorbed into her form?

I am a child of the water, I go wherever you push.

My Dear Ian,

It's so nice to hear from you again! I have been worried about you a lot since you left.

Finally I received your letter today. I feel relieved to know that you got home safely.

Thank goodness!

My darling, I enjoyed spending four weeks with you so much. I had never been so happy before! You made me feel to be cared for, loved and cherished. You touched my heart deeply by your sincerity! I felt very relaxed and comfortable and happy with you. Now I'm pretty sure that I love you and I want to share the rest of my life with you in Australia! I will love you and spoil you forever!

My darling, I know it was a long flight for you. You must feel very tired now.

You'd better not return to work right away. You'd better have some good rest first.

Please try to keep yourself warm as well and not catch a cold. I care for you very much!

Please take good care of yourself for me.

Yes I am back at work. For I took one month holiday when you came, I have to do more to make up my leave now. So I have been busier these days. But I don't mind that. I think it is worthwhile,

I just miss you very much! It take me time to get used to be without you as well.

I also hope you will return to Shenyang as soon as possible so that we can be together again.

I am glad to know you enjoyed this trip and you thought I was the most amazing part.

That's so sweet. Remember everything we did together. I still recall of them when I am alone.

Yes we could communicate but not good enough, hehe. I will work harder to improve my English my darling, hopefully we will be able to communicate better when we meet next time.

Thanks for the photo it reminds me of the wonderful time that we spent together.

Oh, by the way, yes of course I like the new clothes.

Thanks a lot!

Take care,

all my love

Lilly

Lilly & Ian
Mouse & Dragon

(Book Two)

Twelve months of waiting has not aged me in the slightest, the hundreds of letters we have written, each one like a stone lifted from my heart.

Time roles as much as my tongue mixes mud, the glaze of the vessel heated solid into stone by the thousands of words which love plays like a fish on a line occasionally leaping naked from the water to wrestle the hook from deep in the groin. Then the roar of the engine – the roar of my heart, to break free from the world and breathe the fresh air, the fresh air, the fresh air....

The aeroplane is safe like a ship, she flies full of dead whales, each a Moby Dick of tales and adventures. Of stories wonderful, each person's life now at the mercy of the winds, the ticket of us, a little paper kite (in the toilet I found).

I settle back in the safety-belt, secure with my passport which nags my breathless chest, to another world. Back in time to the prehistoric raffle, the chemical tea, the micro-wave food and the empty paper bag. My pulse rises as we ascend, my blood thickens as we sleep, my legs restless begin to walk on the ceiling until restrained by the flight attendant's legs in a very tight grip. Thus they hold me down and thrust the movies down my innocent throat where my wetted tongue slides and tastes yet another engorged hook and cannot speak.

Helpless I watch as men fight other men with guns and attitudes of war. The blood spills down my throat, my eyes go red from seeing. The gore I watch changes my mind and makes me want to kill and slaughter. Why do we watch such aggressive dribble when we are in such a vulnerable space? These aeroplane people are fearless to fly amongst such madness! Where is the grace of watching people suffer even if they are on TV? No wonder people jump in their sleep, these aggressive movies we are forced to watch are disgusting.

I read a Chinese newspaper printed in English. It places a lens inside the government like an externally operated highly charged electromagnetic mirror which shocks and commands to be read. It is digitally dextrous like a platinum robot. Its curling use of the English language is more accurate than a medical dictionary. The invention is stuffy, the colloquial stiff, measured, dry. A group of doctors is trying to do head transplants. Another group has found that after clinical death the brain retains consciousness. Whether it is scripted is another thing.

I will never die, Lilly and I will live ten thousand years! If I die before her we could share heads! That would be good.

Mouse and Dragon Go To Sea

One day Dragon was out in his little boat fishing and Mouse was in the garden planting beans when he thought how nice it would be to make a sail for his boat and take Mouse for a holiday and follow the river down to the sea.

Dragon had heard there were big fish in the sea and he wanted to try and catch one.

Mouse was very excited about going to see the big blue ocean and began to pack immediately but Dragon said it would take him sometime to build a mast and a sail.

In the next few weeks Dragon found some books about sailing and Mouse bought some cloth to make a sail with but Dragon had an idea and said to Mouse that he had designed a new type of sail which would pick up the slightest breeze.

Finally the day came for them to test their new sail which was really a large kite so they launched their boat on the river in a slight breeze. Dragon went up the front and with a great flurry threw the kite up in the air with Mouse holding onto a rope. The wind quickly filled the kite and Mouse was lifted straight up out of the boat! Dragon grasped her legs and pulled her back down and the boat began to move. It soon picked up speed and crashed into the river bank, for the kite was difficult to steer.

Dragon spent the next few days trying to work out how to steer it. He was very clever with ropes.

Finally the day came when everything was ready. Mouse had bought half the garden along and lots of potatoes. She had to leave many behind because the boat nearly sank. Dragon had sun-dried some fish in case their supplies ran low for they did not know how long they would be away. They waited for a bright sunny day and eventually launched their tiny boat and said goodbye to their little house.

The river was slow and smooth and there was no wind at all so they had to row with the oars. After travelling for three days the river grew wider and wider and slowed down even more. Then it became narrower and faster and faster. At one point the water was rushing along and Dragon had to push the boat away from the logs and rocks which threatened to block their way. Then one day the water grew shallower and shallower and the rocks on either side became very large and they found themselves racing along at a tremendous speed.

Dragon listened carefully for he was sure he heard a rumbling sound and looked at Mouse to see if she could hear it too. Sure enough they were about to go down a rapid. Mouse could hear it now roaring like a lion.

Dragon could not stop the boat, there were cliffs on both sides of the river. The boat began to bob and twist and suddenly fall. White water foamed about them. Mouse was hanging on tightly to the front and calling out "Whoo hoo!" and "whee!" when the boat suddenly went completely under the water and Dragon lost sight of her! Luckily the rapids stopped and the boat only half sank. Mouse was all wet, her ears were sagging, "Whoo hoo!" she said again; she was having such a good time!

Fortunately they had not capsized and lost all their food! They spent the rest of the day drying everything out including the kite.

The following day the river slowed and it was hot out on the water. Mouse wanted some potatoes for lunch so she set up her little mud stove and Dragon breathed on the wood to light it.

A slight breeze blew the smoke out the front of the boat. The wind became stronger and stronger and before the potatoes were cooked Dragon threw the kite into the air and immediately they took off.

Now the smoke was travelling at the same speed as they were so they were surrounded by it and could not see where they were going! Mouse began to cough and her eyes were turning red. Dragon was up the front holding onto the ropes and struggling to keep the boat from crashing into the river bank. Just as he smelt cooked potatoes a huge gust of wind lifted him out of the boat way up in the air. That was no trouble for him because Dragons can fly. As he was sailing up and up he looked back down at Mouse who was saying,

"Whoo hoo," and waving. Dragon let go of the ropes and caught the kite in mid-air. He rolled it up and was about to fly back down when he saw that the river was heading towards a huge waterfall! He dived down to the boat, threw the sail in and called out to Mouse to hang on tight. And just as the boat was going over the falls he gripped it with his arms and legs and carried it into the air. "Whoo hoo!" cried Mouse again.

Some distance below the waterfall, Dragon floated the boat back on the water and all was fine. They sat on the white sand and ate their potatoes. Dragon caught a fish which he cooked as well. They slept that night on the sand under the kite a little distance from the roaring waterfall.

Several days passed and the river became wider and slower. Then one day Dragon caught a fish which he said was a salt water fish.

A little while later the breeze increased and the tiny boat bounced through the small waves with Mouse at the back and Dragon steering. The air began to smell of salt. Then one afternoon the river looked like it was flowing in the opposite direction. This was most alarming to Mouse who had not heard about tides, she thought they were going the wrong way! Dragon tasted the water and it was salty.

The river banks had disappeared and now before them and all around was an endless horizon of water. They had reached the sea.

That night a thin moon came up near the horizon and after their meal of fish and potatoes they cuddled up under the kite and went to sleep.

Late at night they were awakened by strange noises. It sounded like someone out of breath swimming close to the boat.

They both looked over the side but could see nothing. Then Dragon stood up and roared a big flame into the sky and Mouse could see that all around them was a school of dolphins. They all disappeared when they saw Dragon's flame.

"We must go home," said Dragon the next day, "or we will never find our way back."

Mouse asked which was the way home and Dragon pointed back the way they had come. Mouse looked puzzled.

"First I must try and catch a big sea fish." Dragon said as he threw out his fishing line.

In no time at all the line went whizzing out and Dragon felt the weight of a huge fish on the other end. He jumped up the front of the boat and hung on to the line. The little boat began to pick up speed and fly through the water.

"Whoo hoo!" and "Whee!" cried Mouse who was hanging onto the back. After many hours the boat began to slow as the fish tired, but not for long. After many more hours Dragon managed to pull his line in so far that he could see the fish and it was huge. "Whoo hoo!" cried Mouse again and added, "You will never catch that it is too big!" Dragon struggled and struggled and soon the fish was alongside the boat.

"Whoo hoo!" cried Dragon and as he cut the line he said,

"Go and be free to live your life in the sea!" The fish disappeared into the depths of the deep blue ocean.

Mouse and Dragon spent several more days in their boat on the water. Once a whale came close and looked Dragon in the eye in a friendly kind of way and some nights the playful dolphins would come about chattering and making popping and huffing and puffing noises.

After sometime Dragon looked at Mouse and said that he did not know the way home after all. Mouse was very quiet as their supply of potatoes was running low.

Later that night the dolphins came about their boat again and Dragon thought he heard one of them say,

"Have you seen the one with the long orange tail and the green wings? He is the funniest looking fish I have ever seen!"

"Oh," said Dragon to the dolphins, "we are lost at sea. Do you know the way back to the river?" Then a very strange thing happened. The dolphins began to bump their noses on the front of the boat and Mouse woke up.

"Throw them a line," she said. So Dragon threw one of the kite ropes in the water and after a short moment the little boat was travelling at a steady pace through the small waves back the way they had come.

For two whole days and two whole nights the dolphins took it in turns to tow the boat. Then on the third day Dragon called out,

"Land!" and Mouse squealed,

"Whoo hoo!"

Dragon flew up in the air with Mouse on his back just to check and sure enough it was their river. When they landed back in the boat Dragon pulled on the rope and the Dolphins came about with their heads out of the water to get a better look at Dragon. They were all laughing.

"You are the funniest fish we have ever seen!" They said to Dragon. "Show us your fire again." And with that Dragon raised his head and roared a big flame into the sky and all the dolphins started leaping out of the water with excitement. Mouse and Dragon called out with one voice.

"Thank you!"

Dragon was very fond of his little boat which he had made himself but he soon realised that the current of the river was too strong for them to row against. With a big smile he and Mouse pushed it back out onto the wide blue sea and Dragon threw the kite in the air. They watched the boat go skidding across the water to drift on by itself possibly forever. As they watched the wind grew stronger and to their surprise the little boat leapt up off of the water and flew far up into the sky. They both saw it go up and up until it became a tiny speck, a little dark dot in the blue.

They turned around and began the long walk home. Past the waterfall and the rapids and around the broad and narrow parts of the river. Dragon caught fish and Mouse still had some potatoes left and she knew the names of many wild plants some of which they ate.

Till one day they came upon their little house nestled in the small clearing just as they had left it. Dragon went in and started the fire and Mouse found some old beans growing in the garden. Their long adventure was over.

The next day Dragon cut some wood and set about making another little boat and Mouse wanted to buy some material to make another kite but she bought some potatoes instead.

Morale of the story:
Love your life and it will set you free.

China, 2013

Deep in the misty night I bounce down again into the cotton smoggy bosom of Guangzhou airport.

Pale yellow space-ship lights stare into the expectant early morning as an embryonic sun yawns within them and pierces into the bus which is a beeping, door sliding, sardine tin full of the multitudes - with the baggage entrails to follow. Whisked into the custom's arms to beep again for the electric smells of bombs and other deathly joys. The whiff of the TV carries on behind. Waiting for the train of people, who like the door-mat are flat and squashed by the millions and frayed. Only pages on people's mobiles flout their squeaky voices to entertain. Now again the airport train on the smooth and polished floor, ejects me, bottoms up, into yet another aircraft bowel where mesmerised by the electric chemtrail-gas I rest in a pre-dawn euphoria.

Soon I will be in her arms, a bleating sheep once again formalised by the electric touch of Lilly – a frail fish or water-reed blown by her hot wind. Tossed like a crinkling leaf into the stocking street well above the knee.

Two in the morning, my flight is again delayed! Then suddenly Shenyang airport and my heart beats faster. She is here somewhere in the crowd. Small, insignificant, hard to find except by her white teeth smile. The magnetic fizz draws me to her eyes.

There she is glowing. We hug and I submerge into her flesh again. Sinking like an aspirin.

What is it in a face, the eyes, the nose, the mouth, the skin? Or is it the skull behind the earthly sags, the tree root-hairs which cling between the stones? Or the fungus features which effuse out from the bone? The cracked, fissured, crinkly skin like the mother's womb or a man's scrotum, all landscaped beautifully. And all is underlined by the mouth, the full stop of the tongue and the dimple on the chin - with grin.

The plane ejects us like ball-bearings at 3:00 in the morning. Lilly's brother Cholong drives the car, after spending some time in the parking station looking for it and still in a dream, I feel the presence of its warm engine even though I have not seen it yet. Yes it is right before us, hiding.

He drives fast, breaking suddenly - the buildings flash by. Lilly and I are in the back being thrown this way and that - collide and rock, collide and rock. The throb of humanity squeezes us closer. Like a river in flood we follow the rush. Bouncing from one edge to the other, the oncoming traffic, our bodies flung through chaos - two asteroids on a mission, all else deflects from our path. I catch her eyes she looks at me sideways with a half-smile. We are together again. Our mute silence surrounds us, so loud and deafening, the cries of love which echo from the deepest chasms of the underground. I grab the door handle and begin swinging like a monkey.

The hotel room above elevates our nest. The bed is once again a garden of delight. Soon we fall into each other's arms to bridge the ancient sea which has separated us all these pinch-gut months.

From the fish bowel I peer out again and down. Then down the swallowing lift to arch and march the starchy street, avoiding the spittle our footsteps on the edges of their pools, avoiding the flood and the drowning of health. On the street corners a few straggling bushes throw their arms despairingly this way and that. They are vestiges of paradise, wispy - of pubic hair still left, cloistered in by the rush either side; knots of wood bravely making their stand and clinging on by hardened roots deep in the teeth of the pavement. Their autumn sags, despondent hopes thrashed by the hot exhausted winds of cars, air-conditioning units, street fires and the breathless gasps of children as they run, run to catch the last bus to paradise and school.

There are potatoes spilled on the road, they are the knuckles of children gravel-rashed by the rush. Rolled rounded stones at the bottom of the river gathering speed with spittle, mucosa and hope.

The same street, shop and cold. The smell of China's asbestos brakes, of concrete and washing powder, steel and glass. We are the children of the wash. Our lives are the splinters of the Beijing sunlight, disgorged from the nail-beds of Reason, of logic - the book of harsh laws. Our lives forced out of us each day. The brain spirals into vine forests where leopard and monkey and bird, insect - verdant and breathing, dance in a green opera.

These things like her, I have missed each day - have fathomed the bottom of my heart. No stagnant pond-weed here through which the spotted green eel slides.

Times hands dance lasciviously about me. The porcelain tide is all around smooth and unblemished, voluptuous and wanting. The women so full of compassion. The yellow fog-smog blackens the beings as they shuffle and scrape, cough and wheeze. The clearing of the Chinese throat is like a barking dog called, "Reason!" Unblemished expressions paint the creative street.

Yes these people are forlorn in times hands, their backs and lungs will be broken by this wretched fearful moon. The innate fear of each other besmirches and worms out like a disease from their innate compassion and is in each person's face revealed by stress and the need to satisfy their government's needs. Such beauty is laid waste by each countries protective mothering instinct commonly called a bank or a library wherein are kept very busy people in one room and government's secrets in another. Black-box secrets or giant robotic mosquitoes waiting to suck our blood.

How can we be their slaves if we know they brain-wash us into this? They spray us with poison and saturate our food then state it is a free perfume they give which we spit back out in the gutter and even in the corridor of the aeroplane where a man explodes his nose like an elephant on the blue-carpet sea.

He alone, with nappy on, is their child screaming to be free. A great symbolic gesture! His cells enmeshed with an evil fear which his government says is protecting him! Why must we be fools in this and not see the dogma of Reason? Reason gives and takes what Reason believes and wants. Moving in and out it makes no noise. Reason is essentially greedy and consumes everything. Its arm is the scythe of time and measures life with a competitive gesture.

Consciousness! That is what it is, that is all! An internal whispering mirror. Thus we give all to this silly thing called God, to be redeemed and by that giving obey the governments of the world. It is this hatred game which is dressed to kill and is like an auto-immune disease which is afraid of speaking out the same as a helpless drowning butterfly which sinks in its own spittle – China, I love you, as cruel as life itself! I give you my body but not my mind.

I watch the people flit past, splinters from a tree, each one an orgasm of light and love -

each breathing each other's fumes and smiling about their hijacked dreams. Like wood our hearts grow stronger and when under pressure our consciousness expands.

China is such a nice place, the people are so sweet. The children play, they are not allowed to cry, if they cry they get so much attention they come out the other end expecting love ramped with buttresses of joy. And joy comes to them as idols of the imagination such as television sets, computers, the ubiquitous mobile phone, big expensive cars, a happy married life, plenty of good fortune and food loaded with the promise of good health. All these material things the soul cannot carry into the afterlife unless humility becomes a blessing of the self or unless we use it all as a fire accelerant for self-immolation.

Two children running dressed like adults, pausing on the pedestrian crossing, boy and girl on the bridge of uncertainty. China will buy them an ice-cream, will make sure they both fall in love and think the world is new. Towering above their dreams the city buildings stand strong with the promise of dripping money to protect them - once I stood tall like them – taller now as I am protected by a Lilly in flower.

Traditions old and intertwining, simply old and often binding.

To really make an impression on the environment and clean up everybody's air we must start with the children. They are the ones to repair and carry on. We must not leave them a worse environment than when they were born. How much can a single person do?

You can change the world!

In India I watched through the window of a school as all the children tore up paper and threw it on the floor of the classroom. When they got outside and had their lunch they threw that paper down on the ground too. They were not taught to respect a clean place. There were pigs in the yard. The traditional sacred cow in the cities has trouble finding grass to eat, there are so many plastic bags on the ground! So they eat paper with organic ink we hope, which colours the milk blue!

Our health is the only thing we own and can take with us on our journey. Each journey is sacred, let it be pure like a mountain stream, fresh and clear.

At last a place to sit and view the passing parade. China again, she lilts, she wafts, she wanders, and I have her still. Her streets laid waste with plastic rubbish - the afterthoughts of love. Her blood is mine, her kiss my food. She is still afraid to let go- to address my challenges – she hides and turns away.

Ah but in the turn embraces an essence in the freedom of the West. Hence her curious eyes descend into mine, yet only for an instant.

The autumn skies before were grey and clothed my hugs and hers with the strange prophetic mystery of tomorrow. Where will the children play when the mists are dense and the streets awash with refuse? Where will love dare to intercourse with the freshness of youth and spring?

I do not dream. My fear is foot-bound, alone with my terror as we both stride about like water skippers, dancing in the still of the reflecting pool.

The city is opposite to love. The city does not love there is no time. Here the wheels hug the roads, the erect buildings penetrate the deep sky and possess the soil. The traffic lights wink at the people expectantly dolling out a frenetic staccato stop start frequency like printing money. They move like puppets, crossing legs, crossing streets. The fallen stranger hugs the ground. The spittle in the womb hugs the Earth as it drapes across her pavements rising and falling, swaying with the car exhausts.

The government possesses the reigns of love, saying not to do this and not to do that. For a long time those government people were able to have as many women as they wanted! Now the rich go to other countries to find to their amazement that the West has sex in special ways, all the time because they are clean, all the time! And that the heart is indeed ruled by the singing genitals.

She is beautiful as she walks, she carries the Earth in her groin – the sun and the moon and all men agree but do not say in any detail! His invisible grasp cannot find any reasonable words.

Shenyang

We venture to the market to see what we can find. Not far down the dusty street past the large boxes and the blank sheds up the hand hewn granite steps, how could we lose our way? Then into a mediaeval world and the raucous reach of time. Shenyang and the smell of rotting chickens assails us - the rubbish piled at the sides of the lumpy walkway occasionally potholed with black watery sludge. The walls of the building thick and unrelenting, white and cold, streaked with the brown and black of many small accidents.

A young man beeps behind us in his motorised bicycle, the carry-all of which just fits between the walls. He passes slowly, nose in the air, his white tee-shirt beautifully clean. He goes inside the building and finds he cannot pass at another point. I watch as he beeps his horn incessantly and waits, then beeps again in obvious anger. The sound echoes throughout the building and I jam my fingers yet again in my ears. People turn to look, his sludgy nostrils black and deep, full of many small accidents.

Across my shoulders the weight of vegetables bears down. Lilly walks slowly observing every possible food substance and asking the price. She goes inside the building which is as dark as an unlit underground. I follow carefully behind avoiding the puddles of sludge - the wet slippery floor. Forward to face the rank odour, the slosh of rotten bones, the yellowing livers and kidneys of the dead birds. On chest-high benches chickens lie turning pale green with their black pupils staring white and their long necks gravity-stretched like pipes over the edge to increase the waterfalls of blood which clots on the floor. Their sister's squirming guts still active as they watch the ground for worms. Their feet and claws hacked off as these are considered the most delicious parts. The thumping sound of the blade makes a slow beat to accompany the raucous rap-gaggle of the bargaining shoppers.

The smell is intense and wafts about the back of my throat. Further on in the yellow dim light Lilly goes on, her floral broad blue hat a party amongst the graveyard. The tables now are filled with red meat of horse and donkey, beef and goat, great slabs of drool slip onto the floor. The temperature is hot and steamy from all the dead carcases. On we walk through these corridors of dried blackness where each bone is still virgin to be gnawed. At the last shop Lilly pauses and pants in front of a warm pile of chicken's kidneys smeared with blood. She says they are tasty and her smile shows her beautiful white teeth. But I say no and point instead to a bag of chicken freshly packed and sealed. She turns her beak sideways to observe them, fluffing her feathers slightly.

In the market the dead fish blindly stare at this grey sea of concrete sky. Their fossil fins and hardened scales, upturned like dimpled frozen waves in time. Their tiny brains pressing to the edges of their skulls trying to escape. Those virgin wishes not unlike our own. Their snake-like smell exudes back through the blackest corridors and reveals the dreadful lust which saw them pick the bones of their fellow fish. Now on earth - we the same as them - walk upright and joust about in the fields and pick the bones of other men.

Back we go the way we came, my feet now wet upon the black sloshy concrete. Past the tank of fish, their last swim in dirty water. Then a pile of them on the ground still flapping. The hack of blade, dead and dull, a single thud of time.

An old stooped woman with extraordinarily large bandy legs squeezes in behind Lilly. One arm swings from side to side, the other drags a trolley through the slush. Such a broad physique I cannot pass! Several times I try but her legs are so wide! Up close behind her now to find a broader passage and soon I am treading in deep gutters of black ooze. The woman is slow her single wildly swinging arm may knock me flat and is impossible to push past. Her split legs carved by hack and age, a formidable spring-loaded barrier. Perhaps she trod the same path when she was young with both arms wildly swinging and a smile as broad as her legs. Lilly's hat is soon to disappear around a corner and completely vanish. The woman turns with Lilly at every corner and soon my impatient youth is paddling in the drain to float past again.

The market goes on and on, the crush of people above the crush of old vegetables. The slight breeze sends the dust about my lungs. And above in the greying sky a dismal sun peeps through the torn umbrellas, the hanging ropes, the decaying canvas and plastic awnings. Having at last escaped the trolley woman I feel as free as a swamp bird with wet feet who has devoured every smelly fish and now looks desperately for a place to either sink, pass out, or shrivel.

As I dip my head to avoid being strangled and picking up speed, Lilly's bottom under the rim of my slouch hat, picks forward. Past the great mound of small dried fish, past the giant carrots and radishes dancing, past the stall keepers with their half-tooth grins and extended fangs like ancient deep-sea fish, Chinese eyes laughing, spitting teeth. And wherever we go the trailing glances of the old and young who point their wishing arms our way and hope that one day they will go to another country and find a young rich man to steady their sway, look after them in old age and give them more than one child.

Two small dogs practice tossing a black dried banana around a pole, the experienced ratters of gang-land, they will not be eaten if love finds them.... perhaps. Past the square water tanks of writhing crabs, spinning and swirling, which are waltzing beautifully together above their exhausted children who clasp claws together in a final prayer at the bottom of the soup. Head down we pick forward quietly, deftly, in fear of slipping on rotten fruit and falling in the drain - the spittle marks our way.

With our modest bag of fruit, chicken's kidneys and mushrooms for Mother, we hoist our umbrella-flag and head up to the eerie. Rocketed back up the building's throat, the lift door opens to regurgitate us out into the red carpet corridor. Lilly has lost her way again within these concrete veins. But we are too late and our door is electronically shut. Back down the lift we go with the heavy shopping to pay more money so I steal another kiss as I brace myself, on the way up, for the anti-gravity pull and the breach-birth into the corridor.

Once in the room we sit to eat our fruit. She spits the seeds out whereas I eat the lot - now crunching like two birds. These seeds, I say, will go a long way to preventing cancer. She observes me, turning her glittering eyes so fast. "Especially lemons!"

With much arm waving and drawings, sketches of alimentary canals, of bottoms, lungs and other physiology, I attempt to describe the foods which are acid forming in the Chinese diet which, in the long term, can increase the likely-hood of contracting cancer. The little worms that come and stay are followed by refuse eating moulds that play and live in symbiosis with other little animals. And if the cell walls are not slippery as in an acid system, all the scavengers stay late for the rotting feast. However cancer is curable I say.....

Since my arrival I have talked much about health, now that I can see the problem, they do not tire of listening to advice. Many say "yes" but like us all, are pressed with too much information. The bottom-line being that the Chinese diet is too rich in protein and the government is not doing enough in its duty of care to inform people of other health dangers in the environment - a few are mentioned herein.

Alone in this rambling city, we spend our time gaping at the lost luxuries of the ancients who had peace of mind, fresh water and many hours to sharpen their spears. We bounce like playful balls from one scene to the next exploring the delights of love.

Shenyang was the second place in China where emperors decided to build palaces. The primary place being Beijing, eight hundred kilometres south. The landscape around Shenyang is flat. Long ago this massive alluvial plane of meandering rivers would make the waterways swell and snake toward the sea according to the snows in the hills of Russia and provide habitat for millions of tortoises. So many that the tortoise–muds are now famous for their richness. Lilly tells me there is no reason to fear flooding on this flat land as the water is soon carried underground and disappears in immense sand deposits below.

In the heart of Shenyang a great river flows. Either side of it are tall building which seem to lean out over the view. These towers are new and have no glass; their eyes are black and blind. The river is deep green and slow with few fish, if any. Close to the river bank is a golf course with rich people straddling, squinting and hitting the whites of their eyes or balls. Only the rich can swing their metal so far and the fish have died from eating too many stray balls full of mercury. Then in between the course and the water a thin row of planted trees before her wet green belly. One cannot get near the water! One cannot look into her depths. Nature is before us - all please refrain from touching her, for in the loving are insipid seeds of destruction.

The nutrient run-off from the grassed area makes the acidity of the water rise ensuring a constant green colour from algal blooms which starve all other life of oxygen and brings disease to the non-existent fish. If fish were there they must be protected by plastic-bag suits and special breathing apparatus. The way to help this river is to begin at its source and replant the river banks, yes banks – clean water is money-soil, with indigenous plants in the natural way they grew long before the Chinese people came. That river could be full of prawns, sparkling with life!

I write to the Environmental Agency of Shenyang and ask if I can suggest a few ways to help the water quality of the river and plant native riparian species. I am told by Lilly's niece who studies City Environments at Shandong University, who speaks reasonable English, that they will probably consider my request a joke! I muse that China has it all albeit round the wrong way or polished to the max until the fog of reason settles and we are back to sharpening our spears.

China TV so colourful, the blue of skies, the whites of clean clothes and glistening teeth, the dark space of deep-time, absorbing the sentimental and the plasticised ethereal cosmos to create a blubbering highly controlled stereotypical infant immersed in either blood or tears. The wars of men, the clash of steel, the broken hearts of the women's wombs, drip, drip.

China is rapacious with its addiction to love stamped out in red uniforms in the field. Yet all the birds and fish have gone – nature has flown away and love with its striving piteously echoes the loss; black eye sockets beside the river reaching out for help like love songs whispered over flat green water.

The news programs on prime-time TV feature the daily criminal activity accompanied by the weeping repentant. Their lives truncated by their evil deeds and redeemed of course, by the hungry jowls of justice. Those criminals are viewed crying as they pitch mournfully for a green thorny garden of red red roses. Ha, caught in the act by CTV cameras everywhere, they blush and turn, turn and blush and turn in their roots, squeezed like an orange drying in the evening dusk – to turn away and possibly never be seen again. Which flesh the thorn pierces only their desire can tell and the sword dissect as the cash registers zing and weigh their organs. Behind those bars of steal, each one an exclamation mark – no words of compassion before the final thud.

The young girl had no money to feed her child. Her husband was sick and could not work.

She stole some eggs and some peanuts, she has no shoes. The young man minds the child; he does not wear a smile. Her face is smeared with tears and grease on the TV. She accompanies our evening meal, just before the jet fighters, the guns and the news.

In the gaping street the innocent flurry past. Sidewalls of huge bill-boards display young girls all dressed the same in vivid red clashed with green, cleaning a public hand-rail. The sign reads,

"Culture." No they do not smile, if the government said "smile" all the girls in China would smile and dance - as they do already. These posters are aimed at indoctrinating young people as all watch the television, the inebriated and the dying. Another sign reads,

"Patriotism-Innovation-Inclusiveness-Virtue." In other words one is not virtuous if one is neither patriotic nor innovative and does not help others, especially the government with new ideas. Throughout the world those who say they care for our bodies and beings feed us the illusion that they really do care. In China everybody works very hard long hours for very little money! And Beijing alone has seventy thousand millionaires!

Lilly spends hours photographing herself in the mirror in the bathroom fully clothed like a child with a new toy camera- she smiles so much I wonder if the grin will stay that way - laughing too. The anxiety about her ill health, her fat and her age all recede with the smile. I join in her play and shoot us together with the camera in front of my face to not show its terrifying age beside her youthful beauty. Her photos are good, her beauty revealed, her spirit is naked and innocent in this forest of concrete. A beautiful woman deserves the right to ponder her beauty before her curious self.

We smile in the mirror for immigration purposes, but Lilly deletes all the pictures by mistake - every single one since my arrival! She is not pleased and demands another massage. I call her my demanding little mouse and say,

"Fat cells do not leave the body they just get smaller!"

Her fat little cheeks will go all wrinkly and the hippopotamus smile she wears at present will disappear. Whispers of death flood my being as I peer down the rifled barrel of the mirror which I rarely look at back home. Grey streaks of offal smear my cheeks and I can hear my lethargic bottom and flat feet scrape across the ground.

Again my card disappears into the nasty little slit of the Automatic Teller Machine, small men puppet-like with large machine guns immediately fall from the sky on long strings. My card slides in like my heart piercing into hers, lost in a forbidden world of chop-sticks, spearing and piercing deep into my ballooning self, deflating flatulence like a spinning balloon emptying into vortex of pussy. Between her legs will I die? Spacious womb I enter your eternity of time, blind and swimming where Reason dilutes to a vapour far away and words have no legs or arms and simply drown – the decorated fall, the simple rot and roar as wealth has no empty-stomach meaning only bad air. Thus the plastic vapour of my burning card comes back out at me from the black-hole.

Because she spends most of her time working she does not know her way around the city. Often she asks our whereabouts and often the people she asks are left smiling or laughing. I find this an endearing quality of her character. Though I do not understand the language her beautiful smile and buoyant personality seems to make people smile and feel happy. She is not afraid to ask the policemen directions, they are very helpful once they see me tagging along, however they never show the flicker of a smile, not once. They are led to believe that they carry the weight of China on their shoulders. Their brows reflect the government's brows which are deeply furrowed.

Lilly is tired. Her ragged body flops about me again as before. She carries the weight of China and her family, rising to cook food early in the morning, going to market to return before 8:00 am, then catches the bus to see me at 10:00. I feed her and revive her with massage which she has done for others for years - but she has forgotten how to relax. Now it is her turn I say. Her desperation is evident with pain in between the shoulder blades and a sore side hip and still her left thigh.

My hands and arms begin to fall off with a morning of vigorous massage.

She takes me by the arm and packs my bag again. Already a bewildering assortment of seemingly superfluous garments and other oddments – and only just arrived! We roll down the slippery lift stealing kisses and tumble out into the bright sunshine. China never relents, her chaos is as rapid as the first avalanche of people who baulk before our step and look again. The women look at me and then at Lilly, she says they are jealous.

We are changing hotels, Lilly decides to take me closer to her family house where she recognises the streets and the market is closer, the restaurants cheaper. The people friendlier with fewer lifts, less vertigo and frowns.

She is so soft, so delicate as she sits beside me at the controls, her face unblemished by pain or hard work. Her yellow jacket reflects beneath her chin. Her mellow eyes drunk in the peace beyond death. Her hands are tender lilies new and exciting like a river before its entry into the ocean - a mountain eroding before its desert grows and melts away with love.

As the coloured lights ascend the distant skyscrapers, the dark descends the same as our rich food. The meal the night before was served in an expensive restaurant and was, by comparison to a cheaper "peoples" restaurant, so deplorable I thought Lilly would say something, instead she said nothing only belched as the waitresses politely said goodnight.

Each morning we walk to the early morning market to eat traditional Chinese food. It is served in small square buildings with small square rooms painted white with oil and spill marks smearing the work-load to the ground. Outside the engine of the market roars as it shears close to the open window, its wheels well oiled. We buy soy milk in a plastic bowl which is covered by a plastic bag. And long thin white bread which has been deep fried in oil to resemble a tasteless puffy thing. Some days we eat the whey from tofu heated and served with sprigs of coriander. Some days we eat dumplings made of white sweet potato flour with garlic chives and shrimps wrapped inside then boiled in water. Thus the day rolls forth past the boiling oil the clatter and the din into the foaming street. Like small enlivened shrimps we pick-step between the protein.

Next afternoon we venture outside, the Mouse and the Dragon, plodding empty-stomach foot-steps. Lilly asks unsuspecting people about places to eat and directions as the meal in China is so important and she is concerned about the price.

In the small smeared white walled restaurant she fingers through the sticky menu like a cat with a mouse. The walls are yellow from tobacco smoke. The meal is ordered and we sit and drink some twenty bottles of beer. Presently the young cook comes creeping back in with his eyes to the ceiling. Stopping and starting, standing for long moments. I am able, at this stage, to keep one eye on him and one on Lilly. It takes me a few seconds to notice his fly swat. His aim is deft, his eye well trained, not one but three flies fall to the ground. He quickly bends down and picks them up with his fingers.

The food arrives with due haste and is delicious and cheap. Black fungus, Chinese cabbage, other greens, tofu, chips, duck, something that looks like it could have been a fish, prawns, rice, boiled lettuce, dried donkey entree, quail eggs, noodles, chicken knuckles and soy sauce with lashings of garlic, tahini, and strange dumplings filled with garlic chives, seaweed and shrimps. Lilly devours all with the speed of a mouse plague. Gradually the beer goes down much like my head which ends up so close to the floor that I can see a little fly dance across and spin around waving its arms and stomping its feet. Then another and soon many more come in straight lines all stamping in time and doing the occasional pirouette.

The people on the street are friendly and helpful, they laugh and smile, though I sense an underlying wariness. The ladies holding hands often wear an assortment of funny hats such as Micky Mouse ears, which are so clean. It would not surprise me if we saw a hat made from Coco-Cola tins for its consumption is on the rise. And if teeth are put in a glass of it overnight they will disappear! Lilly tells me it is excellent for cleaning toilets. I muse and wonder why the people do not wear Panda Bear hats instead! Hats symbolise ones individuality or lack of it and Chinese people love to wear them. Often businesses give hats away - they know how good a hat can be for advertising.

The social media providers know that comedy and flippancy elevates the spirit with comic relief, hence wherever they can a cartoon image portraying an insipidly sweet baby-faced young person festoons every small space. These little cartoon people are a-political, immature sexually and sometimes have simple nonsensical phrases attached. As a result people begin to relate to these little fairies and buy clothes with their favourite characters portrayed. Sometimes their pets are revered the same way. "I love my cat'" was written on one girl's tee-shirt, this may have related to something else as one never sees "I love my dog." The same applies in Western culture however we display demons and skulls and death to satisfy our ancient lineage of aggression conquering fear, which of course creates more uncertainty.

China dances about me her lithe body berry-like in the gentle slope of wind. Her mountains risen while in her underground the dragon turns as I say to her,

"I am happiest when I write and make love to you," each golden note and word fashioned through her flickering eyes.

As the night closes I show her how to mend her sore back stressing that I cannot. That with this simple exercise, she will be able to mend it herself. Before she begins to snore I take the pillow from the back of her head and raise her knees till the soles of her feet are flat on the bed. Then with her hands by her side I ask her to stretch her shoulders away from her pelvis thus extending her spine and to say to herself the words, "relax, relax" and place those words directly within the area of pain. This is guaranteed to work as fast as one teaches oneself to relax. Soon the room reverberates and I cannot sleep for the noise. She lies beside me like a little purring cat.

The longer I stay in China I find more and more people with cancer young and old. Many of Lilly's friends have the ailment. What can I do? I cannot speak the language so I scrape words into the translating machine every day repeating myself a thousand times,

"Body acid, China protein too much, no exercise - food rotten. To alkalize body, morning time - first thing - drink lemon juice and two teaspoons of apple cider vinegar. Do not eat much meat, milk, bread, noodles, alcohol or coffee - makes body acid, no processed food!" Then drink pawpaw leaf tea three times a day if you do have cancer and buckets of vitamin C with plant pigments known as bioflavonoids. Eat dark green fresh leafy vegetables. China take off your shoes and stop smoking! I try to start a website named, "www.chinastopsmoking.today" but soon realise I cannot speak the language and here Google and Facebook are banned.

Steam rises from the gutters as the dragon moves below. They are repairing the underground pipes now while it is warm for in winter the ground is frozen and no machine can dig. The steam heats all the houses if they pay. It is black-fire from Australia which heats the water and pumps it through the tall buildings under considerable pressure.

Lilly's foot goes into cramp; she rises abruptly and shakes her foot violently. The theory is bang your head to forget about your foot. No magnesium I say! Plenty of greens but the magnesium is boiled out of them - the leaves not the foot!

The sky is blue with a fresh autumn breeze. A healthy rush of oxygen as deep as the sea where it came from. The sky is breathing as I watch a small cloud go in and out then hurry along. The TV news talks of America bombing North Korea and shows images of American, Korean and Chinese weaponry. I do not understand the language but gather that China is a little worried and uses the opportunity to bare its breast or chest, "shirt-fronting" as it is so eloquently called. The images of advanced weaponry must fill young hearts with feelings of security, bravery and pride. My own TV was so full of revolting junk I threw it in the dam. Even the news back home is rubbish. It keeps repeating that we are going to war. Then next month…"We are off to war….again!" Then more patriotic brain-washing, "We are sorry for the dead, let us celebrate them!" Will the children look at the rubbish-bin of history and sort the truth from the lies? No, pessimism does not heal the poor and death is very dead and does not hear any praise!

I mention to Lilly that the whole world fears China and America. That if they ever fight the world will end. America has a poisonous bomb the same as many other countries and it is Australia which has supplied them with the organic fuel to make it. China, England, Russia, France, India, Pakistan maybe more I do not know, have this weapon. America alone has twenty four times world overkill which means everything living on the earth would be exterminated twenty four times! When this bomb was discovered the humanoid extra-terrestrial life forms, tried to stop its production by shooting many test flights out of the sky and melting the electrics of others on the ground. The American government has defied this challenge and kept those actions a secret.

Now many of the aliens fear us for we are cruel, they do not want to help.... for a price perhaps? They have given America much technology and America has taken much from them. Weaponry now is more advanced than the simple words within this book could ever hope to describe. Words like Radionics, Psychotronics, Scalar technology. Like other governments they have learnt that a broken tree will grow to heal itself stronger than before hence they milk their respective populations with tyranny and fear and blame and kill other innocents - "terrorists, conspirators" they call them - in the name of Reason which is religion's political disguise. Other names flamboyantly brazened to delude are - social cohesion, God, order, consciousness, all of which - one would hope, would never lift a finger to do harm.

Under the banner of eugenics and sustainability they came marching down the road, the illuminati have flushed us out, our eyes pallid and lost. Our faces expressionless, dragging our skeletal flesh, our brief cases full of pills and empty coffee cups. Our stomachs full of nano-robots like gnawing crabs with national flags. Some have their electrics, their computers their mobiles grafted to their ears with wires untied dangling like monkey's tails behind. Umbilical cords sucking misinformation, sucking Reason's glare.

If I painted the history of Shenyang, it would be a bloody massacre. Lilly does not know like so many Chinese people, that China took Mongolia and the Manchurian Empire by force and more recently Tibet. But every country is the same! The English when they came to Australia massacred many indigenous people who still occupy the land. They massacred many American Indians in America when they took that country as well. Powerful countries have cut up the world like butchering a corpse. Chinese people simply do not know their beloved ancestry, they think their government is innocent!

Why do the old men dance about with sticks on the television? Lilly says they are playing a game. More, it is that they carry on the tradition of war which once remembered is twice sanctified. War and sacrifice should be put on top of the long pole of consciousness or flown in a hurricane like a kite with a severed string and never mentioned again!

We must not glorify the dead, for others will want the same fate. Our time here on Earth is to learn this lesson - to not perpetrate war. Few people understand this, as fear and other negative symptoms are rebirthed to continue. Look up, lookout, study the clouds; the universe is ever expanding with love.

China is dirty, there is no other word for it. Now the water has been turned off for the day in the hotel, Lilly says it is normal. Normal that they do not wash for a week, that they rarely wash their hands, that they spit in the basin others use to wash their face, that they all pick their noses in public and wipe it everywhere, that they urinate and defecate in full public view, same as India and other Asian countries. Ah, the natural world, expanding with love.

Dirty - that the street is lined with spit, that the throat is cleared while eating and its contents spat out sometimes on the floor. That the pavements are strewn each day with refuse and cleaned by orange clad people with masks that cover the entire face and head. That from each tiny crack wafts the smell of rotten tobacco butts and other foods whose fruit skins like foreskins are discarded without a thought for its recycle value or the little old grandmother with the bandy legs who might slip on it, fall, break a leg and land in a garbage bin! That their rubbish is not sorted - the organic from the inorganic. And the soft music goes on and on and gets louder outside the more expensive shops.

Their private space is as small as their breasts and extends exactly that distance out in front as an old woman pushes me aside to get a better view and beat us to a bargain. Here the only butterfly that floats in the tobacco-breeze is a plastic bag. And the market meats are so old and lacking refrigeration - where sagging fresh greens dip their flowering heads on the road.

However having said that it is easy to fall in love with her ways for in all the countries of the world China has a voice loud and clear. I believe that she will lead the way with her love and her feminine compassion. While the rest of the world is still fighting amongst themselves for so called democracy underpinned by oil and a central banking system - China will streak forward as it is doing now and show the way. Fear of slipping into moral degradation is the big hat everybody wears, it comes down and covers the eyes.

She will have to restore her forests, she will have to repair her rivers, her streams. She will have to recycle refuse and pick up all the plastic bags. She will have to build methane gas plants above her rubbish pits. The Chinese people will have to breathe fresh air again like their traditions say and when her waters and skies are clean all the world will follow - they will have to, for if China does not change, all the world will suffer.

Saturday street market, the man with the leopard furs for sale and other small soft animal skins which he strokes and lovingly cleans. All dead before they could produce even one baby - slowly sliding into extinction.

All the clothes are thrown on a thin sheet on the ground, the shoes with animal fur trims and elevated sexy soles. The Tibetan woman with strange writing on the black shoulders of her coat, with the horns, skins, antlers, skulls and dried penises of mountain dear and sheep naked and excited on the street before her. With bone of mountain lion and jade and turquoise stone bracelets from her country for good luck. Her dark skin and eyes like large black beads of onyx whose depths are as mysterious as her journey from the mountains, surrounded by the pure whites of snow. Perhaps she has the blind eyes of a wild mountain lion. She sells and tells a Snow Leopard's arm-bone story, cut off at the shoulder, long and painful, with elbow, claw and tendons still hanging, long sundried, straggling in the dusty breeze - the cooling autumn breath which heralds the past - now dumped in the dusts of Shenyang. The paw has one claw hacked off with a saw, it was powdered and made into a tea. The man who drank that tea is still excited and roams the hills looking for a mate. The other claws are still splayed by the agony of death, with a little tuft of spotted fur to wrap around its needs. Now dead and gone – and I weep for it, as I see it alive in my thoughts caring for its children far above the village, beneath a dripping over-hang of stone.

Next morning we trundle off to another market enclosed in a huge shed close to the hotel. Lilly started at one end, sampled everything and came out the other end fat! The donkey's heads on the black-blood raw ground and the green plucked chooks she nearly tasted too!

Every market has its little ratting dogs which are dirty and very watchful and probably not owned by anybody. Sometimes I am sure they quietly disappear. They are in stark comparison to the pets people own, mainly the poodles of the poodle-people who often seem to have long straight hair opposite the curly hair of their dogs - a particular breed in themselves. There are many other small species which are prettied up like babies saying don't eat me, just like the women. Their little hearts are bonded, in gracious arms they sway and smile.

Culture and words, writing and painting, singing and dancing, all visual images are of the seasons born and speak of a love of nature sublime. Their small dog pets are their only connection with this ancient past when they danced in the firelight and fed these once wild creatures the left-over bones from hunting. In the cities now are plastic flowers and plastic green foliage which exude an invisible poisonous scent which effuses even more in the sunlight. And the dogs are lovingly dressed like fairies or the only child and given meat from Australia while their keepers gnaw gristle religiously.

Dogs feature much on the TV and in the newspapers as the government realises that a woman needs to satisfy her breeding instinct somehow. Hence there are dogs in very human poses with human smiles and human clothes with coloured lights flashing from their ears! Or face-lifted by computer to stare back down their molecular memory into deep time. Some may think people come back as little dogs. Tibetan Lamas are rebirthed as Shitzus for instance, who are little rascals of play resembling small Tibetan yaks.

The cats I see are the opposite. Asia in general does not like the cat and fears their prowess.

Cats in Burma have their tails cut off as they are too divine and compete with the Buddha for perfection. They inhabit the temples and are allowed to sleep in Buddha's arms and there are millions of them, ten cats to one arm! Dogs on the other hand, in Burma, are dingo-like, thin and gaunt and terrified as the young monks take out their aggression and pelt them with sling-shots and nicely rounded third eyes of clay - all day!

To somebody who has come from a rainforest environment to this cement wilderness, this world appears void of nature so I see the culture as striving to regain its control through a poetry of love and appreciation of fine beauty, the branches small and wispy melting into magical forms like electrical conduits - to help feel connected to the real world inside. It is a leap for art performed with the ease of a Chinese acrobat. For the old world has been cut down and rots in the gutters – like squashed garlic and soy-sauce in a dish. Their hormonal soup preserved forever with the ambient sickly-sweet flavour of sentimentality.

Reclusiveness builds an iron cage around creativity and admonishes the loss. Thus their feelings seek to describe the depths of their instincts and measure everything with money which as time goes by is naturally thrown to the dogs.

The contorted masses of metal embracing concrete and pushing impossibly skyward and the flamboyant industry of liquid glass architecture which expresses an intense striving, is born from this passion or battle with the creative self. It is a lunge into orbit, a real frenzy of art, uncontrolled and vivacious, lively and exuberant, wilful and destructive - almost obscene.

We go to a restaurant with Lilly's friends. Her ex-massage teacher and a young student. The restaurant is owned by the Muslim faction in town with Chinese waitresses who shout to be heard, then giggle and start screaming again. Fortunately there are no bottoms being raised here. But then when I think about it this *is* a place where bottoms are raised and filled. The table next to ours is enlarged with great commotion and a family group of some ten individuals comes and begins to order food. There is so much shouting and gesticulating it is like a boxing match. They too start giggling then screaming like programmed traffic lights. The women squeal, but there are no pigs here! Our table is so quiet by comparison overlooking the street with its similar noise. However when the meal is finished everybody smokes! The air is blue with tobacco fumes. My brain begins to forget things, my eyes water from the acrid spew. Lilly's ex-massage teacher has just recovered from a bout of shingles. His glasses fog, his eyes go red, he begins to glow and look distracted as he too lights up!

"Shingles is caused by worry," I say (though I do not mention the little animals which scratch the nerve) and my mind wanders back home into the green hills and the tall trees with the singing birds and the clean air. With the great cloud-making mountain which throws creeks of pure water over its back.

Long fingers like crab nippers slowly extend across the table with chopstick extensions and long finger nails rarely washed. They are rubbed smooth and strong by rubbing other peoples flesh. The table opposite has finished smoking and many now are spitting into tissues. The clearing of the throat is a common sound, ever increasing in the smog and like the multitude of plastic wrappers is swelling in the guttural pavements.

How can a man heal others if he cannot heal himself? For example a doctor friend in Australia who now walks around with a colostomy bag, whose only way, so he thought, to better health was to

"Cut it all out!" But then General Practitioners are not taught nutrition in much detail. Poor man - poor Australia! All his joy contained in a plastic bag! From the image of the drain and the bag I look back at Lilly's teacher's red eyes - on stalks now.

The skin of my hand, by comparison is a little rough where the barks of trees have scraped the skin away to leave the coarseness of stone, gritty and abrasive. It is agreed that something should be done about my hand which will not form a fist nor will it lie flat, the result of a surfing accident. So off we go in a very dangerous tiny tin-can-car slowly as the massage teacher has shingles and may jam the accelerator on in pain. We drive for ages, green to arrive, red to leave, for I am about to find out the true meaning of Chinese massage.

After breathing in a million litres of car fumes and tobacco smoke we fall out of the car in front of a wild looking house in the middle of a building site in an industrial yard. The door of the house has white fly-baubles at the front hanging down and not much movement inside. Then all at once we are greeted by a young light-walking small lady with a glowing smile. And after some thousands of Chinese words she frowns and takes my left hand in her own. From then on my hand has never been the same. Her little wiry fingers dug deep into the old flesh at the back of my hand and tore the repaired bones and tendons apart so they would heel and go back in the right place. My paw had the wrinkled appearance of a Snow Leopard's claw, dried and long dead, old and well-oiled from painful use. She and they watched as I was reduced to tears of agony, which I admit has been somewhat intense for many years. Ah China massage and the sound of breaking bones and snapping tendons.

Then slowly some movement returned. Wiping my eyes and flexing my new hand we left in the little tin-can-car and would hopefully never return. However my hopes were dashed when we went to another place several days later and there she was again. The business she was allied to managed to sell me some expensive green herbs which included a species of Chinese mushroom grown in New Zealand which supposedly contained magical medicinal properties. My hand was grabbed off me by steel fingers and mangled into mush once more, her little wiry beak stooping to grab tendons and straighten them in the cold wind.

My innocent hand became an offering to a crocodile. I did not need the expensive medicines either! However it may have been useful as I passed out after drinking some of their strange tasting tea which they poured all over me. I woke up peering into a machine that photographed one's eyes and spoke to you advising that you were quite alright so long as you had some tea. The lady who ran the place was full of English and needed some tea too! I kept writing little notes to her about governments sanctioning bad foods for the people, cardboard and greasy oil, fast food American style.

The next day my histamine reaction was in full blast. With red eyes like a dragon and pink wounds welling up from inside my flesh. The colour of which was pale and shot through with bilious red veins. From then on I reduced my green tea intake and the handfuls of herbs, mushrooms and barks I was consuming. My stomach was on an adventure as I long-stepped to slide across the same Chinese toilet though always different - often.

Lilly takes my left hand while I am writing and begins to squash it. She adopts a sort of dedicated look and blinks up occasionally to see if I am alive and in agony. If I am she increases the pressure. She is so kind to think that it will mend and she is as determined as a dentist to help - one way or another. Not flinching in China is a virtue of agony.

After a while I found that ignoring the pain helped reduce the pressure and she backed off a little! So she continues – it is like putting my hand in the mouth of a giant mouse.

The general population has lost their resourcefulness and rely on the State, for food, for clothing, for love, for sex, for air, for happiness, for entertainment, for law enforcement and social cohesion. They have the curiosity of small birds being easily excited, easily disturbed. The music goes on and on and becomes louder in the cities. Sport and more sport, what else is there to do, compete in the plasma world for a stamp? Dream sideways, your life is your creation. Grow anew and drift into a sea of joy. There is no pain love cannot heal. Thank you I'll remember that!

The hospital looms dark and foreboding. My memory a twang of tendon and crushing bone. Already from the street I can hear the cries from within. We approach like timid vermin as though we are contaminated with some dreadful disease or have committed a heinous crime and go forth to be cleansed by white coated angels who study books. But then in the entrance a beautiful yeng-yang sign - a mosaic of tiles on the floor. And I wonder at the lives that have come and gone each metamorphosed into a different hue of deep red tile.

The meaning of the yeng-yang symbol in China is nutrition and health.

Lilly has a smile from ear to ear. She may be pregnant. There I sit, placed like a doll, the expectant father already! Yes I have done something wrong! I confess I have fallen in love with a Chinese beauty and she has seduced and raped me. I had no control!

At that moment a nurse comes out of a white door eating a huge banana. Our eyes for an instant lock and I can see exactly what she is thinking. Lilly is here to check her feminine parts to make sure she is capable of having a child, or maybe with child. Many women stand in queue one has a tattoo on the tops of her hips, which are slightly exposed, another has small hearts tattooed on her finger-tips. The unspoken word here is "man" of which I am the only one amongst this forest of strong delicate white legs. Here tree trunks with wings begin to flit before my eyes. They whizz, they spin, they come through walls and levitate above stair-wells. They dodge one quickly in the isles and slip through thin doors like riley butterflies, without a breath of wind.

Then another man appears wrapped around a pale wan woman, his nerves upon his legs as he sits to cross and recross them with elastic zeal. The expectant father has three ice-creams and forgotten where he left the car keys. His wife looks in six bags and he disappears down the stairs floating on her commands. I think he stuck the keys in the ice cream! Three ice-creams for two? Soon with the heat it is running down her hand and all over her mouth.

Then it is Lilly's turn to emerge from the white doors. And by the size of the smile I do not need her words to tell me she has tested positive. Down the bubbly stairs we go but I leave my lips behind as they are still trembling on the floor above. And breaking into English I blubber, "You are?" and "Yes, you are," and "little person coming?"

She says, "Yes, yes, yes!"

Cripes! I am.... I am a father again! Blithering dribbles and I have lost the keys!

The sun and moon have shone into our world and someone else has visited us as we slept. Now my legs take six steps down the stairs at a time and ready myself to take her slight frame should she slip at the end of the stairs and injure the child. But no she survives and crushes me! And as we walk back over the large yeng-yang mosaic on the floor I notice many spirals in it and believe it is the inside of a warm and fertile place. A young man passes us with a plastic bag over his face, quite normal, it maybe raining I cannot tell my heart is in my mouth. Then we pass a man with his suit on exercising robustly in an exercise yard in the rain. Nothing unusual about that! This is China! So we find a space in the broken wall low down where we can sit and not get squashed or trampled. Lilly seems excited enough however it takes me the rest of the day to realise that she has been checked and assured that she **can** actually have a child and that, no, she is not pregnant - and if my legs would stop rubberising around, I may be able to sit down!

Hospitals rise in the morning smog for love like silent war-memorials or cement fortresses to phenomenal heights barren and forlorn, grey and forbidding ramparts. What do they protect? Who do they protect? Suddenly the windows open and doctors clad in white, fire needles from bows at the public. More cement mushrooms billowing upwards from the confusion. Their closed embryonic eyes blindly peruse the street ready to gobble up the unsuspecting crowd. Ready to flaunt their sales on the blue sea and bring good health to the population depending on the individual's wealth. In days gone by a Chinese doctor paid the patient if he did not mend. Now those healing traditions have changed. Good health is an anachronism all over the world. Pay as you die.

If a person is poor and has more than one child as Lilly did, the extra child is taken away. Sometimes early in the pregnancy, sometimes late. And recently a midwife was found guilty of selling young infants on the black market after telling the mother that the baby had health complications and died. What is the price of a life you ask? As much as your parents paid to keep you alive. As much as the priceless love which enjoyed making you. In other parts of China, closer to Pakistan, ladies are sterilised unknowingly after their first child. If a woman is rich she can have as many children as she wishes depending on how pregnant her bank account is.

The young girl is an emissary of China; she launches herself like a missile into the hearts of all men. She is not a miss-guided missile, she believes in her natural urge. The government plays her card, but she may not want to boomerang and return.

We take Lily's computer to a shop to have its English changed to Chinese so she can read it more easily. The heavy metal thing is captured, tamed and squashed in a tight bag – then accidently dropped on the floor. Will it ever work again? The massaged breakfast and the make-love mouse, squashed as well, to bulge at the hips as we make our move and step on the squealing train. In the underground the computer shop is run by young men who speak another language and have no full-stops. The computer splutters and farts and splashes the screen with graffiti. We are left in space as their small minds are enlivened and watch as Shakespeare digs his screwdriver into the brain of the computer. Then out of its robotic depths a thin Chinese whistle like a policeman at the crossing who has swallowed his tune. Shakespeare squints his forehead as he learns the Tao in ancient Chinese text - a strange language from the book of love. She, the computer, is not scarred as she is slipped back into her love-nest bag though now as before as useless as a pig in mud, as I cannot read Chinese and Lilly knows nothing about computers.

As we walk kilometres home to save money we pass a large building development which is to be built in the centre of Shenyang and on the outside bill-boards are photographs of Western people standing in the streets bemused. I am appalled and say to Lilly that Shenyang will be expensive in the future and that such a development will change the city forever. But curiously that is what I want. Alas I find myself in a quandary, though after realise that the collection of buildings will be monitored extremely closely by hidden minds whose immediate thoughts will beg to differ and perhaps cut the tofu unevenly.

So far I have not seen another Westerner in Shenyang. Very rare! I am sure the Chinese would soon abduct me and look after me if I was to lose Lilly in the crowd but then being so raw they may cook and eat me, passport and all!

The Water Tunnel

Lilly wants to take me to see an underground water tunnel. At first I do not understand as she does not describe it in any detail and soon I find myself following behind as usual in the hot grey sunlight to buy tickets to Benxi.

We catch an air-conditioned bus out of town some distance to the water tunnel after racing from the hotel room at 5:30 am only to find the bus delayed one and a half hours! We are not allowed to board until it is time to leave and the early morning wind blows icy from the mountains in the north. We follow the general throng of plastic, glossy-spangled Chinese tourists to be eventually farted out of the city in a dense cloud to a greener, broader, smoother landscape with small rounded mountains covered with small shrubs they call trees.

The original forest was cut down some forty years ago Lilly says, for her older brother and many others were engaged by the government to level the trees! Now the forest has grown back a little and people are trying to revegetate it albeit slowly.

There seems to be water everywhere in Benxi with a large fast flowing clean river passing silently through the hills. The countryside looks old with rounded metamorphic intrusions protruding from the hill tops and in the valleys granite boulders rub shoulders – bouncing down.

On the side of a deep valley low down close to water level is a hole in the side of the hill some ten meters high by fifty meters wide. Outside this hole are hundreds of Chinese tourists gathered like a swarm of bees with cameras pointing this way and that or with heads bowed praying to computers and mobiles. Do they realise what happens if one places a mobile phone inside a bee hive? All the bees die because they lose their sense of direction! Gradually we are sucked into the hole with them and given a large red raincoat as the subterranean temperature is cold. This is the place where dragons sleep and then suddenly one appears accompanied by dinosaurs, brontosaurus in particular - obviously very lost.

Flowing from deep inside the mountain is a crystal clear river and we all travel by a string of boats back, far back in time, eight hundred meters inside the belly of this dragon. The ceiling caverns out and in like a fossilised intestine and we duck the hard cold jabs of the stalactites as they spear down from above. The whole place is illuminated with hundreds of coloured lights from car batteries. The water is freezing and in some places quite deep as many of the lights are submerged. Stalactites hang from the ceiling from every possible vantage point some seven meters long. Row upon row drip into the water and some on the banks of the stream have given up with the drip and clasp hands with arms meters long.

Some have dripped long thin fingers which stretch around the bed to make cathedrals of intricacy. The whole place is filled with a timelessness beyond the reach of words. We are told that primitive man used the cave thousands of years ago. Which is an acknowledgement that there were people here before the present hominoid. The limestone formations have anthropomorphic names such as "Heart Strings" or "Forest of Love."

Lilly sits beside me, she is afraid she may fall in the icy water. I hold her cold hand and say I came looking for her when she lived in here long ago. And added that she was half naked then and we fell in love at first sight. "Deep in the crystal pool I fed my eyes reflected stars and deep firey skies. It was your face and nobody else's that I saw" and added,

"See, it is as I said it would be, long ago, that we would be together again!" Her hand, so strong and soft began to warm.

Out in the fresh air again and down another swirling giant river in an inflatable dingy with some screaming, terrified women. I decided that the water was moving too slowly and tried to turn the boat around for an enjoyable ride and paddle backwards. However another man had the other oar and corrected my sideways push to quell the ladies desperate screams. I do not fear the water like they do.

Everywhere we go Lilly asks people to photograph us for immigration purposes. People are only too obliging and I am very grateful for that. I photograph her all the time. I catch her unaware and blow her face up like a balloon, I don't know why I do this, she makes me delete them all!

After the exciting white-water rafting we were entertained by a singing side-show by what Lilly called transvestites. The stage was set in front of a small pool which was full of crocodiles. Several scantily clad young ladies blasted forth various songs into the audience which I found intensely loud and grasped my ears out of shear instinct and quickly began stuffing them with toilet paper which I had to spit on to make stay in the holes. Transvestites need to be heard!

But I must say these lasses bones did not reveal any trace of masculinity, so I sat and tried to stop my lips vibrating from the sound blast. These nasal noted ladies dressed like crocodiles to kill, exuded a captivating air of divine love. They had large embellished hats and lips which flapped and sang the adoration of something to do with sex, a taboo word in China.

The next act was performed by a young man who danced in the pool almost naked with the crocodiles. He had to poke and jab them with a stick to get them to move. The larger one could have been stuffed or made of plastic. One sleeping creature opened its mouth after three solid thumps on the nose with the stick. Unlike the transvestites they were thoroughly unexcitable. For his finale the man placed his head inside its mouth! Then he ran excitedly around the crowd collecting money and put his head back in then ran around again, put his head in again, again and again!

For the finale all the troupe appeared on stage for a second and then a third time. I looked closely at the man. I am sure it was a man and thought he was very brave to take his clothes off. I think the crocodiles were transvestites.

Lilly and I visited a small park not far away to regain some balance and peer into a small artificial pool. I chose a nice round granite rock for us both to sit on. There I began a detailed discussion on the mathematics of the universe and its relation to love. We took off our well-worn shoes which had also counted the light years though not yet the black-holes. As I reached the part where one atom kisses another a huge snake appeared from underneath the rock and slid slowly over the short grass. It was jet black like the universe and had gold splashed along its back like China and was quite thick. It looked dangerous. It was easily my length and Lilly made a start as if to run. But I restrained her. As soon as she moved the snake turned to face us flicking out its tongue, coiling and rising to strike. But then it turned and slid quickly away. The snake is no danger I said, see it goes - it was bored with my words!

The Grandmother's lore

Long ago, Lilly tells me, it was the grandmother of the family who ruled the roost. To embellish and reward her as a woman her toes were bent under and purposefully crushed and bound when she was a young child, it made women more attractive and was the custom. It was the grandmother who would determine who would sleep where and with whom. I told Lilly that I would not have come to China if she had clawed feet. I would fear that she would grip me by the neck and pin me to the ceiling with her feet.

Man is still the slave in China. He makes the money and pays the bills and plays with guns. He toughens his lungs with tobacco smoke and decays his senses with alcohol. I say to Lilly that when in China I will abide by Lilly's lore and when she comes to Australia she must consider herself my equal.

With this in mind I watch the foreplay of couples in the street. Always it is the lady who chastises the man. As I walk by the river of plastic bags and the little stream I watch a young girl with a man. She adores him and places large purple flowers behind his ears. He is happy with her play and she delights herself with her tease. He doesn't look embarrassed when we pass, only stupid. And another and another, the woman squeals at him and slaps him gently across the face or pushes him in jest and smacks his bottom hard. In the West the women do not do this and never the other way around such as a man hitting a woman in jest, that is never done.

While love watches on I wonder if it is her will that controls all men in China and whether it is the Chinese government which maintains this tradition of feminine control by some of the intrusive processes mentioned herein? And by doing so has actually de-masculinised itself and turned into grandmother in the name of "culture." Now the government prides itself on being able to spy on people everywhere with CTV cameras and manipulate them monetarily as well as emotionally and even has power over the people as they make love in their beds!

There are never any mirrors in a Chinese bedroom, they fear mirrors – too many eyes watching takes away one's power, takes away good health and the surety of self. Superstitious eyes take away the naturalness of freedom.

The government is essentially made up of old feminised grandmothers in trench coats. Or maybe some other gender, who woo the loss of body parts. Do they really watch and care so intrinsically about their grandmother's lore? Do they go back to their own families and relish in their grandmother's control? Was it grandmother who cried "you shall have only one child?"

You are attacking grandmother's womb when you try to fix your pollution by reducing the population. This is a flagrant violation of people's birth-rights. You must let them have at least two children! Governments are responsible for the condition of the skies, the drinking water and the environment in general. As well as energy production. This government is allowing the people to smog themselves to death and taking their children away in a misguided attempt to clean the environment. This is malicious use of grandmother's heritage. It is a childish reaction to an innate problem. Which, it is true, has a considerable amount to do with grandmothers as the problem with pollution has its roots deep in China's traditions. For the more children one has the better one is able to survive old age for the family traditionally looks after their old parents. This is an Asian custom.

In the West if the geriatric does not have enough money the State keeps them and usually puts them in a home where they are visited by the family. In many countries in the East the onus to protect the welfare of the family is based on a sharing premise where the richest person in the family traditionally provides for all.

People in the Chinese country-side may have more than one child especially if the first is a girl. People who live in the cities are allowed only one child. It is said that there are more men in China because of this policy. And I wonder if this law helps create a more pious and domineering male?

We learn from copying our parents. If our parents chop down trees we try to do the same. In China and Asia generally the child is not allowed to cry. They grow up spoilt and wanting everything. Everything just out of reach a child will struggle for. The West has been 'just out of reach' for a long while.

China adopts our science as though it is correct but it is often far from it. Yet China takes it and runs, manipulating it and changing it on the way. When China copies the West it does it beautifully. Once the spoilt child has what it wants, say it is a box, he or she will be hard to convince that the box may have something nasty in it. Now have you looked inside this box at my words or do you just dismiss them as another person who does not understand China?

I don't think anybody understands China. What I do understand is that to let a child grow up without crying, to service everything for the child, makes the parent suffer as well and in many instances they will adopt the child's craving for everything as a symptom of that wanting. Too much security is bad for ingenuity. Security breeds a timidity and fearfulness of anything outside "the family" whereas little security breeds wild rapture.

With something akin to religious fever the government seeks control. There are other less insidious ways to satisfy the curiosity of the child. For instance sharpen your copyright laws and give freedom of speech to the creative spirit which is unique to each person.

Help us fix the planet China, before your children die! You are misguided because you do not want to upset your traditions in particular traditions of child rearing and grandmother's lore. In the West we have our traditions but with every generation we grow on them and change, I believe we stand on our parent's shoulders and look anew! China wants to stand on the shoulders of the West and look anew however in the past communication was unfortunately withdrawn.

Let the child cry for a little while, sometimes they stop themselves and pursue independence and foster an internal strength from which springs a natural creativity. How else will a child learn independence? Your tradition of the family all helping one another is a symptom of government's insecurity brought about by their lack of assistance and the family then having to care for the child's every need. Similarly at the other end of life, a lack of government assistance causes great concern to the older person and the family unit.

In the West we have child care and when we age the government helps financially. The family unit is still strong, we hope!

Teach each child to recycle paper and wood and vegetation such as food scraps. Set up organic waste collection centres which recycle waste into either methane digesters to help warm the cold, the poor, or those wastes could fertilise the gardens which would line the streets and the rooftops after being broken down by worms in private worm farms.

You have to clean the air not only with assistance from the oxygenating trees but by teaching your sons and daughters to be responsible for their own small environment and not expect the grandmother or the government to tell them what to do. It is not only China but the whole world which needs to do this, especially the high energy consuming countries!

Human compassion must not punish woman's womb. If grandmother saw the smog she would take every child out of the country to find cleaner air. Then she would ask you, the parents, to clean up your mess before allowing the children back home. And when the children did come home they would have her knowledge of how important it is to pick up your own rubbish and not pollute each other's space! You have closed the door on respecting other people's space as you were taught that your own space is profound and made more cosy and warm by your loving family. And if you winged enough and your parents were wealthy enough you could get anything you wanted! Consequently other people's space was not important so long as your parents loved you and you had what you wanted! Is this the way your mother wanted you?

Now you find yourself in a difficult situation with the honesty of the internet opening up the world. You have been timid to come out of your shell which is now cracking. Your grandmother is about to have a re-birth and you will see that she can change but you old men find change difficult!

Be responsible in the world, your seas are ours too, our air is yours, your air is ours. Your children are ours, our children are yours. We are all of the one big happy family, do not crap in our nest! And do not blame others for your problem! Honesty is the voice of the people reflecting back to you from the mirror of clear water you should not fear.

Grumpy old men with grandmother's lips for pens, who protect their hormonal banks which are managed by money-medicines and act like wombs. Isn't it time the women stood by their men and began to cultivate a voice for a cleaner environment at a government level? Women nurture - men play with toys, that is reality. Haven't things changed a little since grandmother's days? Is that what is meant by the word civilised?

I find myself looking back at the Australian aborigine and remembering Daisy Bates and others who studied Aboriginal culture in great detail and talked about their highly "civilised" feelings for the natural world - believing that the environment is essentially feminine. So much so that some tribes in central Australia cut their penises along the urethra for birth control as well as the fashionable look of the female genitalia so they could feel the presence of the grandmother's lore always and thus maintain the essence of the Great Mother the Creator or the Rainbow Serpent. This is well documented. The Rainbow Serpent is described in many different mythologies throughout the world. In China it is described in the ancient myth of the fire breathing dragon which thrashed about in the sky for ages. Now it thrashes about in the minds of children, still bringing fear - though now it has adopted a popular masculine gender.

Astronomy tells us that our newest planet Venus, named after a female Greek God, came into our solar system about ten to fifteen thousand years ago. With its entry came considerable geomorphic activity here on Earth. It appeared in the sky as a silvery shower with a tail, and still has a retrograde orbit.

Having said that, the word "civilised" still eludes me for here before me in China is a wasteland of nature in a supposedly highly civilised culture. With few birds or trees and a multitude of people who strew everything into the drain towards the river and do not share their wealth evenly.

Who do not care for their blind and charge huge fees for medical expenses, both conditions of which constitute stress to the internal environment of each person. While the young are not taught anything about how to care for the environment at school. They may plant trees but they are in straight lines with little species diversity. That is not civilised! That is over-civilised! To keep the water and the air clean, to recycle waste, to make methane gas from organic waste, to keep poisons out of food, that is the responsibility of government as well as being honest. Take honesty by the hand for it is the walking stick of civilised man!

The indigenous people of Australia were highly civilised much to Britain's horror, because they revered nature like the Celts, Britain's ancestors, 2,500 years ago. But royalty at the time of Captain Cook who founded "modern" Australia, conveniently forgot about that and thrust their civilising spleen on the indigenous peoples, to the gross detriment of Australia's environment - and do so still! Now China plays that civilised ball and buys land in Australia though we as Australians are not allowed to buy land in China! We are not allowed to make money in China unless we are Kentucky Fried or have a big Mac up our sleeve! What obtuse irony! It is a curious juxtaposition and the little baby ducks in the water reeds who bob their heads so quickly not to be seen know all about that! But nature twists and turns and has a saving grace and that is that the new nature is equally as complicated as the old. But who am I to say which civilisation is more civilised? China seeks to civilise but puts her own soils, her own naturalness under strain.

We grow our own food and give when we have an abundance. Because we give, we should not expect a return. That is a hollow gift and not charity at all. In China if a daughter brings her husband to stay at her mother's house it is expected that he provide a gift to the value of his appreciation. If only a little money is left under the pillow he is considered stingy. Lilly goes to great lengths to explain this to me. And I comment that men in New Guinea buy their women with the gift of a pig or two to the mother's family. I ask Lilly if her mother would like a pig.

Some friends of Lilly's are marooned in bondage because of the over-mothering given to men by their mothers, grandmothers and wives.

Two friends of Lilly's who are divorced have their husbands staying with them and not moving on. There is nowhere to go! One lady after another is forced to live with her divorced husband whom she still feeds and wishes him gone. But he will not go, he stays in the nest like a Cuckoo bird. He will not let another man touch his ex-wife and threatens to murder the man who does. She sits by the closed window and bites her nails. She awaits his return with fear. China is cruel and merciless when it comes to love. He used to go and give money to a mistress and not to her. Now because they are divorced the government gives her a little money for her son's education. She buys food and still cooks for the two grown men!

He hits her, the government does not care! Each day he is in her house he is as contented as though he was her baby. Secretly he fears his mother's power and she never taught him self-reliance and compassion. The lesson of his own mother, whom he now copies, empowers him to dominate and at the same time resent and fear change.

The attitude of the government is the same. The people sit at their windows biting their finger nails and fear that each day will be more frightening than the next. They are in danger of losing their soul.

Benxi

Lilly wants to show me where she was born and meet some old friends in her home town of Benxi.

The train station is crowded and I am positioned at the end of a hundred person queue while Lilly stands at the end of another. Thus we do the Chinese shuffle to see who gets to shout through a loud speaker to get a ticket under the glass first.

The silver-grey misty mountains flash by. From the shining train the narrow foot-paths meander through the dipping heads of the dying golden corn. I peer through their heads into every depression to the exposed soil and view the slow trickle of the muddy creeks but it is not water that I see rather corn syrup, diabetic and sweet. I see the erosion and the wastes of man, I see the money in the drain washing away like soil.

A small woman with a mask on dressed in green comes into the carriage wielding a mop the size of a tree, twice as long as herself. She jabs one poor man in the eye with the end of it and brushes softly over his clean shoes. They were clean before! There are perfectly clean travelling bags strewn across the floor and her eyes, electric, seek the small floor spit-spaces in between.

Beside the tracks and nowhere else the tall thin trees like raised women's arms reveal beneath the brown stain of the approaching winter. The tall chimneys of the brick works on and on, spear the perpetual grey. Through the squeaky speakers a variety of music spills. From Western classical, modern rock, bee-bop, to Chinese classical, clickety-clack. Most people lolly-drop their heads then all of a sudden crickets come from a mobile owned by a young girl with dyed red hair. Though the train bends all frequencies I find it hard not to sleep but the sound of the crickets wakes me loud and clear. The red hair chirrups above the noise; she is a red flowering rainforest tree above a flowing stream.

As my mind quavers in the mist there comes into view a tortoise in a plastic dish. It fights the form of itself as it scratches the sides and damns all the dead around it. In China the tortoise is a symbol of eternity for it carries the world on its shoulders. It is also a symbol of an adulterer, or one who sticks his neck out too far, someone who has unlawful sex and wears a green hat to bed. Such a person is called a Tortoise Man a "Wamba Nanzing!" I begin to see them everywhere. Laws were made to be broken, challenged. Fear's best friend is curiosity and curiosity's best friend is danger.

Benxi used to be a small country mining town, now it is a big city like the ones on the moon. It was occupied by the Japanese who wanted the coal during the Second World War. Today the black-fire still burns in the power station and Lilly as a young girl does not recall ever seeing a blue sky!

In a small grey-brick and mud hut with a garden of red flowers and sprinkled long leaved plants with red veins, she was borne. The straw roof had loose stones and long dead twisted limbs on top to hold it down. Inside the house in the single hot-bed which was heated by the flue of the coal fire going under it, slept four brothers, mother, father and herself. Often in winter the temperature would plunge to thirty below zero and the meter of snow would make it difficult to open the door in the mornings. The steep hills in Benxi covered in ice prevented her from walking so she would slide down them to school on her bottom.

She grew up with the tall nodding sunflowers and the upright corn of the summer months, the friendly mosquitos which make people run and the small neighbour's Pug pet dog whose face resembled an ancient Chinaman, which I am told would not have been eaten when it died - I was so pleased when I heard that!

This was Lilly's home. The young girl on her way to school riding the bicycle for the first time, with the smile for all eternity, dressed in the hand washed clothes so perfectly. Leaving her mother to tend the small garden and water other plants, to wash and prepare the food which was always scarce, to go to market and buy for the family. Sometimes Lilly and her older brother would venture into the hills to pick wild hazel nuts and mushrooms but now they are all gone she tells me. Foxes would come and eat the nuts so people dug up the trees and took them home for themselves.

Lilly's father worked in the coal mines and smoked. Lilly remembers him going down deep into the ground. He would drink a little alcohol to keep warm as he worked. And in the evenings would come home to relieve his aches and pains and sleep in the hot bed. He passed away slowly, grievously, in Shenyang when Lilly was thirty six years old.

It is perhaps not interesting for others to hear of a person's illness but Lilly did not walk before the age of six which was concerning, for in China a person must work or die. However a child will walk when it is ready to and Manchurian legs are pretty strong! Her mother was very worried. Then one day Lilly stood as tall as her body allowed and took the first step.

Her schooling in Benxi was brief from the age of nine to thirteen when she took a job at a huge textile mill and taught her fingers how to move. But her hands developed calcified tumours which had to be cut out and she was impaired for some time. She worked there for twenty three years doing odd jobs, carrying heavy water containers and feeding the workers. Her son was young and she would go every four hours to feed him at a special place in the mill. She tells me now that if a woman has a child she has to leave work and would be lucky to get her job back afterwards.

It was after the birth of her only son that she became intensely weary and had to stop work. She fed him for six months then her milk stopped. Her diet was six eggs a day with lashings of black sugar.

As a young woman she followed all her friends and wore high heeled shoes which ruined her posture and her feet developed bunions as large as hen's eggs. Eventually she was married at age twenty five for a period of thirteen years. However the last few years were unhappy because Lilly was sick and that put a strain on her marriage. She longed to escape her ailing body which she found was forgotten and laid waste. Her heart a strong ship or vessel, with a single unstoppable hole through which all love drained, the oxygen of life, abandoned as she sank in the deepest sea.

Her breasts began to grow painful possibly malignant lumps and her periods were debilitating. She began to eat great quantities of seaweed and then Lilly started to run and she ran like no other, determined to get well.

Everybody looked at her amazed for in those days nobody in China ran at all! She would rise before dawn and run for an hour, then return home to get breakfast for everybody. She ran and she ran, at first not far and then for ten years she would run ten sometimes twenty kilometres a day! She began to dance in the evenings at the village square which she did for seven years and after bought some roller-blades and flew. Her legs became as strong as iron poles. Her health improved, her mother less worried. She began to work with relatives and started a small food outlet. Then one night a man came into her room where she slept with her son and stole all her food!

By this time her mother and family had left for Shenyang and after that night her mother asked her to come to Shenyang which she did. She studied post-maternity physiology and health, she studied acupressure and massage with the best in the city. Her colleagues at the massage clinic said she had the force of ten men and the wisdom of a sage. This I can say is untrue, one hundred men would be more like it and her understanding of the body is profound.

Her son did not have a proper schooling, the husband did little to help and Lilly's family was too poor to afford any school fees.

Meanwhile it is told, her ex-husband's health deteriorated with smoking and drinking and he became grossly overweight.

We venture out on the street again, past the modern cars, around the road-works, out and out further, walking in the middle of the road, holding up the buses and a narrow escape as a taxi nudges us with its nose like a friendly porpoise. Past the clawing crabs as they drown in the square tanks from their spittle, frothing at the mouth. The day is growing cold as it slides into dark, the over-the-shoulder looks in the train station then the late afternoon meal of noodles disappears musically, the harmonics of the single string, into Lilly's mouth. With the usual traveller's dash to the train and the quick snap of the camera, shot from my hips as we streak across the platforms of flat stones beneath the early evening sprinklings of electric lights - to begin the shuffle to the train again after finding a toilet, at last.

In the train standing in the corridor on our way back to Shenyang. My feet ache from walking kilometres on the hard flat highly civilised cement. The ever moving landscape is cascading into winter. The tall corn, a paler gold hangs listless in the fields, tongues out. Acres and acres of them all silently waiting to be moved on, tangled leaves papery singing, rocking. Far off in the distance there are few lines on the horizon just a soft bluey grey-brown mist smudging everywhere. The rattle and surge of the silver train, the clickety-clack to go back.

There standing with us in the crush are five people all men, smoking. Then a young boy at our feet lights up. The air suddenly becomes full of blue wisps of smoke like dragon's breath as the out-breath wafts through and into the carriage where everybody sits. Several girls are also here in the corridor and I watch them as they miserably sink to the floor like spittle as the journey progresses they begin to turn green. Lilly has a frown on her face as I begin to punch in the words,

"I have a friend in Australia who began an anti-smoking campaign with three people at first and then many joined. Now it is illegal to smoke in public." And continue, "Your mother lets your brother smoke in her house around an infant, why?" She answers that the brother would get angry if he was asked to stop.

"Angry or die!" I say holding my breath!

The next day back in Shenyang and for three days afterwards Lilly has a hacking cough and spits and clears her throat constantly. I cannot sleep for spitting teeth.

With time to spare we follow a daily routine. The morning finds us going to the market which is the jungle of the city. There we can find strange wonders to excite the taste buds, to dose ourselves with new coloured worlds then try in vain to lose weight. As we swing about the rafters bargaining is generally a quiet affair. We bargain with the many well trained voices which one finds in the parks at sundown singing loudly. The market is the giant stomach of all the people laid bare on one big fat table. Each section maintained by a particular personage. The carrot and vegetable man, the mushroom lady, the garlic man, then the fish and meat sellers. The hundreds of eggs and the pupae of moths squirming in acute agony, all doing small circles with their heads all pointing out like little Chinese penises stacked neatly and put to bed.

The floor of the market like an old book, now black with sweat then frozen in winter with ice, always slippery always with a treasure. I bend awkwardly to pick up money off the floor, a dangerous act unless done quickly - Lilly does the same. We buy our walnuts and our flat corn bread, our jujubes and the big white peaches - peanuts and plums. The arms fall off from the weight of the shopping and the legs develop a permanent shuffle in the queue. The hotel is kilometres away around the whole of China. Through the "bring....bring!" of the bicycles past the cars, moving out, far out into the middle of the road, dancing through speeding cars - legs begin to move as cars nose in close like a cluster of inquisitive children! Legs-not-long-enough to move!

Now on the bed nibbling like a couple of domesticated, civilised rats returned by bus. Our teeth cracking nuts with Mother's nut cracker. Staring at the washing on the floor. The faint smell of tobacco smoke wafts under the door, we are not alone. The laundry here has mirrors all around, sentinels of virtue, her eyes come and go - treasures of engagement.

We catch the train to Benxi again and unfortunately may have to stand once more. Lilly has a friend whose son works in a dental hospital and will check her teeth for free. After the ordeal with the tobacco smoke Lilly goes inside the carriage this time and starts talking to an elderly lady who kindly offers her a seat on the edge of hers. Lilly sits down and is soon fast asleep and begins to flop all over the place. I try to support her as best I can while standing next to her in the corridor. She ends up with her face in my crutch which is not a good look. The train is slow and old, many people get on and jam down into the stomach of this metal monster. One overly large sweet-selling lady shouts through my ears and pushes her way through like a rag in a rifle bore. Couples jam together being careful to avoid alluring positions. Human after human comes surging through and squeezes past until I am leaning over others and embracing them somewhat intimately myself!

As the train begins to move and bob and sway everybody falls asleep. Bodies flop everywhere, even those with mobiles phones and tablet computers begin to doze in the stifling air. Most have two layers of clothing on like ourselves for the temperature outside is zero degrees, now in the carriage the temperature soars to around thirty.

Beads of sweat form on many faces and those who can open their eyes peer through tiny slits. Then another sleeping woman crashes into my crutch somewhat insensitively, must be my lucky day - momentarily waking to straighten her hair and pick her nose. Another young girl stands to take off her coat and accidently punches an old man in the glasses, he is taken aback and does not smile. Another young man with a small back-pack comes and supports himself by leaning on my side and the side of another woman. He produces a tablet computer from his pocket and sticks earphones in his ears and immediately loses perception of where he really is. There is plenty of space for his body a little distance away but no he comes and uses me as a steadying post! So I let him lean on me with increasing pressure and when I think I have all his weight I pull away quickly. We can't have these creatures of modernity leaning all over the place and forgetting where they are! Who only communicate with others who grow electrical cords from their ears. The poor man is totally thrown off balance. His computer crashes to the ground and he looks at me. However to my dismay he regains his intimate stance.

Perhaps he is a product of the one child policy who thinks he has a right to lean on people, or perhaps I am an old grumpy fastidious man with weak knees?

The train slows as it comes into Benxi and all the young people jump to their feet and charge for the door. People sitting on the floor in the corridor are trampled. The young man who lent conveniently on me relinquishes his seat which he quickly grabbed after a passenger alighted. At last I sit down and watch the rolling hills lit by the afternoon glimmer turn autumn brown and my knees go back into place as we screech back to Benxi.

We are met by Lilly's old school friend and forced into a taxi much to Lilly's annoyance, who always wants to save money. Round a multitude of bends all beautifully kept cement pavers, smoothed by many feet and bathed in much protein. A great big smile reaches out to us full of wondrous teeth as large as fingers and glowing eyes. It is little wonder her son is a dentist. Later she insists we drink beer and finish each bottle. Our teeth do not clash as we spend much time trying to get the translating machine to work. Since it has been washed and dropped many times it has a broken wing. But it does work and she was delightful like all the women in China. Hands talking with frenetic gesticulations and voices rising to trail off just at the right time, squealing decibels as laughter soon bubbles along. Eyes wide again and almost an argument, then the rising phonetics as long as your gnawed arm - all I see is teeth, then comes the chuckle again signalling all is fine.

As we stagger out of the restaurant we are swept up by a thousand roaring buses and standing within one amongst a sea of upright Chinese, like sardines in a tin, I reach my gnawed arm up like one who prays or cheers and notice an unpleasant underarm odour. After a while people seem to clear away and finally I am awarded a seat for my bravery. I decide never to wash again.

Lilly heads for the dentist who works in a huge hospital. There are garbage bins lined up out the back for we arrive that way, through the back door - no not in a garbage bin. They were full of teeth.

Before she sits in the tooth-removing chair we both visit the toilet. As usual there is no toilet paper or soap to wipe one's bottom with or wash ones hands. I ask Lilly if this is normal in a hospital and she replies, yes. I ask further if everyone in the hospital has dirty hands and a very dirty bottom and she says, yes. The kind dentist puts his listless hand into mine to shake and gives me a plastic bottle of toxic mineral water and offers me the couch to alleviate my stress. Here at least I have paper to write on. I wash my hands over the plastic flowers.

In the dentist's chair nearby, head bent back and neck exposed like a chicken before the slaughter, is another man with a very strong young female assistant down his throat. She has strong thick arms and is as determined as a Chinese gold miner - I watch her fiercely thrusting. She jabs his mouth incessantly with screeching scratching metal implements and occasionally barks or coughs in his face like a dog.

Then all hell breaks loose as both the man and Lilly begin to clear their throats. The sound is like a pack of dinosaurs gargling and spitting rocks – blood and spittle everywhere. I cannot sleep.

Dentistry makes similar noises as an Englishman eating. In the old days it was found the metal fillings picked up mobile phone waves and in some instances the rattling teeth interfered with reception.

In one case a man with many metal fillings could hear an echo of high frequency like a woman screaming when he answered his mobile phone. The sound was the same as an approaching train on screechy tracks. He began to think it was his wife playing a trick on him. After sometime he realised it was his teeth. So after many frustrating phone calls he decided to do an experiment. He took his ear phones and bit down hard on the jack. To his surprise his wife answered and the reception was exceptional! After that he decided to have the metal fillings removed and he kept them beside the bed. One night his wife rang to say she would be late home but it wasn't his phone which rang it was his old metal fillings! From then on he never paid a phone bill and carried his fillings in his pocket everywhere. Unfortunately he found he could only receive calls as it was too difficult to dial numbers.

He also discovered that biting down on the earphone jack with a mouth full of salted-peanuts enabled clear reception and turned out to be an efficient method for charging his phone. Better still if one takes out a filling from an old tooth and hammers it flat then inserts it as a battery in your phone it will last for years!

We climb the mountain behind Benxi. The meandering track has seen Japanese foot prints as they hunted the locals with guns. The stones of the track rumbled a language as they tumbled chaotically to rest eschewed and lacking braces. The small wispy pine trees are singing gently as we reach the cooling summit. Far out into the distance of ancient China the smooth hills roll around us as though we are on an island at sea looking toward a rough horizon. Benxi below spears her sky-scrapers through the smog and somewhere far below another little girl is born who may never see a blue sky. Amongst the delicate trees young men flex their muscles, flicking their eyes our way, wishing that the sea would recede so they could walk amongst the green hills without their weapons and find fresh meat or hazel nuts for free.

Approximately thirty five years ago all the countryside was owned and controlled by the government. Now it has been divided up and given to persons who are concerned with growing food. These farmers when they age will be given very little money from the government. If they are poor and fall sick and have to go to hospital they will not be given sufficient medicines and simply die. People who live in the cities and grow old get a little more money from the government to survive. People in old age do not like to think that their children will have to look after them.

On this mountain there is nothing left, no birds or animals to cook. Though I did see a small terrified bird which looked out the corner of her eyes at me as I looked a little different. Also there were monkeys around the corner of the hill enjoying the best real estate in Benxi. Sitting up like old warriors in the early morning sun sipping their favourite tea. Meanwhile on the other side of the hill the humans stalked about hunting invisible forces and after smoke away their fears. Many bounce around exercising with radios strapped to their belts to increase the pain. "No pain, no gain," should be written on the bill-boards. The monkeys laugh at them then look a little grim.

Why are humans so afraid? One follows another like a line of insects. Their conformity will be their undoing. They will not explore the new and like a school of fish in the sea are guided haplessly by their grunting stomachs. Will the rest of the world survive China's lust for greed? No – China devours all. This plague of people, this servitude to the ill health factory – few will survive the regimentation of the young in those red uniforms which guild comfort and integrity, direction and a glimpse of eternity.

On the way back to Shenyang again in the crowded bus and then the crowded train station and then the crowded carriage, after breathing the perpetual crowded air, with the heads all crowded sideways looking my way - vacantly looking. Lilly cleverly barges to the front of the boarding queue determined to secure a seat. Her manner of moving through a crowd is well honed as she lightly pushes through. I on the other hand will refuse to push and rather stand and wait. I tried pushing before but found the people were not standing on their feet properly and they all lost their balance and fell before me. It was obviously a bad moment for everybody!

The carriage air is hot and full of tobacco smoke again but we discover several empty seats before the main throng arrives.

Lilly commandeers what turns out to be a man's seat behind me. He approaches her and asks her to remain seated while he smokes a cigarette at the end of the carriage and thus intimately wraps his lungs about us all. For some reason nobody approaches me though I offer to give my seat to two young ladies, a family with small children, a man who grows electrical flexes from his ears, two old women and two old men who looked like they may have needed to sit down. So I have gained a seat after all and begin to look back at everybody sideways in the glass. The night outside is cold and black. The windows are faded and dirty, they reveal mere shadows of the workers.

An assortment of ticket inspectors come around to check tickets regularly which by the time we get off the train, they have looked at at least five times. I watch one of them dress in his little booth. He watches the reflections all the time and notices me watching. He changes his stance and wriggles his neck. His tie is perfect, his hair - too much to worry about and difficult to keep clean, has been shawn off long ago. His coat dusted, the buttons polished and gleam like yellow stars, his index finger is polished like steel for guilty pointing, his trousers pleated, his hat a masterpiece of card-board and his teeth, hands and bottom, I presume are absolutely filthy.

Highly experienced are these people at detecting would-be ticket dodgers as they - not one but many - shuffle and push past the innocent treading on their toes with their over-sized polished hard black shoes as they parade down the corridors like ominous black sparkling night skies. I watch them go stamping down the aisle crushing feet as people suddenly jump indicating a well-aimed stamp. Sleeping passengers are wakened dramatically with this manoeuvre. I muse that if one commuted each day and dressed like one of them one would never have to pay!

As the journey progresses I can hear Lilly and her company mentioning the word Australia many times. Then she taps me on the shoulder from behind and says she is off to the toilet. No sooner has she disappeared than the man who gave his seat up to her comes suddenly from behind and presses his face at right angles into mine. All I can see is his sideways eyes and twisting mouth with the rank smelling loose tobacco teeth.

"Ore-talli-a?" he questions.

I say, "Hello, Australia," in Chinese. Then he replies something indecipherable and I say,

"Confused!" in Chinese.

Then he says, "Blah, blah…," in Chinese again…..indecipherable!

And I gather my breath which was taken by his and answer in Chinese,

"I do not understand."

He replies in, "blah, blah…." again and I say (in Chinese)

"I do not speak Chinese!"

Everybody from seven people around me deep, is now entranced and the poor man looks bewildered and disappears as quickly as he came. A little while later I reach up for my bag and the translating machine and with everybody's eyes on me I write,

"Hello, I am the grandson of the Queen Mother of England" and pass it back to Lilly who cannot stop the many faces looking over her shoulder to read. To my surprise there is complete silence. A trickle of a smile washes over Lilly's face as the brakes of the train begin to squeal with excitement and we slowly slide back into Shenyang.

As we alight from the carriage I notice a galaxy of black sparkling ticket collectors all talking together. But as I pass I notice they seem more interested in watching people's feet. People give them a wide birth.

China's smog is caused by an acute greasy uncertainty of the natural world and too many people. Their excessive eating is caused by a fear of not having enough. Many however under eat and are too skinny. This is an eating disorder brought about by the same reasons. They will over-eat and over-smoke because the government, by blocking communication with the West, has given most a feeling of insecurity, isolation and inferiority. This is one of many reasons why the TV has weapons of war on every news program, martial arts fighting, regimented adults and children and close circuit television which spies on people's privacy everywhere. The main viewing time on TV shows criminals up close who have been captured, their faces smudged and smeared and unrecognisable with the same greasy mix. Bombs and rockets or lavish talent shows of singing and dancing have underlying values disguised as traditional creations but from the seams oozes a competitive control and intimidation equal to no other. The governments mandate is to give people sport, the ability to communicate and music and they don't need much more to be happy they say.

This competition does not teach respect for another individual. But who will stand and say such things? Even the government in Australia acknowledges that "China shows the way" for making money and controlling the masses. And yes they do! For in each room and on each lonely mountain top the people with their electrical devices listen to the music of soft quavering love songs or loud blaring electronic white noise which has love as its underlying theme. It is everywhere and considered a delicacy. One will hear it in the wildest places for there is a distinct fear of being isolated. Content with the small and smaller, each generation born blind to feel their way.

Everybody wants to belong to the broader community of the world but this has been discouraged by the government. I believe this attitude is too severe and intrusive and reeks of disrespect for the individual. Meanwhile at the closing ceremony of the Asian games on television we read in large red letters "Diversity!" written in English on the ground and viewed from a plane. Diversity has been sucked in through thin lips and digested till the political body grows fat.

Chinese people give generously to beggars, one elderly gentleman outside the Shenyang railway station was memorable as he had only one maimed arm, no legs and stood in a round dish only three feet tall on the side of the footpath. He sang his plaintive lament to the ladies with a deep well trained voice and was truly amazing. Why is it that man takes with him all his pains? Some believe it was in previous lives we accrued our sentences.

Every night Lilly washes her clothes in the shower. Not often in the wash basin. The art of washing clothes changes markedly from country to country and region to region. So with that in mind I presume Lilly's method is the same as most Chinese. First the clothes are wet through and a neat round pad of the cloth is made by a spinning action. Then the other hand grabs half the cloth and squeezes and twists in the same movement. The type of garment matters hugely. This washing is quiet and quick and uses little water. I make sure she wears cotton and not short circuit-breaker nylons which, through static electricity, suck magnesium from the skin.

One can stay in a hotel in India and at three in the morning all the Indians from around will begin clearing their throats and washing their clothes. Their method of washing is to use a bucket to rinse the clothes after hurling them around the room and smacking the ground with them. A poor excuse for killing flies or malarial mosquitoes. One ends up with a remarkably clean spot on the floor, the walls all covered in dried soap, smears on everything, an unusable mirror, no sleep and the gut feeling of being flung about the room.

I know very little about the history of homo-sapiens movements in the rest of the world or how the Asian people came to be where they are today. These are "secrets" made more intriguing by legend and DNA sampling. I will not elaborate further only to say that the washing machine is by far the most efficient method ever developed for washing clothes and a highly civilised male is the key to creating a clean and happy wash.

Lilly's stomach is cold, her kidneys are sore. I massage her stomach, rub her back, bottom and hands. It is more than her food I think. She has a gremlin in her nerves. Or something is confusing her calcium levels - body cold? Perhaps early diabetes?

We decide to go for a holiday and catch a plane to Beijing and then on to Yunnan Province some five and a half hours away. It is a honey-moon really. I want to see some tall trees and rainforest. I long for a green hilly landscape and the smell of leaves.

Late night supermarket, the haste to buy the food for travel. Food and its acquisition is a security issue, as one day forgotten is one day hungry. All the supermarket shoppers seem to be overweight. All roll their trollies which have calories like over nourished cumulonimbus clouds inside which overflow like their stomachs to the outside as they rest their flesh on the handle bars billowing out in front. Behind us the apples fall and roll automatically on a mission to save the breathless fish whose ice tears long dead evaporate up my nose. Breast and leg, fingers and foot of chooks rest, sleeping in the morgue, waiting to be chewed, spewed, used and abused, fermented and exhumed, sacred beyond the magic and into the pottery-pockets of the afterlife. What on Earth did these poor chickens do before they were born on Earth, to suffer such a fate? Through the checkout the forest of beings quietly now, only the ruffle of paper money do I hear and the beeping of the cash registers like a colony of green frogs.

Early morning seeps into soul – she is awake and strides towards the toilet. Hesitant I whisper, "Time, taxi already there" waiting in the blue light, red and shining. The first fare of the day, half an hour early.

In the taxi she takes my hand and pounds it into powered rice once again. The pain is intense. Past the tall sad buildings, the civilised womb of China rocks to the ineffable universe of wah… wah…wah! Cement hearts beating for the baby and the love - square and rigorous into the distance never ending.

She dances about me, eyes wide, her smile from ear to ear. In the airport she charges around with our passports out in front asking people directions and getting lost often. By the time we have checked in and are waiting in the lounge she is utterly worn out with excitement and has everybody following and guiding her through the right door. Airport shuffle to a waiting blue chair in which she soon sleeps from the exhaustion of keeping her Mother's and my shoulders broad. Lilly the lion who saves the world is curled up asleep in a her little blue sky.

Lilly's first flight. She goes to sleep in the airplane after eating half my lunch as well as hers. Her feet hoisted up on the seat in front, her twisted torso curving like the half-smile. On arrival, after busses and taxi she is besieged by a smooth female sales-rep for the local tourist guide's bus service. She takes Lilly by the clothes and hoists her well up in the unexpected air like a flag, shaking violently. Then my turn and miraculously lots of money falls from my pockets and Lilly loses her half-smile. She is concerned that we spend so much and I bite my bottom lip and say that it is our honeymoon and I don't care about money. Before long we have signed up for a week of travel along with a bus load of others. The sales-rep is down on her knees half smiling, picking up money.

The first night we rattle-bang out from a crowded bus depot at 8:00 in the evening and travel flat out till 1:30 in the morning. As we are tearing along Lilly wakes me, I am not allowed to sleep, the tourist guide has a deep smoker's voice and the volume is unbelievably loud. Again I have toilet paper stuffed in my ears. He says that because the bus is climbing up a mountain that it is foolish to sleep as the "brain may explode!" Lilly believes him and keeps prodding me thinking there will be a big mess everywhere. The bus is gastric hot. Close to midnight, I say that she sleeps in aeroplanes and her brain does not explode! And people who drive cars up this mountain have passengers who sleep and do not explode. She looks confused. So I meditate. She is horrified and prods me again and again expecting me to explode any minute as the whole bus is wide awake, but I say I am meditating and talking to somebody who sells special helmets.

Miraculously the bus slows and we are bundled out and put in a room with a cold shower and a double bed. Lilly and I crash. The bed is cold and I produce a long green hat which I am accustomed to wearing to sleep in the cold. Lilly looks at me aghast and says,

"No go bed with man in green hat. No! China say never go bed with man in green hat!"

"You explode?" I ask.

"Wamba nanzing!" she says. So I turn it inside out revealing its virtuous white interior. It is now gleaming with purity and all is fine.

We are woken at 4:00 next morning, a quick breakfast then off again. The day consists of driving at great speed and being entertained by another sales rep who gets on the bus fifteen kilometres out from the factory and yells at us. The bus then pulls up in front of the factory and we pile out and buy, buy, buy! And we all did exactly that! Thankfully we won't be yelled at for another hour at least. Then hopefully after the next siege we will stop somewhere and jam food in our faces with madly clapping chop-sticks as lunch is an eat and run affair - as fast as the passing wind. And we all did exactly that!

One of the first stops is a large Buddhist temple. The largest in China. A truly magnificent spectacle with a huge golden figure of Buddha rising half naked into the sky. The sun glinting off his shoulders as he bears the weight of all men and women. Inside the cloistered rooms are paintings and lavish decorations imbued with the magic of the modern world. Before we are allowed to kneel and pray we have to buy a candle and a small offering. I am not pleased about this. I will not give money before the eyes of the Buddha. I write on a small piece of paper that Buddha would be disgusted to see money being exchanged in his house and hand it to the priest. He looks at my loin cloth, my beads, my braided hair, my naked feet, my bare chest and says in beautiful English, "Each man to his own."

I kneel and pray. And a tear wells to my eye and falls upon the lavish red carpet where it turns into a cut diamond which nobody sees.

After three days we scrape ourselves out of bed and claw at the mirror. How could we have let ourselves fall for this money fanatical bus trip which tortures and starves the happy holiday makers and turns them into mean and nasty frigid ATM machines? Soon the rest of the crew drags themselves, battle wearied from their galloping breakfast to gallop again to catch the runaway bus or be left behind! Then right behind she roars with the early morning cold metal of her interior as my chin sinks beyond the condensation on the window and bangs on the steely sill. But I was awake an hour ago and then I had dinner or was it breakfast - but now what time is it? Is this China or the war?

Thus we stumble into a small valley, eyes on stalks, with a system of streams cascading down and a flying-fox cable, squeaky, clogged with sleep. We peep over the edge of the cliff to see briefly into the butterfly of our beings and backing off am asked would I like to throw myself off with this metal string attached to my precious left leg for love? My immediate answer is no. And Lilly looks at me as if to say, go on I will die for you. So I relent and say, if you come. Knowing that she would fly and I would fall. But we are told that two cannot go, so I am saved by the flimsy little wire string and I do not have to show my love is true by leaping off a cliff in China! And I ask myself why should I want to fling myself off a cliff for love! Lilly looks a little saddened as though she could jump off any cliff safely with me. I decline as my passport is too heavy and would break the steel rope, fluttering down.

Further descending the many stairs, the rooms and the old tribal areas with their circles expanding - now only their words remain and remnants of their fashions, swallowed by the modern Han multitudes. We are entertained by the local people who still retain an amount of compassion for natural things and put on a bird show for us using Australian birds as China has eaten most of their own. Pink Galahs, sulphur Crested Cockatoos, some Budgerigars, Cockatiels and an Emu called John Howard which ignores everybody and lastly a Macau from Indonesia. Then further along a huge cage full of butterflies - it is too dangerous outside for them to fly. And further still an elephant show in the courtyard of a large pavilion.

Over the tops of the black haired heads of people we could see the large grey forms of the elephants as they sat and swayed and rolled over. Around them one thousand people were gathered under the verandas with much enthusiasm and clamour. Six red-uniformed young elephant-trainers ran around in the pen with six elephants all dressed with hats and behaving like each other - drunken rascals, swinging their trunks around and eyeing the young people smiling. Even the elephant trainers were well advanced at behaving like the animals, swaying sideways with their loose arms. We staggered in sideways too and used the jam-push method of moving through the crowd.

I followed Lilly, to find a seat way at the back however when the action became serious everybody stood on their chairs and began to sway like the elephants, so we could not see anything! Have you ever seen an elephant spin around on one leg? We did here! Have you ever seen an elephant blow a trumpet backwards? No not here! But what we did see was that the trainers had more than a circus up their sleeve and had a fine sense of entertainment. The elephants even looked happy! Waggling their heads, jumping around, looking very boisterous, even though their beautiful white tusks had been cruelly hacked off.

Three young ladies were chosen from the crowd to stand in a straight line and were asked to raise their index finger at a given moment and waggle it simultaneously. Next an elephant was chosen and made to sit on a stool and cross and uncross its legs which it obviously enjoyed doing. Then a huge pair of sunglasses was placed over the creatures head way down low on its trunk and a funny hat to top it off. The elephant then put an elbow on its knee with one foot under its chin. It was then made to wobble its head from side to side, lift its trunk up in an ark and smile at the ladies. The girls were asked to wag their fingers which they did, much to the crowd's amusement and flashing cameras.

The effect on the elephant could not have been more profound as it became sexually excited which was visually apparent as its member became the animals sixth leg, counting its trunk. This fine automatic extension was dexterously used to help push a large ball around the yard. The excitement of the oohing crowd matched the excitement of the elephant rising rapidly to a fever pitch as everybody frantically began to push and shove and kept falling off their chairs in the struggle for a better view!

Then suddenly like a great climax great surges of grinning people rushed with their arms outstretched to get that special shot, holding flashing cameras and ducking and weaving to avoid the falling bodies of their friends in the trampled crush. For that instant falling and floating in a dream, remembering the tusks of the elephant in its moment of wild glory which was now showing the crowd its pride. Girls were squealing with excitement and giddiness as they kept rising and toppling off their chairs. The red-dressed keepers kept up a fast rate and pretended not to look as all the elephants started charging and swaying everywhere like mad young children. Eventually things slowed down a little as things receded and went back to normal. The relaxing sigh of the crowd was audible.

Another sales-rep steps on the bus and screams into the microphone her tonsils bouncing around the claustrophobic windows before nestling in my toilet paper ears. She announces the upcoming jade shops which have slabs of jade cut so thinly and large they covered whole walls. Round and filamentous full moons with light shining through. Intricately carved fish and huge circular slabs with holes cut out of their centres, smoothed like flying saucers, revealing a highly polished technology. We did not buy, merely admired.

Loaded into the bus again and after the fast-food lunch when we were all snoring, another sales-rep stamps up the stairs and roars into our ears. She bludgeons us into buying expensive tickets to go in a cable-car up to a dragon's cave. She makes us put up our hands if we are keen. Those people who do not put their hands up have the loud-speaker pointed directly at them and she raises her voice. The cave is half way up a mountain and was inhabited by ancient man. As we ascend like wingless plucked chickens hanging from heaven we strain our necks to look out across the sky blue lake far below to the south where the haze is densest. In that direction lies Australia but this land is mine too I say, as we arrive and turn to go into the Earth.

The cave is deep and in places narrow. At every turn it has the polished walls of time as people pass and caress the stone. But on closer inspection I see that the walls are jade, brown and green with a slimy wet lustre. On a small ledge a small water urn has been carved from the solid rock. Then an opening with a vista of the snow fed lake far below. At every vantage point the hand of modern man has etched his money making claws and clings to the slightest whiff of commerce for small shops like bird's nests have single individuals covered in their trinkets as they hang by their talons to the narrow ledges.

I wonder if this is the same cave an English anthropologist came to study and found a tablet inscribed in ancient script which read:

"We crashed here 5,000 years ago and are just waiting for them to come and pick us up!"

A film I saw from the NASA space shuttle revealed similar shaped discs as the round moons of jade with pulsating holes in their centres and curious square sections cut out of their rear. These discs materialised and flashed on and off. One of them was measured at some 20 kilometres diameter as its light manifested.

Well these people may wait a long time! And when and if their friends do come back to Earth to collect them we hope they take back a bus load of sales-reps!

Lilly entertains the bus, gets to know everybody as each is curious about us. She is smiling all the time, even when she sleeps. I have come for her, I will take her back home.

Yunnan is close to the eastern border with Tibet and the architecture has a distinctive Tibetan influence as does their colourful dress and welcoming custom.

Dry and thirsty, more like starving and empty, we are blown like dried leaves by the gale of another loud-speaker into a building which show-cases specific Tibetan customs. Lilly being a doctor in her own right is soon face to face with a Tibetan doctor and keen to hear his diagnosis of her cold arthritic-like sensations. He inhabits a small dark room at the end of a corridor which has Tibetan deities and Tanka paintings lining the walls. He garrulously takes Lilly by the arm and feels several pulses up to the elbow. Reaching across the table he then grips her throat to feel her pulse. It is an alarming gesture done by a "doctor" who can sense her innocence and finds he is able to dominate aggressively in a most obtrusive way which was unlike any Tibetan I have ever met.

We leave penniless after paying for the crushed jewels he recommended we buy to fix Lilly's partially blocked carotid artery or that is what I sensed he meant.

Out on the street in the bright sunshine again and we are accosted by one of our bus team members who whispers to Lilly that Tibetan doctors are sometimes superstitious about their health and quite often wrong with their diagnosis. A twinge of pain shot through my hand as a crow came and squawked above us and I looked up far above to the towering snow-capped mountains with the cold clear air and the frozen stones - the Himalaya and felt for Lilly's hand.

Beside the lake are small low-roofed houses with corn and great upright slabs of transparent stone, chips from the moon, in the front and back yards, not aligned with the stars, rather for sale – a small good luck charm to promote and guarantee better health, to tie around one's throat.

Not long after the roaring fast bus spat us out across a busy road to a restaurant where we all sat at large tables with huge rotating plates in the centre to engorge very thin bird-nest and fish-hook soup with long thin chop-sticks which kept crossing their legs - awkward in the extreme! In my bowl I found long thin fishing line noodles, plastic trinkets and a small alien shop keeper from the cliff face, Lilly found a piece of plastic and a single shoe. Half way through this chin drenching exercise we are told to get ready, finish and go. Lilly complains looking around the table and says that I am staving after a week of quick lunch stops because I have trouble eating fish hooks fast. I know she says that because everybody at the table looks at me with pity.

Just then the flies above the many plates of food decide it's time to eat and begin landing on the table. People wave them away alternately. When they come over my way I swipe at them. Then one lands close to me so I wait a little while then take a superfast grab at it and pretend to swallow it and resume my meal. Suddenly a woman across the other side of the table bursts out laughing. She has a fish hook stuck in her throat and swallows backwards and is gasping for air and laughing at the same time! She is quite uncontrollable and the people sitting next to her seem worried and her ask her why she is spitting soup everywhere. In between her hysteria she explains. They then look at me unsmiling and bob their heads silently. I tell them that I will share the next fly with them.

"Ni fungsa ser va." They quickly resume eating and the sound of slurping ensues, quiet and serene, punctuated by the lady's uncontrollable spluttering outbursts, her friends look concerned as I begin to look for flies.

Presently there is much commotion outside as a woman is run over by a motorbike and may have a broken foot. The driver does not stop. There is blood everywhere and she is dragged onto the steps of the restaurant where she is given a cold drink. With the last few moments savoured I slurp my meal and squeeze outside beside the bodies and the wall like an escaping fly.

As time progressed we were, more and more, treated like money-sponges. Back in the metal beast the loud speaker did not relent, movies flashed by, carpets of dreams splattered with Chinese idioms, trees, low hills, mountains of time wasted in a frivolous grasp for our pockets. But lo, the China person relishes the "spend-mania" and is soon swallowing bars of soap, jewellery and glass frogs as mementoes of the spending spree. Another brain washed shopping trolley, whose pockets have been ratcheted open like a womb of innocence. Obese and sloth-like in the bus are now blowing soap bubbles and snoring.

Up early to be hauled onto a stubborn horse in the teaming rain and walked some two kilometres along a slippery clay track and back again. My horse stampeded into a drain and had to be rescued because I tried to open my umbrella as I was getting wet. The silly thing did it again when I tried to photograph Lilly in front of me. It must have had eyes in the back of its head! Lunch consisted of cold wet fish after which we were hauled onto a sinking wet boat and paddled one hundred meters out on a shallow dam in the icy wet hills before they decided it was a wash out. Along with the farm dogs who helped us eat our small lunch we engorged our own melting spirits - cold and hungry and penniless again; they charged us extra for the raincoats! Suffering severe hyperthermia Lilly and I returned finally to the luxury of the thumping arse-jamming bus and the touch of Lilly's warm arm, bright smile and soft cuddle.

After seven days of the same Lilly and I are ready for a holiday. Towards the end of the trip the other Chinese men on board were looking at their empty pockets and beginning to realise that it was not a holiday but a commercial venture akin to mountain bike riding where one is constantly on the edge of something terribly bad. Like going to a hospital full of Tibetan doctors. I watched them from a distance plan their revenge, a grumpy word shot out like a mobile phone in a sling shot. I hear murmurs about rocket launchers, ballistic missiles and dead crows, worse still the grandmother! Like all China, slow to move, difficult to act.

We came to Yunnan hoping to see some rainforest as was advertised back in Shenyang. One stop brought us to a small valley with what looked like newly planted trees to twenty five meters tall. In the valley was a small stream with the yellowing marks of pollution by its side. There was no old forest. There is no old forest left. Perhaps way up in the hills on the steepest slopes where tourists dare to tread one may find fragments like shards of crumbling cloth hanging on for dear life. A place where eagles rarely go.

Yunnan is now only the memory of the cold showers, the rapid meals, the elephants and the river boat ride with more bosom wobbling transvestites where we were shot many times and offered the photographs for a price. Then all of us composted together with mounds of food on a boat with more transvestites who were thumping out loud dance tunes which precipitated many sideways glances from the women and belches from the sea-sick men. From all this - and the fruit tree orchards with the jack-fruit forest and the silver and jade shops; the wet horse ride was the most intriguing.

Until finally we spiral back down the roaring maize, back to the crowded bus terminal from where we started all those centuries ago. With the dirty dry bitumen and the shouting people. To breathe with relief from the sagging hardened backside and gasp the new hot unconditioned outside air. Then to the airport and the blue sky, breathing again the air-conditioned silence of the safety-belted seat.

Floating through her electric blue, the wheels again to throb upon the soils of Shenyang city where it was raining hard. The street lights few, the glistening black road, our way confused as we both walked round and round avoiding the giant puddles. After asking directions we returned to our original position and caught a bus wherein we soon resumed our "under arrest, stick-em-up" hands-up hanging position from the roof like drying monkeys. Finally at home where familiar streets do not seek to rob the poor and merely smile, we squelched and secreted ourselves with abandon, then enter sideways, primitives at heart, beneath the door of yet another hotel room.

There is a marked difference in etiquette between the table manners of Asian peoples to those of the English. While fingers excavate food from the plate in India to load up the mouth and long pointed chop-sticks everywhere else in Asia, the English relish in the stab of the tongue and the lick of metal. The hard steel tastes like dentists water, the clash of iron on tooth reminiscent of ancient armour and the mounted rusty bangs of battle lances.

The left hand in India is used for somewhat intimate bottom washing and not for dealing money, shaking hands or eating. The chop-stick encourages one to eat selectively by making it easier to pick special dishes which one likes from a long way across the table and mixing the food in a small bowl of rice or other. Hence many people merely nibble here and there and select the savoury and spicy dishes which may take hours to consume.

The English meal is served with three courses in mind. The first is soup or an entree, the second is the main meal followed by desert which contains the vitamin C. Iron and calcium compete for absorption and use vitamin C as an enzyme for their uptake into the blood.

The protocol of the Chinese meal presents all the dishes at once, usually many plates of strong rich food and quite a few different meats. There is very little vitamin C, or orange coloured vegetables (for vitamin A) and very few salads or fruit in a typical Chinese main course. Traditionally fresh salad greens have the living daylights boiled out of them.

Reduced sunlight from clothing and over consumption of calcium rich foods contributes to a lack of calcium as it is constantly being deposited in strange places in the body as it is unused or excreted, depending on the amount of vitamin D and not absorbed. One eats a breakfast rich in grains and protein same as the main meal in the afternoon which is also rich in protein then fruit is eaten separately at night or in the afternoon. English people like to eat fruit and grains in the morning.

Having said that there are people in China who care about what they eat. Some disobey their parents so their diet is not the same as an ordinary Chinese diet. A friend of Lilly's does not eat anything with an eye. But I argue that a nut is an eye because it watches the sun. Chop-sticks therefore are responsible for inventing considerable diversity among tastes and food preparation.

The Chinese rarely touch food with their hands. Their sense of personal hygiene they believe, is superior to others. This is the custom of the English as well. For in England I found many examples of a blasé defence against germs, the lift for instance was smeared with snot and was absolutely disgusting. The same insular attitude is apparent on the streets of Asia where there is little curtesy only a mad dash to see who can get to where they are going fast! Others have to clean up your mess as everybody copies the hygiene of each other - one follows the other.

Few stand and say, hey that is a dirty practise to pick your nose or hold one nostril and blow, hence they are afraid to shake hands in greeting. Consequently it is the dusts of our ancestors that we, the living, imbibe carelessly. In one nostril we sanctify their souls and nurse their ideals and from the other thank the doctors by exacerbating their work load by shaking their hands gratefully before running them over.

A Japanese person will turn a tap on and leave it running, for hands once washed will not touch the dirty handle of the tap again. Hence a fear and dread of germs invades the sanitised home so people buy every conceivable poison, long banned in the West, still available on the supermarket shelves here and in other parts of Asia. It has been found that hospitals are actually filthy places for some hardy germs enjoy a sterilised environment. Germs arrive on patients, doctors and nurses. Chemicals create mutations and can kill friendly bacteria which leaves a space for invention. Sunlight is the best sanitising agent of all. And lemon juice cleans silver and benches, intestines and blood beautifully.

Personal cleanliness in India is considered vital and many times a day one's various orifices may be cleaned often by others for little money. Ears, noses and eyes can be fastidiously emptied of their toxic contents which are otherwise exhausted by not touching but blowing loudly or if one is poor by a long golden fingernail delicately grown for gouging.

Those feminine hands of men, those deep voices of the women. It is little wonder that with so many chemicals in the environment men are becoming more feminine and women more masculine. Isn't it wonderful how hormones can either make one miserable or feel on top of the world? Imagine women with hairy chests and extended sex organs. Men as we know them will be doomed in the future and may begin to reverse any outward growth. Their love dominated by sentimental introspection.

One day China will realise that a man to man or a woman to woman marriage does not produce babies and that in many other countries those same sex relationships are becoming common, whereas fifty years ago they were taboo. Our hormones are changing, it is not our fault that science is mutating and sanctioning foods with febrile endocrine altering tentacles. Future babies will come from phials of glass and will cost money as sperm will be scarce and many men will be sterile. Come and get your vaccines, your sterilizing agents and your use-by date!

This is part of the world-wide de-population agenda. Eventually one man may father millions and all will be brothers and look the same. Mr Right will produce the crowds and they will all salute the flag. He will be paid handsomely for the service. He will have the smoothest palm, the richest skin and the correct genes and probably stalk about in the bushes fighting invisible enemies. The woman will never know what a real penis looks like and instead be sexually aroused by a machine as many are today!

The male will mirror the desires of the medical fraternity of each country and disguise his fear the same way governments use vaccinations which produce horrendous diseases far worse than they were "designed to control" and these days few of their manufactures would allow public scrutiny as to the contents of such concoctions. International Patent Laws sanction that. Other toxins such as fluoride in the drinking water, poisonous tooth paste, alcohol and tobacco, monosodium glutamate (a neuro-toxin which is widespread throughout the Asian cuisine) all help bring senility, autism and apathy to the crowds. Neuro physiological symptoms are becoming more common as we imbibe those ion chains of pseudo-life which grow tiny robots in our beings which feast off micro-wave electricity.

However one of the worst "poisons" is sugar which has a higher addiction rate than heroin. It is this substance and consequent invasion of the pancreas by the pancreatic liver-fluke which is causing an epidemic of diabetes worldwide. All those necessary poisons to keep the money rolling in by dumbing down the population and keeping them ill. Sounds like genocide to me, but not here in China!

With so much white noise around it is little wonder most of the population is too busy working to be creative or think there could be a better life. For the brain cannot think clearly with so many sensory neurons occupied. At school the children experience subliminal multi-tasking which destroys one's attention to focus. This becomes evident as I am often asked the same question several times, having already given an answer.

Perhaps it is the way of the new world to create one brain with the creative strength of the many - melting into one. Whatever it is I want one with a set of new ear drums to assist my hearing and other attachments such as an automatic aural translation service. Intelligence is measured by an ability to connect.

Mouse and Dragon Find a Super Market

Mouse and Dragon were up early, the sky was cloudy like the days before. They had finished their breakfast of home-made bread and eggs, porridge, dumplings, bananas, potatoes and fish and were sitting quietly on their small veranda in their rocking-chairs sipping tea and looking out across the river.

They were both very happy however Dragon's back was sore. He had always said the mattress of their bed was too hard. This day they decided to go shopping for Mouse wanted to bake more cakes and they were running low on flour.

They jumped in their little car and were off. Mouse loved going shopping but did not like Dragon spending too much money. As they were coming closer to town they noticed a new building with the words "Your Super-H Super Market" written in large red letters out the front. The building was not there two weeks before when they had last come into town so they decided to go and have a look.

It was huge inside. People were everywhere pushing trolleys about full of shopping. Dragon put his glasses on and began reading all the labels of the food on the shelves and started to throw things in the trolley like everybody else. Mouse was looking at the prices and began throwing things out of the trolley as she was sitting in it having a ride. There was everything for sale, from toothpaste to soap, vegetables, fruit and shoe-laces.

"We need some flour," said Mouse wobbling her whiskers. Dragon was attracted to a large fridge area which was selling all sorts of meats.

"Oh," he said, "I like the look of this, and that and this." He began to fill the basket again so Mouse had to get out.

When they arrived home they found they had ten tubes of tooth paste, ten packets of frozen chicken and other packaged meat, bread and biscuits and lots of shoe-laces, but no flour!

Dragon was hungry and decided to eat some chicken, bread and biscuits. Mouse ate some meat. It was different food to what they were used to which was vegetables from the garden and fish from the river.

Dragon looked at the tooth paste. Some was red, some blue and green with orange stripes running through it. He wanted to try it out so they both grabbed their new tooth brushes which were so expensive and went into the bathroom. Dragon's teeth were huge and Mouse's were little. Soon Dragon had bubbles of blue foam dripping from his chin, then red then green! He had never cleaned his teeth before! Mouse was laughing so much she jabbed herself in the eye with the tooth-brush!

"We will have to buy some flour next time" Dragon said scratching his chest. With full tummies they both went out into the garden to look for worms to go fishing. They found a few but did not want to go fishing as they had eaten so much. So they went to bed early, Mouse was soon snoring.

"When are we going shopping?" asked Mouse the next day at breakfast. "When we have eaten all the food" said Dragon as he held some bread up and toasted it with his breath then smeared it with butter. Then added "Lets clean our teeth."

Over the next few months they began shopping at the Super-H Super Market and changed their diet to include chicken, meat, bread, butter, milk, sweet biscuits and sugar which they found like everything else, came in either a brightly coloured box or a plastic bag.

Mouse looked at Dragon and thought he was so clever to buy all the food and had a very soft handsome face .

In the bathroom Dragon was looking in the mirror, his chest was itchy and his eyes seemed to be sagging at the edges. He thought he was getting old or perhaps he was putting on weight! Mouse came in and began to clean her teeth. She looked at herself in the mirror and saw another face! Her chin had more hair on it than usual and her eyebrows were turning bushy and black! She scratched her chin and looked at Dragon in the reflection and noticed that his head had a pile of dust on it, or was it hair? She reached up to touch it and sure enough it was hair!

As time went by Mouse began to put on weight and grow a beard! Her chin grew such an amount of hair it was astonishing and Dragon advised her to shave! Mouse looked up at him. His hair had grown all bushy! She scratched her chin and said she would have to cut Dragon's hair and added with a frown,

"Dragon's don't grow hair!" Dragon was silent and pouted his lips.

Over the next few months Dragon's hair grew so long it was down to his shoulders and frizzed out like a tree! At first Mouse refused to cut her beard but after a while it was so long it dangled in her food so she trimmed it a little.

Back shopping in the Super-H Super Market Dragon bought some lipstick and Mouse bought some big boots! Dragon raced home and was pouting his lips in the mirror again and applying lipstick when in walked a very tall Mouse in boots.

"Oh you do look beautiful!" she said scratching her chin. Dragon scratched his chest and replied in a little high voice,

"You look pretty good yourself!"

Dragon's chest had been itchy for a long while now and since Mouse was just high enough to see in the mirror they both had a closer look at Dragon's chest.

"Ooh!" said Mouse, "you are growing bosoms!" Dragon looked again and blinked, he didn't say anything, just kept combing his long hair, pushing his lips out and applying more lipstick!

Over the next few months they bought a large mirror and put it in the lounge room where they could watch each other change. Mouse grew a long beard which she eventually cut and Dragon had a number one hair cut! She had so much hair she stuffed several pillows and made a new mattress for the bed!

They were both quite happy as they sat quietly on the veranda in their rocking-chairs looking out across the water as they sipped their sweet tea, grew their bosoms and beard, with their very clean teeth and red red lips and their very long hair. With their stomachs full of chicken and meat, milk, biscuits and bread which they bought every week from the Super Hairy Super Market. And Dragon's back was no longer sore!

One day Mouse found Dragon in the bathroom looking in the mirror. He was banging his lips with the rolling pin which she used to use for rolling out flour.

"What are you doing my darling!?" she asked.

"All the better to kiss you with my dear!" he said pouting his lips and showing his big white teeth.

Moral of the Story:

Love is the connection between dark and light, it has no sound yet it roars throughout the universe.

Now all over the world, art, that voyeur of science, has become childish in the extreme. It is either a splash of intense pessimistic grief bludgeoned with tobacco smoke or other drugs or it is repetitious, big-eyed and obsessively cartoon-cute and sugared down like a neutered baby boy who extends a feminine aura, who fights in the ancient tradition to allay the fear of demons while pretending to be tough.

In the West our equivalent is Batman or Superman and more recently Spider-man, all with special tooth paste in their pockets and properly vaccinated. While talking to a friend he translates through his phone that "the West has bad self-righteousness" so I guess we can all breathe a sigh since we all *do* need protecting.

The small creature within her belly will bring China to her knees and maybe the rest of the world. It will manifest from the compounds of grandmother's dust long blown about in the streets – her bones we breathe. Or maybe it will be some health antidote which "backfires." Blasted out the back with careless distain. But China will go first because they never wash or clean under their finger nails. They bath or shower communally once a week. When they use the toilet they do not wash and they use chop-sticks which are often poorly cleaned, as tooth picks then spear dishes of food communally, thus spreading germs.

Chop-sticks hold their custom to the tradition of eating communally. Medically they are used for extracting difficult tonsils and scientifically for inserting things inside atomic reactors. However people's stooped positions, the "noodle stoop" at the eating table is another reason the massage business is thriving and few Chinamen grow beards. They sneeze and cover their mouths with their palms then touch the handles of public utilities or sneeze carelessly above dishes of food and spread germs like toxic clouds.

Studies done in India comparing the longevity of children who played around wild pigs in the street to the longevity of children who grew up in neighbourhoods without pigs found that the children with no pigs were more susceptible to diseases than the children who grew up with pigs. The reason being that pigs have particular bacteria in their gut which assists food and nutrient uptake in humans and also once ingested raises cellular immunity.

Ascaris, the round worm, survives in the dust and hatches in the lung then lives in the stomach and spends its life cramping and generally mangling the health of humans. Worms…. worms, from pigeons and pigs to dogs to cattle to human. Every species has its parasites. And quite often it is the excreta of these pathogens and the moulds which come to digest it that causes further health complications such as cancers. These creatures, the worms, infect Western people just as much as Asian people though without chilli Asia would be sicker still.

Chinese women do not kiss as they know that mouths are full of spittle and have the dust of the roads mixed with green slime down their throats.

They do not make natural love as they are afraid the government will see. In the West it was the same one hundred years ago but then it was the Church which pointed the finger and lasciviously watched, secretly wished and often did. Here people do not explore their creative spirits for they have been taught not to. Only survival skills such as how to kill everything that moves, birds and dogs, for they love their protein, their red red meat.

They have little sense of personal space. They will wake you from the deepest sleep. Scaring the daylights out of your dream. Their space is ultimate and fast, one has to run to catch up or slow in order to do the Chinese shuffle.

The family is bonded and talks about money and food. Many burp and fart and care not that others are close and take the smell which, it seems, is reserved for special people such as husbands and family. The crescendo of flatulence is a childlike reaction to domination by a higher force. They literally fart away their fears as a creative embellishment to their downtrodden existence. At least soy sauce is a pro-biotic however it can create a full sail-away, contrary to the English whisper.

Alas it is the same in the West but this is the nature of man. He is wretched beneath the bowels of Reason – we drink and smoke and fart away our fears! We are sprayed and toxed severely and fed rubbish and chemicals to eat. Our bodies are so full of preservatives when we die we do not rot! And in the hospitals we are pumped too many chemicals which bring death all too quickly. An old person in China is in their mid-eighties, ninety is very old and many die twenty years before. But some who live private lives with their beloved, usually in the country, live to one hundred and thirty years old!

The personal sacrifice is to see one's children perish in order to save the world from overpopulation - that is the game all governments play, that is the dust they sweep beneath the carpet.

China and the West the same. These two balls I juggle. While blue smoke goes in one ear and out the other. Little wonder they teach love. On all earth it is the only flower left to admire. We live, we cry, we love, we die.

The family is the unit of security. The house its shell, no money, no house, no family. The family in that sense is a closed social unit and within that spiralling vortex are complicated social morays mostly unspoken though often whispered to others, uncompromising and severe. The China family echoes the State in this regard. Its progress on the social stage a downward slide to a rabble of personalities, uncertainty and retreat to the family home. Difficulties arise when they all sleep together in the one house and in the one bed. No wonder these difficult decisions are left to the grandmother, she rules with an iron fist! Who washes up, who cleans, and who takes out the garbage? The regimentation begins – without it there would be chaos. With up to ten persons sleeping in the one hot-bed in winter, all snoring and in the morning spitting out the same dream. For dreams to them are worrying aspects of the mind and rob the body of good sleep. Their dream is fast, in step and quickly forgotten.

Dreams come in a flutter of the black wind - possessed by peculiar demons. To us in the West they bring stories and divine messages. She is there, the snow of sleep melting from the stone to hold me in her arms.

The iconic happy Chinese "fat man" is at every street corner his body rubbed with gold, the yellow light glistening off his roundness, with a big grin on blubbery lips, smiling at the crowds. De-natured of love and sex, his genitals mute. He is a symbol of the money which he eats to survive and to a woman he is the fat baby, immature in a masculine sense. He is at once the smiling Buddha and a baby of the world. However I wonder what small chested woman would give her breast to him? He is full of rice and noodles already and the animals of his alimentary canal are hypersensitive, hungry and over-active, they need rather to be succumbed to sleep with an overdose of sugar.

October winds blow cold from the north, over the mountains of Russia and down. The temperature drops to minus five. We dress with extra clothes, two pants, two shirts, two jumpers, two socks, two coats, two hats, too the supermarket we go as civilised as we are able. Too fat and two of everything! People are caught off guard in the icy wind, some look absolutely freezing as they stand in yesterday's clothes. The rain comes down and many get wet. People are running everywhere the wind is strong and almost freezes our ears.

My shoes get wet but my body is warm. In the supermarket there are people with their shirts off as yesterday's air is so hot and stale. The white-ice tables with the yellowing mounds of dead chickens, the fish tanks with the live fish, the crabs all weeping for mercy their mouths foamed up and dribbling, as they look about - is obviously too much for them.

I try to describe what happens to the body when the air is full of carbon dioxide such as here in the subterranean air. It becomes more acid the same as our muscles after poor breathing during exercise. The burning of energy produces carbon dioxide which, if not exhausted by the breath, goes hard within the muscles and when cold it crystalizes. This cuts and tears nerves creating sore muscles and joints. The same effect occurs in our sleeping bodies as we breathe the stale air in our bedrooms with the windows closed. The window of the bedroom is the exhaust for the out-breath - keep it open, open, open, to help de-acidify the blood. Hardened cell walls are bedrooms of mould, engines of glug. Through the windows of the body we will float on life's wings and explore the night world and dream of a future of good health and wisdom.

I receive mail from Australia which shows students in Hong Kong demonstrating for democracy as they are dissatisfied with rule from Beijing. Not since 1989 have such demonstrations been so large. The people want the electoral system changed so they can have a say in who will control them. There are mass riots with an estimated 80,000 people gathered. But the people have not grown up, they still wear pretty dresses like children and Micky Mouse ears, Superman eat your heart out! They watch TV all the time and have no sense to think long-term about how they could achieve a better life. They are sheep dressed up the same as we in the West, but even more so. It is a terrifying force which rips our hearts out before the crowd and eats it raw which was an ancient Mongolian tradition of war. Thus is people's honesty tested and ignored by the status quo until frustration spills.

Now the politicians advise the TV stations not report on the Hong Kong uprising, instead they telephone them with threats and say that if the riots are reported people may lose their jobs or maybe something else! For the government has the keys to every family home and infiltrates like a serpent and slides into each bed while the people sleep and swallows them whole. In the morning they wake inside the belly of the serpent and believe they have been dreaming - that Micky Mouse is real.

A friend in Australia sends me a newspaper clipping of the demonstration and is worried that Lilly and I may "get caught up in it." So I write to the newspaper back home:

"The government in Beijing will not change easily; they are irresponsible in their duty of care towards the health of their nation. They have their ancient traditions which they consider sacrosanct.

There is no mention of the demonstration here on the mainland however micro-blogs are getting through. Unfortunately such a change in China may mean much spilled blood. And we know who will "win." As in the West the problem is overpopulation which governments are now using as money making disease factories.

The problem is in the human mind world-wide and will not be resolved through politics. With a dead environment China will rise to gobble other environments much as she controls the internal natures of her innocent people. Dumbing them down to a Disneyland of ill health with tobacco, Coco-Cola, fluoride, MSG, traditional acid foods, preservatives, smog and much geo-engineering with an assortment of concoctions including metallized aerosol "chalf" as it is called in the West.

If they do not want Washington to interfere why do they allow Big Mack and KFC in the same buildings as their big banks!? Yes they hide, and they take from Western science, believing we have the brains but not the culture. We are China's fools and we know that.

Yes, China rules the world! At the same time China is splitting down the middle – mitosis. The government has invaded women's wombs with the one child policy knowing that her women are the weapons of China's future. It is the great feminine migration as they all want to escape and unwittingly take China abroad. God save the environment of the world!"

The message bounces back; they have blocked my internet again! But no I am wrong - my computer is wrong as well? Cripes!

I am sure my computer is being watched, both by China and the CIA. I do not blame them! I am an alien who struggles beneath the heavy bough of nature, at every turn I will fight for her heart wherein we all find a clear stream of unpolluted water which gives us food. She will hold my hand for in her being all men come to learn and not to fear. Will man ever learn that an appreciation of the natural world is far greater than his flowery words and lust for power, wealth and technology? Deport me then, fast. Let the rest of the world know that your natural world is breaking up and that you disappoint others with your banality and your silence. All men are equal, come take my heart and eat it raw!

I find myself looking out the window observing the comings and goings of the garbage trucks. Thinking that the hotel will be raided at any moment by masked men. I plan my escape after leaping five stories into the back of one and covering myself with garbage.

In the bus jammed in like coloured fancy dressed monkeys going to the ball - in the black glass reflections of the past - all with our arms up in surrender - old monkeys off to find the new. We are the "followed generation." There we hang pretending to be lovable, adorable, adventurous and wise. As though the ripening fruit is ours to pick and consume with toppings of fat which now in the bus is being a little jiggled.

Pale and glorious the childlike China face, simple, beautiful amongst the rough faces of the old. The bent sailors, sod-plodders, city-wise pen-pushers and ancient mothers in their grandmother's tradition - in the dusty breeze, courageous with a never ending pride, gravel-rashed deep. Then the tank of bubbling water and the huge frogs inside, with green skins like ladies shoes tastefully shod and waiting to die - clasping each other and wiping their tears with pink socks.

In the clusters of city mirrors I see my body grow from a flower to a shabby rose under the siege of the heavy air. One's brain resembles the hot dipped chickens, boiled a million times and the mind too has many vaporous wishes to be preached then deleted like a vagrant cloud. Dressed in a speckled drying skin, taught in the howling wind yet becalmed as though anchored by the balls. Washed by waves of blood-red through the great pump above the twirling gut. Eyes sunken back so deep with overgrowth of mind to red pools deepened by the weariness of travel.

Lilly goes regularly to her mother's house to do the shopping and help cook food. This day she comes back to the hotel with a huge vibrator with her eyes to the ground. She uses it in her work and says it helps reduce fat. She is growing large around the stomach possibly because I feed her so well. Another reason perhaps is that her three brothers would have consumed so much as baby boys Lilly may have felt she must eat fast or miss out! That urge may continue to this day. Eating patterns create diseases often attributed to genealogy however many pathogens invade through the window of food habits which at times blows open in a cruel breeze.

She lies on the bed with the roaring machine. We know I am not strong enough and my hands are breaking. My left hand is crippled but then I compare it to my right. Both hands will not make a fist. I watch horrified that I have been usurped by an incredibly loud machine! Ousted from the care of her body and her health. The machine is automatically warmed and the whole bed vibrates. I am concerned that it will damage soft tissues and express this with my hands with crosses and cut off heads. Lilly looks at me curiously. Who would dare to come to a massage house and be attacked by such a weapon? Only a fat person is my reply. Such is the spoil of advertising that it can induce phobias and feelings of uselessness and anguish about ones space by defining the beauty of one's outside form to fit into a nice thin little box in the end like everybody else. The lucky ones are simply stamped and sealed by the government. This ideal beauty is measured on the stock exchange before being buried or burnt.

The world has closed around me, enveloped in a Chinese eggshell so close and growing harder. Lilly's grin of pleasure pierces deep as her stomach rolls about like a frothing sea of oil. Spitting up large swells, foaming at the top and cascading down into drops of viscus ooze. The sea is mixing grease and internal bleeding. This tidal-wave of dislodged fat then confronts the liver and spleen, those islands of good digestion, before it is released from the body in a single blast or gushes out in a toxic flow. For days she does not eat, her liver intoxicated like a sea bird covered in oil. Washed up on the rocks, slightly breathing, a victim of somebody else's scheme. Her kidneys play like two children in a sand-pit, sifting time.

The air becomes thin as she lies there panting. Her fat rolling in hot juicy slides and pooling at the vortex of her navel. Amazed I watch as kilos are sheared off in moments and she is well like a child with a doll. The walls shake and the roof shudders as my shell begins to crack and an outward flow pools before me, half of tears and half blood mixed with rotten sebum. My buttery emotions melt before me as her China wisdom will not change.

"Fat cells do not disappear!" I repeat to the walls, "They just get thinner!"

No use reiterating my words. Help will not come unless she stops eating so much. Unless she is satisfied with "less" rather than "more." For in China the greed of the gut is a sign of wealth but who can enjoy good health if wealth means a ride on a fat horse? As I look in the mirror my jowls begin to tremble and to my surprise a neighing sound comes out! Lilly answers automatically above the roaring din as her body rises momentarily on hot air.

The Park, Shenyang

In the evenings the street vendors emerge with their three wheeled shopping trolleys resembling mobile dragons created ingeniously from bicycles for cooking corn and sweet potatoes, some with ancient steel pipes, swivel doors, strange levers, tops and boxes to protect and carry the charcoal and wood flames. Anything to control the beast. When stoked their eyes glow and chimneys thrash like tails - can shower cars and people with fire and the burnt remains of food. Many long iron troughs full of hot coals warm cold hands and smoke strange meats such as offal and bones skewered and smouldering. The alleyways clot dense with smoke and will cook you if too close - the same as they have done for thousands of years. Many people sit at small tables in the smoke and drink beer, smoke tobacco and eat these often expensive meat treats like confectionary to help feed an excessive protein intake which contributes so much to their acid bodies and ill health. The traditional cuisine becomes a stooped affair under the weight of indulgence.

We go to the park at night to see some friends. Under the overpasses, along the bitumen roads we slip like fish in grottos, in a smoky black swirling sea of lights. Tall buildings on either side alight like long vertical troughs and engorge electricity exhibiting spinning colours up their flashing sides. These are displays of wealth as precocious and alluring as the long smooth naked legs of the ladies in the blinking lights, all bitterly cold and raw, though a little smoked.

Only car headlights lined up at the crossings compete for brightness. We lunge across the pedestrian crossings like startled pigs from the undergrowth for the lights once changed bring forth a wall of speeding cars which jab us with their eyes.

Like a herd of charging bulls they shot out at us then some like fish bent to lead the way around us as we startled stood and regretted our first step. But the people dance sideways through these crossings, some one hundred yards wide. If caught half way the traffic miraculously slows, bends, beeps and twists and though most drivers have only had cars for a decade or two their driving ability is well advanced. In Australia we would crash or run over people in the middle of the road. Insurance will pay for it, no use worrying! Those who are poor have compassion for others, money encourages greed and speed. That is why insurance companies exist, to sweep the shattered remains of compassion under the carpet out to sea.

As we draw near the park the cement road begins to throb with the deep heart of beating music. Crowds of women all dressed in lose fitting uniforms pale blue tops and white pants like English pyjamas stand in perfect lines fifty by one hundred deep and dance for the exercise. The music is loud and the beat strong and constant, thundering through the earth like an army on the move. Lilly steers a course directly through the middle of them and embarrassed by my strange nationality I follow. The women fling their arms and stamp their feet in obvious enjoyment and my step follows their time so as not to be punched in the face or kneed in the groin. They do not turn their face to me though each eye pierces to my being. There is obvious love and joy here in the beating heart of Shenyang.

Many other battalions of dancers flaunt the concrete stage all flinging their arms around and uniformly gesticulating or performing some other simple exercise. Hundreds of people dance to the squealing high pitched electronic whizz. Often the music is played at high speed so the voices sound like dying cats while their feet the lowest notes stamp out. Many afterwards have chronic flat feet and squashed spines as their toes are rarely exercised. My own feet begin to flatten like a ducks and yearn for a mountain and rough ground.

About the feet of these dancing ladies the children play and out, far out, in the half-light their older fathers and mothers scurry and talk, laugh and dance like slow moving crabs their backs deformed from poor health and an unusually strong adherence to the old traditions of preparing food. All the people are beautifully dressed each with perfect shoes. Take the shoes off a Chinese foot and it will not walk on the hard ground for fear of pain - whole armies would refuse to march! Feet are revered as much as the opposite end of the body; any hardened skin on the foot is scalped off. The foot is then smoothed and placed in a plastic shoe.

In this "park" which is a raised cement platform one and a half meters high by five hundred long and three hundred wide are ten huge circular glass pillars which are thirteen meters tall and a meter wide. Their transparent interiors are alive with swirling avalanches of brilliant ever changing colour. Close by a fountain of some one thousand spouts, ejects frothy water intermittently ten meters into the sky which is shot through with reflected colour. The whole place flashes from green to vivid blue to brilliant red then mauve with all colours in between. The people's faces suddenly alive with colour as couples dance their troubles away with English waltzing, to a zappy step or frenetic nasal Chinese music with much arm waving, bobbing and spinning.

The moving colours spiralling up the giant cylinders, the squared blocks of regimented women flashing with colour, their arms waving with ever increasing speed and the deep throb of the music which shakes the ground, is a spectacle to behold – for this is the heart of China. They may be brainwashed like many other races by the TV and the roadside placards advertising toxic soap, toxic food and medicines to "cure" but here in this park are the people, the beautiful people, all exercising and touching their natural bodies with exhilarating excitement.

Every night the same pounding tune, every night the same bright eyes. Here on this hard hard ground they absorb their modernity through their rubber soles as many through the day, spend time sitting down in an office, their bottoms rotting from lack of exercise. Now escaped from the squash they fling their thin little mushroom-stemmed arms and stamp their bottomless legs like string-puppets or mannequins flowering joyously in a psychedelic field.

Kites with coloured lights touch the electric universe way up in the black sky above and children on skates and roller blades slice through the thick crowds. A young girl on a small mono-cycle speeds about as though she was born on a circle. The whole place is alive with the overwhelming throb of humanity.

Lilly teaches me how to waltz and with great self-consciousness I try. My feet uncontrollable tread on hers, however after a while I think I have got it right but we both stumble and I fall. There lying on my back I look up at the luminous green glow which changes to the music far off in another land. I pretend to be dead and not until many people come to look at me and one old dear begins to look like she may try mouth to mouth resuscitation that I quickly stand up. We resume dancing after convincing one hundred women in pyjamas that I am okay.

Lilly is well equipped to hold and all I want to do is hold her close and whisper in her ear! The bright neon lights have raped the vitamin A from my eyes which feel puffy and red. On the way home I step on the gutters edge, up and down to regain my levity. The crossings are deserted, the cars seem far away, the sound becomes muted as we talk our private language and discuss quantum mechanics and dried fruit. The bed like the cars seems a long way off.

With the last breath we rustle the keys and prod the hole for entry. Back in our safe nest where the only eyes are hers and mine. Then the single flickering eye of the great vibrator reveals itself again and crashes about Lilly's stomach. The whole hotel rattles like a ship passing through a choppy sea. I grab the wheel but the lilt is unstoppable, the waves above the gunnels, washing sleep.

We visit another park regularly just on sunset. People in blue charge around in quick-step with arms swinging and pony tails bouncing. Their radios squeal loudly like a thousand squashed piglets. If one stands in their way I would think one would be trampled. There would definitely be a pile up. Then on further we see young and old holding hands and spinning around, the boy is twice as tall as his grandmother. He is being trained to hold a woman and his glasses keep fogging up. They all wear the big-black rimmed glasses which makes them look and feel as though they are under water. Their beautiful eyes are not accentuated as they think they are - they are lost. Unfortunately the grandmother nearly breaks a leg and her hip looks like its gone - they stagger off stage.

One man with huge tonsils is determined to shout the rest of the music in the park down. His small accompaniment of people with traditional musical instruments is completely swamped with his profoundly loud agile voice. Many people clap and the ground shakes with a palpable fellowship. Far above in the winds of thought fly several kites with lights in the smog, they are ancestors on strings partially free, held aloft as examples of birds and tethered memories.

Further along in this cauldron of humanity we come across an exercise yard where humans are expected to pull muscles and stretch tendons on ingenious metal racks of torture. Lilly throws herself at an iron and chain monster and thrashes the daylights out of it. It ends its aggression as a mangled form twitching slightly - is definitely subdued below her. On another machine she pushes her own body weight up twenty six times, I can only do seven! Out of the corner of my eye I am watching some young men practice martial arts. I look again as I see one young man spring from a lying position to his feet. This is well applauded by all the bystanders. Then the man who is training the others does fifteen push ups on his thumbs! Every time the men finish doing a movement they would spring to maintain some awkward stance and look mean as though they were trying to say something. On another metal rack men leap up to grasp two metal bars, but before they do so they shrug their shoulders furiously then look around to see if someone is watching. If they fall the ambulance nearby has arms and spare shoulders for sale.

Stepping to avoid the human exercise-trains which bend and lurch along the narrow cobbled paths over-hung with frail vegetation we come across a small round space with lots of human size rocks standing upright in the middle and many swords sticking in the ground. These are empirical statements about the virtues of logic which reach skyward to the realms of the magical. We pass the silent stones and the quiet old men who speak softly amongst themselves. As we approach together and pass close by some stop talking to look at us and I can hear them breathing like the sound of a distant sea. This is a place where ancient dancers come to talk about the various styles of martial arts. And now that they are too old to jump around they come here to finally say what they have always wanted to say, to express again their wonder and admiration of the beauty and force of the human body. Their bent wives who have withstood their various love-making throws are in the shadows hiding, waiting patiently for them to return home and reiterate the memories of others concerning youth and the wounds of love.

Lilly begins to sniffle and sneeze; her sneezes are ear-splitting and dangerous. I fear she is about to contract some terrible disease and become bedridden. The machine is an addiction, a vibrating exclamation mark of civilization. It is not used for pleasure completely the opposite. If massage is not painful it is of no use.

My brain begins to see red...and we can't stop now! So we decide to go out, she wants me to meet her mother. Mother! Sounds like the matron of a hospital. So I ask about shoes to wear and things to take and how far it is and what shall I wear? I think she realises that I must be terrified of Mother and think she may be tall and domineering. Lilly takes me by the arm and smiles at me sideways.

Family

Lilly considers my worth sufficient to introduce me to her family. It has taken some time to break the ice. After all we are off to Beijing together again and Mother is very curious. It is not allowed in China, to have sex before marriage - I suppose I am the luckiest man amongst the one and a half billion others here. I may be tall but my neck is not as long as a tortoise's.

She takes me not far down the road through the cold streets, past the pools of black water and back in time once more. Though perhaps my perception of time is wrong and I travel the wrong way. The street is dirty with plastic refuse but each day it is swept down to dirt. Lilly has a stern expression on her face and a strong step, determined that I am the one. She knows deep down that her traditions will have to change and I explain to her that she as a leader amongst women will open many doors.

As I follow close behind I see her picture as she appeared on the website all those centuries ago – as clear as if it were yesterday, her smile and her internal fires burning, branding my being. Now the final step draws near, the streets grow narrow with the tall cement blocks of flats squaring every corner, preventing the warm touch of the sun. Presently, surrounded by steep walls with kitchen windows peering out over a small square courtyard with some straggling greenery, is the landscape, the garden. And turning sharply am directed to a crumbling opening like that of a cave. A closing chapter as I ascend the dark cold steps of the grey building to Mother's house.

At the top of ten flights of stairs and through two steel doors we come to a small well lit apartment of some five rooms. There her Mother greets me with her eyes unsure and her body language slow, she is stooped though not too much. She is a small frail lady of seventy six years with a genuine welcoming smile from ear to ear. Though she is small she has the strength of a horse and the will of a lion. As I enter she offers me some house slippers.

Unfortunately my own shoes are tied up so tightly it takes me some time to undo the knot and while standing on one leg lose my balance and step forward. Unknown to me there is a small child on the floor behind Mother and I step to avoid treading on him. My foot swerves and I tread on his plastic toy dog which lets out a terrible squeal then a loud pop as its whistle is blown out of its body. I lose my balance totally and fall forward and land under the dining table. Standing up I bang my head on it and fall again! Embarrassing to say the least! The small child wails, Lilly is laughing and Mother is running after me with the other slipper.

Lilly takes control and I am offered all sorts of small foods by Mother with a fraction of a frown if I refuse - she insists I eat. I express my joy and stamp out many small phrases on the translating machine such as,

"Your daughter is a wonderful person and she loves you very much." And, "you have done very well to produce such a big family." She bows and smiles from ear to ear. She knows that I love her daughter and will look after her as best I can – I say that too.

I am family at last and Lilly makes me feel at home. She will come to Australia and be my wife, she will walk in my footsteps by my side and dig my garden. She will be bitten by the same ticks, leeches and mosquitos and eat the fish I catch. Who knows she may even bear my child!

I show her mother my father's art work on the computer and a picture of my own mother's sweet face. The curious silence is leaden, pregnant – she does not know what to say. Art communicates like a string of planets connected by gravity through the cosmos. We all follow mute and afraid that we see the intimate whispers of another being.

Mother married Lilly's father after her brief two years at school. They were so poor. Father never went to school his family had no money - always too busy finding food somehow. He would wade the low tide near the broad sea inlet near Shandong looking for crabs using stilts in case the tide came in. One day he did not return after a high tide and grandfather became very worried. How did he survive the rush of water in the dark with stilts on and armfuls of crabs? The love of Lilly's mother kept him afloat, he could not swim.

Somewhere in Mother's old face I see her youth and her husband's memory as she half-smiles and looks deeply into the computer's flat face.

It is a wondrous thing but I swear that Chinese people float. One sees them on escalators rising or falling then outside travelling at the same speed - floating.

Like coloured kites in their embroidered shirts and capes and hats. Then airborne as they advance on the enemy or address the great congress of love. Lack of lordosis in the lumbar region and the resultant stiffened gait makes the head remain somewhat in an unmoving horizontal plane. Thus her mother comes and goes like a patterned leaf now blowing in the breeze. She is happy deep down for her daughter but does not know how to displace the worry for her family. Go forth I say and invent your own time, where mystical memories fill the spectre with everything. And leave no stone unturned for life takes, comes and goes, before you look and feel. Life travels fast, one must record the memories for the family. You will not worry about them when you make them smile.

How can words explain the fathom of the mind, a life once lived recorded freshly for others to breathe? To walk hand in hand with a stranger then together share the wonder of a startled bird or a glorious sunset.

The day ends with much introspection. I was as much a mirror of her Mother's husband and her own youth as Lilly was the butterfly reflected in her Mother's eyes.

Out again our stomachs lead the way, like blind sheep we follow doing the belly-dance and bleating. The cold blast of the day greets us as the morning shopping sharpens our wits as we buy some fruit for Mother. Then plod the grey hard street to ascend her tall square mountain to the small flat of little square cement cocoon-rooms. The stairs are tall and cold. One stamps one's foot to make a light go on, night and day. The hairy bicycles at the top of the stairs have cobwebs of dusty chemtrail-smog joined up to make small curtains. Nobody cleans them anymore. These were their strong steeds, their only transport, nobody minds as they decay. Here the people are all a little old. Through the iron doors with the squeaky hinges, with the Chinese writing all over them and on the walls outside - little sticky paper advertising. Nobody minds that the advertising is old. The steel doors are rusted and force outwards on their frames. Sometimes they remain stuck and one has to exert all one's strength to open them. Mother one day may be shut out by their age and hers, unable to get in.

The five rooms with four small windows opening out are blinkered by long curtains. On one side of the building is the vista of the howling trains and a view of the pollution and the melting sky-scrapers not far away. On the other side is "the landscape," which is a small courtyard like a cherry speared with light.

Then deep within this tall nest of steel doors Mother greets us. Today she is pale and wan. Her head is yanked to one side and her eyes are having trouble straightening. Lilly immediately charges into the bedroom with her and begins to massage her shoulders and spine. I can hear bones cracking and for an instant see the tiny body of a little girl wrapped in silk at the bottom of life. I creep into another room and begin to powder rice grains on the computer. No noise comes from Mother's room for one hour. Then all of a sudden Lilly charges out and goes into another room then returns and closes the door.

I have visions of severe injuries as a result of some mad wrestling match. But no, totally wrong. After another hour I decide to visit the toilet and while on the way Mother's door opens slightly and I can see Lilly inside with a drill and a canister taking blood out of her mother's neck. About half a cup. This is the old blood, dark and clotted; it will be replaced with the new. Another traditional healing method. Finally after two and a half hours Mother appears her head at another angle altogether. With a kind of static smile and a strong assurance that her neck feels a heck of a lot better.

I look in her eyes in a flash and know that she knows she is losing her daughter.

After the day of repair we descend the stairs but Lilly has forgotten the umbrella. As I am waiting a floor below for her to return another steel door opposite creaks opens and a slow shuffle, loud knock and heavy breathing is all I can hear. The sound is growing louder and I am curious to see what it is. The air develops an electric fizz as the light goes out and a peculiar odour exudes. In the dim light I can just make out from the top of the doorway a large head with long straight grey hair, it has a dirty bandage covering one eye. It is neither man nor woman, however it has an overgrowth of beard. It looks at me with a piercing eye. The head then is followed by two massive shoulders which are pushed up awkwardly by massive crutches and slowly the enormous body of an extremely large human dressed like a woman comes into view. She pushes a great plastered broken foot out in front and is stooping to avoid the top of the door frame. She would touch the ceiling if she stood up! How she will get down the stairs on crutches is a mystery. Lilly comes floating down just as the woman begins towering over me. In a flash we skip and vanish down the stairs.

As we are rounding to the bottom level a terrible crashing sound comes from above followed by the low growling of a deep human voice. I am in half-step to return to help but Lilly takes my arm, it is her crutch.

I remember reading a book on Mongolia years ago written by an Englishman who studied the physique of those tribal peoples. He mentioned that there were people who stood some nine feet tall. We know so little about other races which have been on Earth before and whose reality is still hidden from mainstream view. In the world and China there is much to learn.

Wandering the flat endless street landscape, I look up beyond the tall buildings. With a piercing eye I float off into an unusual never ending blue. Lilly's hand brings me back. It is the hand of an infinitely warm time-machine.

There is a Marlin in the market! Huge - it bridges three tables. Its great fin stands above the throng like a static flag. Its grey sweaty skin, dark and still alive, has swum inland one hundred kilometres from the sea. Its eyes sunken, its spirit gone back to the tides. No sound of water moving, rolling or wind across a fathomless blue. The market of men, the twitter of ladies, the sound of the horn, the gears, the motor and the swivelling electric eyes. Then the flood of people all in dark clothes who mob the fruit and meat stalls, robotic spenders with pockets as deep as the sea. Splayed horse's thighs lie baking in the smog - dank air. Lilly finds money on the ground it has good fortune. I found money in the taxi it will not buy us a fish.

Amongst the grey, beside the market sprinkled beneath a small shrub and in flower, a small smear of green and on closer inspection I recognise a cannabis plant not far from the police station. As I look I find more and more. I show Lilly saying that it is a Chinese medicine plant which it is. I comment that it is illegal in the West. Lilly knows nothing about it and wants some for Mother's neck. As time goes by I see that it is naturally growing everywhere and finally I ask somebody in Beijing about it and they say it is legal in China and that many people eat the seed for its health benefit. It is called Dhar-ma which I believe is an Indian word meaning "the flow of a river" or "life." The ancient Indian Sanskrit translation of the word cannabis means "the teacher."

Alcohol, the destroyer, cannot make brick walls and build houses, cannot make bio-fuel, cannot create peace, cannot make rope or strong clothes, or cure cancer like cannabis can.

Next day mother wandered, as she usually does down the straight flat stairs, twisting to the very bottom, then sat in the sun for a little while chatting to her friends then returned back up the flat-mountain stairs to her fifth floor. It took her a long time to ascend the stairs and when she got to the top she nearly lost her way and kept going up another flight of stairs! She had enough energy to run.

Lilly mixes food on the small table in Mother's house. Sprigs of green and spits of flesh fly about like missiles, inter-ballistic and dangerous for flies. The huge TV screen massages her pineal gland from behind and the phone sparks a conversation with her flimsy underwear. A glossy magazine has wafted in on the lonely smog-breeze wherein the little doll-like women hug two ounces of flesh to hide their bones. The clothing is skimpy and tastes like lemon juice, black-sugar and cream. The colours beautiful as the TV reflects red lips and little plastic bits down on the same pages smooth. Then walking like a lord, the great emperor of the stage across the glossy landscape, with chest so smoothed by cranky raiser. His spidery gait, puffed out through caution and acute self-consciousness. Across my page he walks, hugging an ounce of projectile-flesh which he caught in mid-air in his mandibles. There he goes, a denizen spider well trained to live in this China house, luckily he was not found and murdered by the grandmother with the broom! So I gently pick him up with the slippery page and pass him on to the outside world where his reading ability will come in use as he scans the smooth walls of the building looking for a delicious mate. Nephelia species, I know you well, just the same though different in Australia. Here so pale and white, tippy-toed walking, with red lip-stick, meek and afraid as though birthed in a fridge.

Lilly's thigh is sore, her neck, her feet begin to interrupt her mobile messages with static marching. Through the square streets, to the square houses with their square rooms and square doors. Which when demolished crumble like skeletons falling in the dust. One is mistaken to measure time in China, like measuring the age of mortar. The air is full of radon gas which cement gives off as it loses its compression strength in about one hundred and twenty five years. Cement is alive and the radon gas has no perfume and is carcinogenic.

In a ritual befitting an Emperor, Lilly's brother Cholong takes us to a shop in his car after using sign language and polite gestures. He guides me up the stairs of an expensive multi-story fashion boutique and then asks me to take my shirt and pants off to try out some clothes. My top was easy to take off however my pants are difficult so Lilly and he hold my arms. I try to tell Lilly that I broke the elastic in my underpants this morning and they may need holding up. She does not understand at all and backs off when I grasp her other hand and thrust it down my pants to help pull the broken elastic out which I end up doing. It came straight out like a long white worm. I don't know what her brother thought was coming out of me! He quickly stopped grinning and looked the other way. Finally I emerged from the shop looking like a real Chinaman in my quail-grey speckled dark trousers which were three notches up the status ladder and as long as curtains. The matching coat which seemed to puff me up at the back like a hunch back transformer, could have been worn by an ancient Chinese Emperor!

Dressed and back in the street I humbly smile, nod and wave goodbye as Cholong drives off in the sunset. However I am not the happiest person as my underpants have fallen half way down my legs. And we have about five kilometres of walking and ten by bus and twenty by train to get back to some private place where I can lift it all back up.

Our exercise pace quickens and we are soon leaping across roads stepping on car roof tops as they speed beneath us, horns beeping and testicles waving. A woman in a taxi has white gloves on like fresh clean clouds which grip the wheel as she fights the male aggression on the roads. Her white gloves protect her hands as heaven guides her into the masculine din. Suddenly from out of nowhere she narrowly misses a couple of acrobats who chance to be skittled, but we are on a mission again, floating above and unstoppable.

Beside another great maternity hospital is the "un-gloved shop" with the golden rings. Here the openness of love is wrapped in romantic highly polished glass boxes - those polished letters, as feminine as her wedding finger, tender, soft, virginal, as the golden moon slides on. The zero of all things, as final as a crescent moon which loves to fill her circle. Impeccable virtue, spit cleaned by a volley of shop attendants with little sweaty fingers and great big giggly smiles as they glance up to the maternity hospital opposite. I ask her to choose and she goes immediately to the most expensive one, as heavy as my pocket while a big fish caught on a wisp of curling black hair. Now committed to the great woman – she wears my ring – it is a ring of golden sunlight sprinkled on bright sea water. Her smile like tiny waves ripples across her lips and dimples her sandy cheeks. Uncomfortable to say the least, my underpants float about my knees.

We hang in the bus again much like my underwear, arms up, under arrest. Surrounded by the music of the crinkling plastic bags as painted nails engorge the ancient contents and flash-fingers chase rabbits across their mobile screens - those scratchy dreams. As furtive glances fill the space, each man his pocket bulges with their games. As noise pollution fills my ears, my heart longs for the silence of the bush. My new attire is restless on my body as at last I waddle along the small street to the salvation of the hotel.

Rising early we visit the supermarket. Down the floating metal stairs we ascend from heaven again to spend money and grovel under tables and peer at the lively fish who peer back at the dead people through the glass. Lilly grabs and strangles a bunch of greens and jams them, dying, in a plastic bag for Mother. Then we peruse the ice-boxes for real yoghurt which is all laced with sugar, impossible for Mother's diabetes. Back home, the golden orb leads the way. Then the meal again laced with the shavings of the dead finger-nail spices. After the meal, the white rice, white bread, white sugar, the dead corn hangs its head for the diabetic slide as the multitudes of energised particles thrash the pavements looking for a sleeping space to crash.

Back home in our honest bed we thrash the pages of the translating machine and put the baby computer in its little dropsy bag to sleep. Deep in the dark as the spider steps along, so quietly now, I am woken by the thin sound of fire crackers far off in the distance. A high pitched whizzing sound softly ending with a bang. As I listen closely the air grows scented as China air often does and I realise the sound is Lilly with her happy dreams farting through her new golden ring.

We have come all this way and searched Shenyang for a venue for my father's paintings and my mother's books to be displayed and published. As Lilly says it is not a city which revers art, it is an industrial city. The people are too busy to have the time to appreciate any vestige of the higher realms of creative freedom. Creative people here put their energy into making money.

Beijing is the place and we were fortunate enough last time we came to secure a place in a large Art Fair in that city which is willing to allow us to exhibit his work.

We walk to the railway station one afternoon to buy tickets for we are off to Beijing for the exhibition extraordinaire.

Beijing Exhibition

In the train to Beijing she sleeps by my side, the half-smile shows me she is happy. Outside the train in the deep afternoon a miraculous pink sky quivers frail and exhausted like the surface of a silent sea before the familiar white streaks zebra across it cutting deep into its logical fibre, the geo–engineered mathematical squares of Reason. Ah those Climate Scientists are at it again, they know exactly what they are doing! The fine metals they use in the name of Solar Radiation Management will stop global warming. We will all be saved!

As I lie there alone staring at the train's ceiling I muse that she is not close to me again for she sleeps on the bunk below. However I say that the night will soon pass and we will be together again in the morning. In the night I dream that we are one and in the morning I tell the ticket inspector exactly that.

Relishing our own freedom, we fly into the big world the two of us joined at the hip, with pieces of paper, phone numbers, addresses, government personages, bodies, boxes, ammunition such as words, lots of pens and socks and other types of adhesives - glued.

The roaring in my ears is the sucking sound I make as I descend into the swirling hole of China's lovely face - eaten alive. She is ever youthful and delights in watching me carry all the luggage as she knows she will get a good nights' sleep as the pack-horse will be well exercised and exhausted. The wheels on my giant bag have a mind of their own and keep wanting to go the wrong way. The bag is impossible to lift and like a blind dog on a lead keeps wanting to wrap me around poles.

The early morning Beijing smog assails us like the thick humidity of a storm at sea. The silver-iodide (or other) smog sprayed over the city the day before, cold and calculated, crazed and insane, clangs through my veins. The iodide clogs the thyroid, depressing the immune system and is toxic to fish. Suddenly as I sniffed the air I realised it smelt like metal, not asbestos as I first thought.

Our enthusiasm began to melt as our destination became ever more remote as we couldn't see the street signs nor recognise where we were in relation to the tall buildings. The subway trains go one way and we walked the other, the same as the floating stairs one comes up to ground level on, one twist, once around and one ends up backwards-front. And the stairs suddenly stopped in the middle of their flight due to the weight of our bags! Miraculously they started again and slowly, ever so slowly with a horrible screeching sound they just managed to reach ground level as we hurled each bag clear at the top. Fortunately the escalator started up again as quickly as before.

Feeling like two fish in a slippery sea after walking two kilometres and crawling six I spied an island of security and headed for that.

Starving and exhausted she runs off in the rising swell. Not knowing where she is going as usual, or so I suspect. I stagger to my knees and hoist my bones up onto a warmer ledge which seems to have more of an early morning-smog-red-sun glow to it - away from the cool air. However the bag with the food is back down on the ground so I jump down and haul the heavy bag up onto the ledge and climb up again. But the food is in the other bag! So I jump down again and haul that bag up on to the ledge, yet more exercise. Just as I scramble back up she returns with news of where the hotel is. It is quite close, just around the corner she says about three kilometres so we share the last mouthful of our rations of dried fish and salted cabbage with lashings of Beijing smog. In this dark oppressive "weather" I expect to see animals out feeding, wallabies or small bandicoot. Who would think that in Beijing there are no scrub turkeys, no birds to eat or hunt only people, people? Where do they go and how do they survive this smog!? I sit on my awkward bag and Lilly steers my body- bag along the Beijing footpath for three kilometres!

The hotel is called the "Yi House" and is near a railway station. It was definitely the cheapest Lilly could find. She inspects the room and finds it to be crawling with cock-roaches; she has dozens of traps set immediately.

Morning wakes to find Lilly blowing smoke rings of pollution. She lies there at peace with her life, snoring like a baby. As soon as I move her heavy arm bashes my side and begins to hold my imagination down like a recurring jingle.

Rolling sideways the arms to the sides to bridge her gap as the martial artist in me brandishes a sword while she her reckless wound unfurls.

As the moments pass the day splatters itself over us like wet paint. We shower together we wash each other; we drink from the same cup to the wisdom of our time. Alone in the world we descend the stairs again and scurry off down the street like a couple of Beijing rats.

Beijing

Beijing smog engulfs the sun till it is a red angry ball, a ballistic fat man ready to burst. All day the other sun, the light of perception - the red dragon's eye, has already fallen blind from the sky and wrestles now on the ground with the throng as they dream tormented dreams of red-giants which will not brighten and let the blue of day bleed through. Such a patchy repairing sky would allow the trees and flowers to again feel the seasons as they were felt before, but now their flowers are confused – already blind. Thus the smog shades the heart with despair. The dry cloud is weeping; those ragged edges of our disease as they fling themselves from horizon to horizon like torn shreds of toilet paper.

The river smells putrid, the duck meat the same. One thousand people smoking in a restaurant and the beams of light pierce through but not the oxygen. Across the river I can hear the music of the evening as those pyjama ladies are here too, having jogged from Shenyang. The heavy smear of the smoky evening smudges their minds as they dance to the jittery music and inhale their exorcisms profusely. They don't look at each other because they can't *see* each other from three meters away! Alone with their music, somehow connected.

Across the river on the other bank a large front-end-loader fills a lorry with garbage.

The smell wafts across the wet mud as we walk in the pollution after our evening meal.

We do not walk far, we cannot see! A torch shines ahead through the smog, it cuts a straight narrow beam like a lazar shining through an Australian bush fire. But this fire does not smell of eucalyptus as it smoulders from the bowels of those in power! And that smog will not lodge from our lungs!

In ten years, Beijing, your hospitals will be screaming desperate places saved by one beaker of fluid and one needle of salvation. And your one child will feel lost and angry as he/she searches the exhausted river for young companions!

Twenty yuan to see art? I say "no" as I have spent a lifetime looking at art. Life is love not art. Art does not warm your bottom or pay for itself. It is dead life, a vision from the past repeated, reworded, revisited. Art tries and teases Reason. Life moves all over the place like a giddy circle, looking for love. Without love of course there would be no life. Love is a circle, designed to hug its invention.

The wind plummets down and brushes the dusty street. The leaves stand up and roll like plates, papery singing, swaying from side to side wondering where they will spend the night and lie flat, circular and silent. The sun burns through for an instant, strong and drying, crisp and clear; reminding us that the universe goes on out there beyond the trodden clouds.

Lilly leads me on I know not where, through the never ending streets of Beijing. At each corner we pause to fling our eyes down another street, reminding us that we are at times alone and unattached. Together we march on, together always. I stare into the gutters looking for coins and diamonds, one leg shorter than the other. We walk as the one animal, four legs four arms and one head - she wears my skin.

From the gutters of art and the tall straight cement corners we turn a bend to be accosted by a sculpture of steel pigs which grope about a solid rusting table feasting on people's sanity. It is a definite social expression regarding politics and the gap between the rich and the poor. Some pigs are ill, others drunk, some passed out, others rule. Not one pig is happy, they all have cruel scowls, their upper lips are twisted as their bloated stomachs ache. Around another corner another steel table with Marlins using their beaks as chop-sticks to tear up the remains of a human. Curiously they all seem happy. And more, around another corner, another steel table with young fat male babies feeding on old men and women in uniform.

We have to get thirty two copies made from original art works blown up on good quality paper, three of each, and have thirty two framed to hang in the show. Think of that! So far away, glazing in the distance.

Far out the sunset way behind Beijing is a flat land with few trees. Fruit trees are few, corn fields are many. In a string of straight cluttered single-rooved dwellings is the master print maker. He does not understand a word of English. And there in the room is a beautifully dressed lady customer in vivid red who interprets for me in pretty good English. My God she was another beautiful woman all painted, her bright red lipstick lips kept opening and closing! The cylinder of prints would not flatten! When finalised the print man kindly drove us through the endless traffic to the railway station. Somehow we found our way back home to arrive well after dark.

We are off to the framers. Our large role of prints, white and virginal rests gently across Lilly's thighs in the jamming bus. Three busses later and already exhausted we fall out onto a dusty gutter full of listless people who peer lugubriously, blindly, up at the sky. Soon we are pointed in the right direction. Far out over the flat land, the concrete strips the veins from our legs as the plod replicates incessantly restricting arterial air. The only exercise besides the shuffle is the rapid climb up the stairs of the overpasses for a better view then down the stairs on the other side squashing ducks.

Out the back sunset way again, deep in the quagmire of market stalls, furniture whare- houses fruit stalls, shops, tents and canopies is the small room of the framer which opens out onto the flooded street.

Here in this little nest of straight lines and colours his family survives. Clouds of tobacco smoke waft by as we determine which colour frame and mount suits which print. It is not long before we are all photographing and hugging each other in appreciation for our ability to not understand a word of each other's language yet are able to achieve an outcome in the name of art. Each print lies on the floor splayed wide and enticing the eyes to wallow in the frightening reality of the nude. Strange murmurs rebound through the floor as each tries to control their natural curiosity. The middle aged framer tries to understand my gesticulations and his wife who looks well pleased about everything I do and their only son, who whispers to his naturalness,

"Ah, that is what they look like." Then the wife whose modesty is uncovered realises she holds the key and triumphantly throws her arms around Lilly then me as my eyes try not to smart. Finally the anatomy lesson ends and I shoot them all with arms flaying, squashing breasts and shoulders, weighted down. The son holds the camera and proudly bites the lens spitting little spits of glass onto the floor where once she lay as fragile as a slipper, as taunting as a young bride.

Tip-toe we go back into the fresh wasteland. Lilly hand in hand with the lady who now knows her son knows all about the female form. Such a luxuriously easy education!

The small spits of rain wet the pages of my father's life as the remaining prints are tucked neatly under Lily's arm splendiferously.

We set a course by sniffing the breeze and begin again the up and down struggle over the innumerable overpasses and along the flat, flat squares. Then in the middle of a huge road crossing where six busy ways intersect, Lilly cries something indecipherable and high pitched. The traffic stops. She holds the prints in the air and as they catch the smog filled afternoon breeze we are blown back the way we came. To return again to the framers to get a receipt saying that he has thirty one prints to frame.

The evening air grows raucous as the traffic honks below the overpasses, under the passes, over the passes around the long way, to forget our way. The peak-hour roar and blast of the anxious horns freely vents through cracks like those family ties again expressed with special admiration. Who's polluted reciprocal breath we all have to swallow. A dying orange light caresses one side of Lilly's gentile face. And I follow silently like a shark behind a wonderful sailing ship which is blowing in the horizontal blast of China's petrol fumes.

Lilly leads the way past the flowering trees - beyond the reach of the blue sky, across those long cement bridges in the traffic breeze of sunset. The roll of prints, white and unblemished, the story of my father's life, wrapped tightly in a China woman's arms.

After the struggle home in the peak hour jam we roll into familiar territory feeling like jam ourselves. The jump and leap of the bus as it travels over new road numbs my knees and the monkey-arms physioed above make the body stretch and stay stretched. I walk the street back home with a bobbing stance with my arms still stretched above my head, fingers trilling. Lilly does not look at me as I follow behind like a baboon.

It is not the first time we have to go back for something. Forget me this, forget me that. I will not forget to take my China girl home! Now the bags, the receipt and then the mobile, calling in the empty room, no signal in the murky mind's transmissions, free at last to slowly die, its power a little black dot of energy before eternity. So we return to aid its heart and answer its bleating questions and demands.

The dark deeply grooved barks of the Beijing street trees and their fine fingered branches trail off to single yellow orange leaves, we twist our necks to see. Past the small bicycle stall with boiling oil and soy milk. With other flames and simmering pots, the bang and clatter of the caboose as it rockets the workers to work. From her dress the hem of which is the gutter of the street we look far up inside the walls of the concrete cliffs. With small turrets and windows draped with utilities such as plant boxes, washing lines and steel bars. The finery of life - curving branches and in the distance the sound of the birds in the rustling leaves above is echoing the clear water stream as it rounds and smooths the black stones.

Lilly translates my father's website into Chinese for a poster to be put up at the show. The wording is endless with the complicated detail of Chinese writing as rich as each meal, the cooking of traditions as tasteful as the tea. Lilly is totally dedicated to its exactitude and rouses a storm in the poster shop to get the job done beautifully. It is their job to serve the customer and her effort is well rewarded with a superb poster. She has detailed every small stroke and there are thousands, every full stop and comma, every nuance of inflection.

Outside in the street, colours of grey green and yellow blend with the flickering bodies of the people. The ladies with their woollen coats, their fur frills with the white sunlight splashing on the cold road. The yellow autumn leaves falling like cigarette butts in their thousands to be swept up by orange over-alled people who are ladies with masks on, brooms for tongues. Old men with fat bellies hang from dilapidated bicycles which have the power to stop the roaring buses. The paper and cardboard stacks on the backs of trucks and bicycles beeping and beetling along. The poodle people passing nonchalant, the young girls in love with their fluffy dogs. The small boy pulls a toy car on a string with sirens and flashing lights, his father clearing a path has forgotten how to play. No insects, no birds, only dogs, cats and people. Cars and flashing lights beyond the wash of modern sounds, machines wheel and squeal in adoration.

The silent body beneath the many layers of clothes - warm and yet frozen to the flesh. The caps, and knaps beneath the black eyes, bridled by straight hair, long waterfalls of black cascading down backs to small bottoms and narrow hips. The three wheelers slowly turning in the pit of despair floating on the hunger of commerce, loud and deafening.

Angry men are few, women arm in arm laughing tippy-toe as if drunk on women's secrets. Hand in hand, arm in arm, laughing and playing in the pool of love - great China, febrile, fecund, luscious, sprawling, happy! Happy in the freedom of personal expression. The great confession of the testicles as they hunt the wild womb of the street. It's a flotsam and jetsam world; it's a world of deep introspection and learning.

Amongst these grey concrete buildings the wind whistles, it is the ancestor's thoughts from long ago blowing. Here the white snow falls about the whites of their black-pool eyes, welling tears like rain. The orange leaves of autumn are falling eyes lashed into sleep, the rain washes in and out like the beat of waves on a crimson shore. The wind is a growing hunger like the rising sun which taunts the leaves to burn in the quietly rustling feminine breeze.

The wind is soft and fresh with the portent of ice. But do not breathe too deeply!

The underlying bite of cold through the mountains restless blows and drapes itself about the skeleton buildings and shivers about the fat of the finished ones. Many autumn leaves still on the trees not yet yellowed and dropt, the orange clad street sweepers now have work to do as the carpet is woven and turned by the weather, their stems pointing inwards where they are flattened like Chinese paper calligraphied into cracks - drinking deep. We shuffle ourselves like penguins back in the dark to our "house" as Lilly calls our hotel room. The poster will be ready in the morning.

Exhibition

Clear skies above Beijing followed us to our destination. Then at midmorning three aeroplanes sped through the blue high above and released white lines. Madly I photographed the lines as they dissipated and become misty clouds. And on our way home the sky became a sheet of filamentous white. The mist began to thicken till we fell down in the fruit stalls and embraced the fish tables. Until we began to shuffle again like people in the drains with masks on and watch each other's eyes from a hungry distance. These masks are becoming fashionable, they cover the whole head, only the eyes show, blinkered. But we too are dead donkeys. Then in the evening still, a cold shuddering calm as the white "smog" lumps down. Next day the face masks are out, the pretty scarfs wrapped around, as many people don their blind-fold protection from the lifeless artificial "smog."

Don't they know they are being sprayed? Did they look up to see? Don't they care that their government is assisting the pall by doing this to us all! That air we all own do we not?

It is *our* air they play with at forty thousand feet! Do they want us to get sick and pay money to "their" hospitals and "their" pharmacies?

Of course they do! Another reason why we are kept in the dark about the health effects of mobile phones which cook the brain so the government can trade us when we lose our senses and take our money for the "medicines" which the government brews like old female witches who stir large cauldrons of the stuff to keep us just on the edge of death. Our brains are weighed on the stock exchange and we are sectioned and sold by the dumb-tonne kilo.

All our throats have frogs in them! Slowly we die, slowly we shuffle to our ill health and try not to believe that people could do such a thing to their own people. "Neagh!" we say like donkeys. But it is happening world-wide. These brews, concocted by scientists, are released in the jet-stream airs to circumnavigate the globe. They are turning us into machines and laboratories, controlling us and altering the climate, this they know.

It is the new way and they cannot stop it. Do not talk about climate change until you study the "clouds." It is the crime of the century perpetrated on Mother Nature, the grandmother and our children. I am told by the World Meteorological Organization that over forty different countries are doing it. And that lately few countries are submitting detailed information about what they are using because disclosure is hidden behind the protocols surrounding International Patents. The World Meteorological Organization informs me that as there are so many variables associated with the weather and few reliable controls many countries are trying out everything including grandmother's washing powder! Alas the clouds are not the same as those that I saw in my youth! Each cloud a sheep, like you and I, cotton-tailed, ragged around the edges and dumbed down. The particulate matter or condensation nuclei as it is called, has lowered the atmosphere because it is heavy.

Cloud seeding with metallic dusts is yet another forced method of making people sick and we are told rightfully that climate change is caused by man and his addiction to oil and greed. Nobody in the mainstream media tells the truth, that weather engineering is real. The metals increase microwave reception and transmission for mobiles and computers. But why do they spray our skies with poison? Because we let them! Don't you know you and the Earth have been gassed by your respective governments to feed our addiction to communication? Is that the game they play while throwing our good health to the wind? Bye bye blue sky.

We all can live to one hundred and thirty years old. We all could do that if we were not forced to battle with illness and were informed by our "responsible" governments about health and proper nutrition.

The Agricultural Centre is the venue for this four day art show. It is a metal barrel vault building with a cavernous high roof and thin-skinned walls. The temperature inside is much the same as outside.

They have given us wall space which we pay for by the metre. Lilly looks at the plan and complains that it is not the same shape as what we paid for. One wall is in the wrong place and must come down, she is adamant that, in the eleventh hour, it must be changed!

She organises this with great alacrity, with her hands firmly in her pockets. Then the neighbour on the other side of the wall asks if he can have one of our walls for free to hang his art because he has brought so much from Sweden and quite obviously thinks his is better than ours! Lilly looks at me sideways, eyes rolling, her jaw drops to the floor and all her teeth fall out like little peppery sparks. She does not say a word. I can see little fists forming in her pockets.

The opening ceremony, where shadows of beings all dressed in black crack open bottles like themselves and evaporate through the spluttering loud speakers and the popping balloons. The ritual opening explodes in the car-park under an ominous painted sky. People google at themselves in the black reflections of the polished black stretch BMW limousines, Mercedes Benz and Rolls Royce cars. Eyeing their black wealth and pouting their pink beaks as they frizz their black hair, afraid to step beyond the naked flame of their black-zappy fashions and freeze. All too afraid and whispering in their sleep, groaning in the womb like young children showing-off, peeping out from the uterus of wealth, with a view to everlasting youth.

Through their black-tied throats their vaporous words extoll the virtues of being colourful and creative. Transfixed I grip their seeds tight in my fist and squeeze their saps. How their wealth turns them into skeletons of flesh, mortals grown and flowering on the wretched stage. Forever poor and supposedly unblemished by their own fortune which rallies from others the adornment of their bare chested egos. So now their age is beyond their childhoods when their poor mothers changed their honest nappies and taught them to believe in the virtues of a kind government. Suddenly cold white eggs begin to fall from the sky like hail. Then coins and money splash down like blood.

Many people with cameras crowd around our table feeding us brochures and mixed advertising material. The drawer is full and about to be sick on the floor. As the day progresses I am curious to know where these people come from and why so many. They seem more interested to give me bits of glossy paper which advertise their galleries and merely glance at my father's work and snap it with a camera. Many also fish and trail their hooks through the other alien's display booths.

I have asked galleries and the organisers of the show what price I should sell the prints for and they agree that the price should reflect the quality of the work. However I would like to sell them cheaply as they are only prints. But they say the price should be a little more to make people think they are getting something worthwhile. Many people ask the price, the work is good but the price too high.

As the first day draws to a close we peep outside where the snow and sleet is falling once again. Then timidly from the warm clutter of this huge exhibition hall we scramble for warmth and plastic to keep away the icy wet. It is most unusual weather for this time of year! Then afraid we launch ourselves into the early night stepping paddle-free to find our way home. Lilly turns right defiantly in the wrong direction and like a blind white rabbit looks for the white underground station in the white snow. After a little while she realises it is the wrong direction, we are soon wet through and she is lost again! I turn her around to face the other way. She is not pleased and grits her teeth and yelps like a small puppy stranded on an island. But I lead her on, she follows my train. She is angry at the weather, her mouth turned down at the edges. She talks in Chinese and when finally home pulls my frozen socks off and bangs my brittle toes.

On the second day people linger through, fingers blue, some talk and do the pink-lip wobble, or wobble pink-lipped. Squelching about with frozen wet feet I busy myself distributing DVDs to the organisers of the show about weather control and geo-engineering. Strange that it snows for the next two days after which the show ends!

The wrestles morning wakes me with a simple tune, albeit blast, which embeds in the brain for millennia. With a flash of lightning I rise and start the grind of the computer screen. The machine is stubborn it will not upload nor download. It stares at me blankly and refuses to move – a blind sheep I stare back, it cannot talk. Thus we are frozen together. Mute and impudent, flat faced, the bloody thing stares back at me again! Its face has squared quiverings of fear as its verve grows slower and slower. I muse that perhaps it has a disease or Chinese gremlins? The blind who lead the blind. We are beings of this computer age; China the wild wind follows you.

She shaves me again like a mother cat and flicks my penis sideways saying, "No, no." Then studies English by playing, north, south, east, west with it until it is thoroughly lost and suffering hyperthermia. She massages herself, her arms, her feet, her stomach; she pinches me and pushes me in. I look at dead cockroaches that struggle in the sticky paper and feel the same. Then write in the translating machine,

"I love you Lilly! Take my love and give it to the world!"

Then suddenly she is alive. The little flashing lights of her mind beam from the stars – as if stuck on a download of great distant knowledge from my friends in Australia whose fingers are long and politically bent. I type my messages on her face, tattooing her lips into fractions of screaming pleasure. She is mine at last, her womb is open the vortex grows unafraid. Above its gaping hole we balance our words on the equator.

Lilly sleeps, her snoring voluptuous body-brown like a little berry with no seed and thin skin, warm and enticing. Opposite to the rapacious computer which rapes my mind, from the euphoria of love to an unsureness of being. From our warm room we descend the stairs into the cold flat faced silent secretive underground.

The whispering day has dawned long before and idle workers brandish their umpteenth cigarette. Crossing swords their words meander through time's little bosoms.

The bright light of the street is aglow with snow and ice. The rain is hard and cold. Cars are draped with white, melting, dripping. Rain and the sound of car wheels through the water slicing paper on the way to work where they tear cotton sheets. The gusty wind is freezing. For thirty years at this time of year, this kind of weather has not been seen. Lilly is aghast. Her shoes and mine not waterproof as we step carefully through the ice. The trees their leaves hang down with the white weight, the ground a slosh of white water curdling brown. Thus the zebra stripes come down!

On our way to the exhibition with her mobile glued to her ear, Lilly is lost again like a wayward bee as we crawl out of the underground station which we could not find the other evening. She stands with her mauve umbrella and flimsy shoes far off in the middle of the white field. Far off I can hear her talking to herself in her high pitched squeal. She has forged her own path and for a moment she finds herself alone as she cannot see long distances. My own path has eroded into an abyss of deep snow, where frozen toes bite the prospect of danger.

The sound of cats fighting issues from the roof tops, it is a woman singing through her nose. Her tradition of music is based on the authority of the single string - quavering, lilting, vibrating, plucking, racing, crying, squeaking, talking. She cracks the ice like a mirror. China does not have many traditional instruments compared to other countries and I confess I know little about the derivations of many instruments in the world though such a study would be intriguing with the Western orchestra topping the list for diversity. She is strong of voice I can hear her whispering far off in the cold orchestral wind.

The mauve umbrella like a beating heart or morning glory flower far off, a dot of purple on the white. I call to Lilly in the frosted morning, beyond the car-park like a baritone moose, but she does not see me only the white field. Through the smog, coming closer she sees me waving from beneath the black plastic garbage bag she made for me into a raincoat. Look I say I am a frozen corpse waving! The wind bites my fingers. My camera slippery in my metal grasp. She follows, her shoes laced in frozen white. The puddles deep as ice runs about and between my blue toes - there are black-holes in my shoes! She is lost so I lead the way like a silent black-plastic wolf leaping from tree to tree.

The director of the Art Fair comes to talk to me. She does not know my shoes are full of plastic bags. She could not sleep last night - the wind so strong. She lives at the top of a sixty story building. I gave her a DVD on the use of metallic dusts for weather engineering. Another piece of useless information for China and I feel the magnetism of a pessimistic despair as I suck in the junk and spit out the nails. I confess my brain is full of metallic dusts, my transmission awry.

We drink tea together, discuss the role of the earth, the etiquette of politics and the lack of copyright laws in China. She admits she feels uneasy about people coming into the booth and photographing everybody's work. Many admired though few asked if they could shoot.

My father's naked ladies are hot on film and some photographs were painstakingly and suspiciously executed. I was told that they could go away and reproduce the picture and put their name on it and we would never know and not be able to do anything about it!

"Aliens," as tourists are so lovingly referred to over here, have no legal rights in China. The tea is poured in one tiny glass then another then another, it too is painstakingly executed. The flavour is mute; the water is from a plastic sterilized bottle. One click and it is all gone.

The art show is a flop and mirrors the sky. We do not sell anything! I find out later that it is not popular with the government for aliens to make money in China. They can make money in our country though and many do! The organisers of the show are attached to the Cultural Arm of the government. They have charged me a considerable amount to exhibit. Many Nationals are also exhibiting and Lilly asks many if they pay like we do. She is horrified to find out that many are sponsored and are exhibiting for free. When we booked the show I was told that because I was booking early I would get a discount. This discount never came and it was only after considerable harassment from Lilly that we eventually received half the amount they said they would give us originally. They must have known we would not sell anything, our prices were too high. Yes I was forced to the put prices up to raise the kudos of the show!

"Two days rain - you come all this way - no sell anything." Lilly is upset. The tears stream down her face. She sits on the bed beside me silently weeping. Her pain drips on my leg as I throw my arms about her to cushion her anxiety. We have not sold any prints. We have worked hard to find an outlet for his work which I thought the Chinese would appreciate.

The expression of his line, the acrobatics of form and space, so eloquently rendered. The nude figures, angelic, float out of the paper, now displayed throughout China on digital screens, shot through the glass and misty like impossible dreams.

All the framed prints we drag back to the hotel, up the four flights of stairs in the snow at night. Next day we carry them down the stairs and far off to another venue, a print gallery where photographs of paintings are sold. It is run by an opera singing Chinese lady who trained to open her throat and gargle in New York. As we help hang some works she begins to yodel in the cement compartment of the small gallery. Soon other works are flinging themselves off the walls in a rushed attempt to find and block their ears. She is kind and admits that Chinese people are embarrassed by nudes, though she likes the works and will do her best to sell them.

Outside in the courtyard a sculpture of a man and a women embracing, made of polished stainless steel stroke themselves as they rise up to a single rapturous point and try to touch an idea so imbued with self-pity it sickens and reflects a stultified expressionless government which shows no mercy or compassion. The feeling is cold and not happy, the reach too perfect…but I like it!

Cars belt out pollution as the grandmother thrashes the old carpet on the stairs while grandfather tinkers with his engines in the garage. The dust rises again in the blue and after our meal of chicken's feet, frog's legs and pig's kidneys the air goes grey with desert as the frogless smog descends. Lilly now strengthens my resolve to act as she leans to kiss my brow, her resolve slow to grow as though an ancient force drives her underground.

Ah but there is nothing like a bottom massage to get the blood circulating! And in the cracks stress reaps a harvest as the hapless cigarette butts fall and the cost of living rises. What worthless sacrifice is a life without love or a life without art? Self-pity of the drowned soul singing like a lonely cloud.

In the early morning we walk the waking street and through a small steaming doorway are surrounded by the loud voices of the feeding multitudes. Here a single family cooks and sweats from four in the morning till nine. Their breakfast feeds half of Beijing and is cheap. Dumplings with garlic chives inside and shrimps bobbing gloriously in a thin soup of more shrimps surrounded by patterned green seaweed. Boiling pots flinging their steam like angry arms to the ceiling. Long white bread dipped in hot oil and zeppelined on the plate is wrestled between two sleepy chop sticks before being punctured between our teeth, hissing down.

Market people old and slow, their shuffle reduced to a toe-walk, as they squelch through the muds of times merciless claws. Their noses in the air looking for a bargain but it is late in the day and all the frogs have died and the kidney-train has left - all the tickets sold, all trapped beneath the silent smog to kiss their final yuan goodbye. Above in the wrestles trees the yellow leaves drape across the clouds awaiting a breeze to carry them on. The squash of people adorned in clay as the day recedes, smooth and round like the new wisdom of the world, changing tides. Young children stand tall as they spin the DVDs along the gutters, spinning and singing, turning the old into stone with the fires of their new wisdom, moving on in the clouds to forget the spirit people long dead. For at the back of our throats a sound like laughter grows stronger as the seasons change. For time will not wait for the sentimental who freeze as they try to embrace the warmth of yesterday.

The space of time where the tune awaits, is filled with oceans of freedom. And what better vessel to float on that ocean than the heart-beat of the imagination? The butterfly of love awaits the warm sun and the shifting wind to embrace again the nectar of the flower.

Lilly has gone into the city to visit some friends and I decide to remain at home and rest. As I walk alone beside the river, all the birds begin to sing. But I know they fear me as I am a stranger perhaps a predator as they loudly warn their friends. They do not sing for me. Then not far along on the other muddy denuded bank a man with his flock of fifty large sheep scour the ground for food. Further along a work crew has cleared the straight even-sloping river bank of weeds and left the muddy soft soil exposed to wash into the river. The naked soil is a common sight all over the world. I fear its message and search for answers.

Further still a herd of cows comes to greet me. They walk up the newly made road which is one kilometre long and covered in thin plastic as a finishing process for the cement. The plastic is now breaking up and blowing in the silted river. And nobody will reveal the rivers form beneath this transparent dress.

The cattle stop some distance ahead and eye me with caution. Then another snake crosses the road before me, side winding on the smooth concrete. It is a beautiful green colour with a shimmer of red around its neck. A small distance ahead a group of men are building a stone wall, they are the only people around. As I pass they do not look at me, though look indeed they do, so I walk silently past. The river is thirty meters across and in places the slowly moving clear water is only twenty centimetres deep. Though it is in places clear, in other places it is opaque with a thick green slime shimmering around its neck and edges and where the slime is thick it is wriggling, swirling like an angry venomous serpent. Large giant lotuses are pushing their great green leaves wide in the afternoon glimmer - large colonies emerging from the wet mud drape across her plastic belly.

A few egrets feed, a flash of white amongst the green and grey. The planted trees on either bank are placed in a dead straight line and equally spaced to the centimetre. They are to ten meters tall and have large flat leaves and sing to me of the cool papery north wind. As I walk the notes of a tune come filtering down. Through the clutter and rabble of China I hear the "Sound of Silence." Then I remember clear as day where I heard it last. It was in the train with thousands of people clambering for fresh air and doing physio on the way to Benxi.

Lilly will not shower without me. Whether it is to save hot water or something else I am unsure. She insists I scrub her back and everywhere else. She is a slippery fish and likes to pee on my feet which turn white between the toes and begin to show signs of rot. Meanwhile she is the opposite between the legs and comes out as clean as a whistle. Her nice round bosoms with their black tips are as smooth as China silk as the white suds drip and run. As my age is apparent compared to hers in every way, it seems natural that I should begin to rot from the feet up like an old tree standing in acid soil. And her feet, twisted and deformed by hard streets and difficult shoes, always wear sandals in the shower – anything to escape the rising tide.

My hand is still in pain, throbbing like the rest of me after a night of sleep and waking in her arms. The breakfast air attracts us out into the noise of clutter, to join the city melee. Suddenly I am amongst the trees back home and the birds talking, then back to the food placards on the outside walls of the tall buildings, appearing subliminal, flashing like TV screens, never missing a taste of red - smeared on wall or road. Showing mixed red and green food stuffs dripping with a glistening Martian sauce. Then bumping into the old grandmothers who stop in the morning to discuss the days' fruit prices. They form a clot on the corner of the road; their little read society must be avoided by all people in vehicles, for the women will not move. Then inside the restaurant old men hoist their morning flags and smoke wispy noodle-rings into the corners of the room. A young girl operates a broom with blackened noodle tassels on the floor, dissecting the grime from the grime. The dead flies are no match for her well-made soggy sweep which thrashes flies in mid-air. The servery of rotting food in the kitchen is well loved by the traditions, such as a unique soy-sauce revealed after being uncovered amongst the ancient clay warriors. Now contained in glass is splashed liberally with salt to make the sternest warrior feel proud. And the clay which melts about his feet, the cook will reform to sate his taste whatever noodle delights she offers for breakfast. However, whatever the delicacy, afterwards we will all make a toxic mess.

In the evening a small young girl with a bent neck, long fringe and pony-tail serves us in the restaurant. She has a loud voice like a man and shouts the orders through my megaphone ears. She seems to run the whole place and is perhaps only thirteen years old. The cook in the boiler room starts the gas furnace which sounds like an aeroplane taking off. She looks at the translating machine close up as though she is blind. I show her how to use it and say "hello" to her in Chinese she laughs and pokes her little triangular face squarely into mine. She has such a happy laughing smile, all the children do! Meanwhile Lilly is deep into selecting the meal from the glorious photos in the glossy menu booklet. There are cats on the chairs keeping them warm which occasionally leap off to chase rats. They, like the Chinese government, feel they are helping the young girl by remaining on the chairs to perform a duty. And while on duty they found up high was the best place to smell the cooking and let a few rats escape so the girl believes one story while the rats ration out the scraps with the cats. Now we come to the restaurant to mind the chairs for the cats.

Early in the morning I rise to view the scene which I find I cannot see as the "smog" is so bad. I decide to collect some deposits of it in a bottle and take it home to have it analysed in a lab to see what it is composed of. I take a swab off the window sill and a thick black glug fills the small tissue with one wipe!

Lilly says, "What is the use? No good! What do?" She, like everybody else is smeared with the same heavy glue of inaction. This is the fear of the dead who succumb to ineptitude before they go.

Back home in Australia some six months later I have it analysed at a government laboratory. The breakdown per litre of water is as follows: Aluminum, 256 milligrams/L. Cadmium, 0.015 mgL. Barium, 6.93 mgL. Strontium, 2.31, mgL. Aluminum is the main metal they are using in their Solar Radiation Management programs. It smells like asbestos and many say causes memory loss and possibly alzheimers disease. While Barium causes acute neurological disturbances. Thus honesty blows in a cruel wind. Bye bye blue sky!

Some people wear a face mask, fools smoke and walk in the orange field, many exercise in their own stagnant cloud and all cough and quickly give up.

Lilly does not understand when I say,

"You must change China, you ladies have put men in power but they have grown bosoms and like many women spend all day looking in the mirror and not helping the environment!"

Today the orange sun bleeds through the turbulent sky. A "Red" day is a day to stay indoors according to the government. Schools in vulnerable places will be given monitoring gauges to advise pupils not to go outside and play on such days. Fortunate for them!

When they grow old and open the box they will see that the weather engineering is causing the pollution.

As I write I learn that the World Health Organisation has recommended that China ban tobacco advertising on TV. Men smoke because they are afraid woman may think they are feminine if they don't and by smoking they join the fraternity of brotherhood. 'Bottoms up', rather than 'hot-tips down.' At last the Chinese Legislature is considering banning tobacco advertising on social media - I decide to start giving out masks to school children as they leave school. But Lilly says no and I agree. Those masks do not stop fine particulate matter. Everybody stay inside - better to go underground and live in cement bunkers. Tobacco is a known neuro-toxin which may speed up cognitive abilities and then kills you.

The restaurant has some silent frogs wishing they were dead. Now climbing on one another to get a better view of the aliens. They peer out at us and think we dress funny and why do we wear large black rimmed glasses and blow smoke out of our chests? We eat from plates and use pointed sticks, we talk and do not croak.

"When we die," they ask, "will they take us back to the water- reeds, back to our families in the mud?"

On the table pig's kidneys gallop and whisper amongst themselves. They too ask about the afterlife and long to be back home. Perhaps they will be used again and after the meal is over taken for a walk beneath the starry sky. And in the morrow together with the frogs to watch the blue dome open and the single misty eye of the sky rise above the orange rice paddy.

We walk and we walk, to where I have little idea. All I know is that there is a medicine shop somewhere down these streets. Led by the nose I follow an angel whose engine sniffs and spits and farts for the future of mankind. Somewhere in this monotone labyrinth is an ancient tradition sprawling with remedies for the up and coming youth. The shop we find has a thousand clones. A whole street of fungal remedies - bags and bags full of strange exotic mushrooms, dried lizards, caterpillars which are crushed and eaten before dawn and deer's penises aroused and snap-dried awaiting China's youth so they may discover their youth! Here is the engine room of China's natural medicine. Some of the fungi have other newer fungi growing on them! Here is where the ancient warriors came to be restored and nursed back to better health. Lilly watches them come in, she has eyes at the back of her head as a result of eating some extremely good fungus. She floats angelic for ages, entertaining the worst afflicted first for the greatest medicine for a man is love to keep his youth alive.

Then she finds me out on the street my sword bent and barely able to move, exhausted by the flatness and hardness of the ground which I hug. This natural world will not heal my wound, Lilly's mountains will! How can I explain that the hills create joy as the water is cleaned by the rush to the sea and then the rush to touch the sky from where it naturally falls and cleans the street, the bowels and the brain? Her white clouds come over me as her mountains show a small amount of flesh. Rushing for her shelter I am left to scrape my reflection off the road. Thus a woman will exhaust the man with shopping then feed him medicine to make him well.

She buys volumes of something which looks like dried chokos or little old ladies dried bosoms. They make one sleep soundly for fifty years, I am told.

Lilly fingers her mobile phone and I gape at the eternity of China. We leave today after a rushed morning of breakfast at the market. We endured the slippery walk on ice and the steely melting snow which is still in white frothing mounds around the bases of the small frozen trees. The breath from people steaming out in front melts the icy air but no, it is cigarette smoke! People dance and clap their hands to get warm, fingers are pink and brittle as they extend from hands uncovered, icy cold.

Suddenly our bus to the train passes without us noticing, in the flurry, the fizz, the flamboyance and the tripe. In a mere fifteen minutes another bus stops and we sardine-travel again on a monkey-mission to Mars. The grey mornings' smell of the asbestos brakes falling from the sky compliments the delicate tofu soup as it rasps the lungs. And fast to disappear - the small words "Sex Shop" flits by. Our bags heavy and huge block the isle. Ascending travellers climb the first step and spurt into the bus like noodles. The fast bus-driver rockets us all awake and soon many small people are squashed beneath our cascading bags. They lie on the floor squirming and writhing. A little green lady with a long broom enters and pokes one of them in the eye and sweeps the others into cracks. I have seen her before, she is well trained and accurate. Now I notice she has improved her fashion with a red eye on her forehead which flashes on and off like a traffic light.

Lunging forward, stopping again, lunge, stop - we eventually secure seats and sit with our arms stiff, still up in the air. With legs crammed and our toes bent over, crushed and bound to save space.

Beijing railway station, the deluge from the trains sees people flooding, swelling and moving like waves of flesh, dressed in monotone garb. People are sleeping on blood red seats beneath marzipan ceilings which float above every flavour money can embellish. With 1950's chandeliers embroidering the frothy dreams of architect's signatures. The red seats lined up never ending, a million bottoms a day. The bang and clutter of bodies, bouncing bones as they ricochet from wall to wall, room to room, train to bus to bed.

As we sit in the passenger lounge blood and tears on the TV screen drips and runs towards us on the floor. Women advertising flaunt sexual poses, leaves dropping like plunging necklines, China has it all. Lilly is wide eyed for a moment then fast asleep beside me.

Only a few young children scurry underfoot. They have risen early from their expectant clouds and excitedly chosen the wealthiest parents to pounce upon. Old ragged men with long hair and grey beards lounge and snore in an agony of forgetfulness having spent the night in a chair. One young child squirrels over her father's shoulders in delirious bright red, her black eyes piercing. Meanwhile ladies dancing on TV screens explore the superficial loud beat of their shoes. And another music violins into squeals to pacify. Romance looms around every corner, before the train rushes in.

Beijing is humming in the distance as two doves nestle and coo on a perilous edge. She is timid and fluffy yet monstrous and full of underground trains, bleating people and buildings like shafts of gold which rise to tickle her weeping skies. These Beijing days floating through the streets on her wings - she leads me on. Then the mango shop with its splashes of yellow and orange moons on parade. Voluptuous delicacies rolling off their chairs to lie on the deck, ripe and enticing to find a hungry mouth. But the vendor smokes and fills the shop with pollution, the mangoes all slide to the floor green with their tongues loose, their seeds tight lipped. The ice on the road, as slippery as the spittle around the railway station and the muddy people put their luggage on the beautiful seats then walk about to save their bottoms. When they return two pigeons are asleep cooing on their possessions and there are arguments. Some yell and others form a crowd. The crowd grows like Beijing itself till the electric eyes venture in and continue the hum. The flock dissipates and sleeps to grow wings and preen in peace.

Voices coalesce the crowd and sends them marching forth to form clots of bones before the small door. A man dressed as Batman takes the tickets and chews them like a rat and hands them back. Women stand black-coats, red-pants-tall, to attention on the railway platforms their little batons disguised as brooms, their electrics inserted. Magazine ladies flick eye-bright through the windows, their red uniforms call to attention all high healed services for sale - our water and our food. Stoic in the extreme, they all ache for normality as they wait for us to enter before lifting their legs over the moving threshold.

Next stop north, eight hundred kilometres, Shenyang.

The whispering train thumps on the tracks, brackets of metal, a never ending tune. Shenyang is home, away from the wild encumbrances of Beijing. The pale grey landscape flits by. The pale yellow gold of the cold winter strips the ground. We pass tree after planted tree. Each one before had a clump of leaves balancing on its spindly stick, as square as a box. Now the boxes have fallen and spindly fingers draw eloquent lines in the space.

As I squint from afar from the roaring air-conditioned train, the fading horizon has the fossilised trunks of abandoned apartment blocks. They rise in grey silhouette on the horizon. They are the giant ghosts of the old forest. Once the hope of the cement-box-people and engineers, who fashioned the skeletons inside from Australian steel. Rusting metal cranes on their tops look like the feelers or antenna of insects on dead consumed skeletal remains. They scan a static flat landscape of mud, turned and irrigated a million times. A road runs along beside. Small square trucks on rubber wheels beetle along but we go faster - images of China. The tracks run beside the field, the wheels of metal sing, in the yellow field black crows rise, Lilly's eyes are closed, rocking gently she tamps my shoulder into numbness.

Flecks of ice speckle the horizon of the bus window back in Shenyang as we launch upon another swinging journey to our hotel. I write in the translator "the age of war is over, now the governments of the world try to change the weather to make money and have more power."

Back again to the wash of familiar streets and faces. Those faces which study the street and never look up. Who mill together and gather people in their arms, so close all one sees are the backs of their legs.

The great wheel turns and the belly roars as the blood begins to thin. Off to the market again to eat breakfast in the small food splattered room away from the snow and ice, the donkey's heads, the bicycles and the backs of people's legs which we follow everywhere. The little room is full of the gastric breath of the morning song. To pinch and wrestle again with the deep fried bread, the tofu soup, the clanging pots and the roaring gas. Outside a man throws a snow ball at a leafy tree and all the small leaves fly away leaving their branches to draw in the air. They were birds disguised as leaves, they all had red socks on and black hats, they were waiting for him to turn his back so they could raid his table of fruit. He laughs - he has uncovered their disguise. Little does he know that each carried a mobile and a pair of sharpened chop-sticks - they will be back.

Through the narrow little alleyways she leads me, in the early morning light. The early smells of Chinese soy and garlic ratcheting the snot-smog. Past the fruit stalls already open and the man who pumps the tyres and mends the boots. And he who makes the tiny wire sculptures of small people riding wobbly bicycles. The grey streets of the workers - the drab colour of sameness. Lilly walks between their bodies like a martial artist through an army.

It is hard to keep up without bumping into people and knocking them flat. But then the air clears, there is a hole in the crowd, I can see light and hear her voice, high pitched nasal and angelic. To be birthed by a crowd of market goers - to come out with two eyes, strong shoulders for carrying all the shopping and a bare head as everything gets knocked off. Around a few more tight corners and we bear down a strait with only ten people beside me and four thousand up front.

Everybody can cook in China. The cooking lesson at the supermarket is closely observed. The cooking can take longer than building a fifty story building and even longer to eat. Lilly is mesmerised and convinced that the stainless steel wok which they used to demonstrate with is a necessity, Mother must have one! The money comes out of my pocket like a forgotten meat pie.

Then one day she wakes with pain below her stomach, only slight but she notices it enough for her to say something. We go to eat breakfast across the startling road, she is watchful of me always as the traffic still goes the wrong way. She is not hungry and feels tired. We buy some fruit and head back to the hotel. She is lazy and sloth-full with no definite plan. It is as it should be. That every day unfurls without the stress of unnecessary concerns, that life one day will create the next and the next.

I am eager to live a childhood dream and travel to Lhasa the capitol of Tibet. I want to take my love to show her how much she looks like a mountain girl with bright smiling eyes and a joyous happy white-tooth-grin and beautiful skin. With hair as black as a yetis and deep snow leopard eyes. I want to adore her and lavish her and give her the life she has longed for and dreamt about. I tell her so and she confesses that she has fallen deeply in love with me. We have written over three hundred letters to each other, two a week for two years each translated accurately. She knows me well!

I sit up in bed and type "travel to Lhasa" into the translating machine. She frowns and looks at me sideways. She does not understand so I explain how I went to Tibet in the seventies and fell in love with the vast space, the colours, the people, the loneliness. But then I could not go as China was about to invade and make Tibet another province. I glimpsed China from Ladakh in Little Tibet where the Indian military were defending the border, also in Nepal, exchanging fire. I vowed then that one day I would see Mount Kailas the sacred mountain and the Potala Palace, home of the Dali Lama in Lhasa.

Lilly is worried she turns and squirms. She tries to distract me by putting my hand on her stomach and saying in Chinese "harder" but she soon drenches herself in sweat. She asks me not to go. She is afraid, "there is trouble there," she says. I reply that the Tibetan people are friendly, that she will be by my side and that I will protect her no matter what. She is ever more concerned and looks away searching in the rubble for the machine. My hands redundant, no use, she turns it up and buries its head down hard where it engorges fat. However she soon puts it aside and looks distracted.

"No go" she says, "China person make trouble" and adds, "you no understand!"

After a short while I say okay and leave it there. I am her water-wheel, if there is no water I do not spin, she is in control.

I am unable to wash to where I want to go sometimes. Her decision has perhaps saved our lives as many times I have only just saved my own. At the helm now, she decides my life - our life. Being together is more important to her than a possible tragedy which she has imagined would happen to us in the hills.

Mother's house

We step outside in the snow the two of us alone, to a frozen bicycle landscape glued by the flakes of ice which clamber up snow dripping fences. Lines of white follow wires and other small ridges clinging on like Lilly's arm. Now Mother is near and our intimacy I fear will be studied again in detail. May all the snow melt and in the gushing warmth fill each being with the spirit of joy.

Mother's house is small with each tiny space filled with a thousand memories all cleaned and sorted many times. The small kitchen a clutter of woks and pots. The cupboards groaning with time. Small extended balconies reach out dangerously to shake hands with the neighbours but steel and potted plants and regal clutter prevent many a view.

I try to source long vegetable growing pots to place on every window sill so she can eat fresh greens. But Mother would not be able to move them they would be too heavy and she likes to sit there herself in the sunlight her bare legs waving in the warmth of the flickering sun, five floors up.

We shop for Mother, she feeds a multitude and every day Lilly cooks a huge meal which is composed of many small dishes. The table is small and we take it in turns to sit and eat in threes. Lilly, Mother and I eat first. The morning market provides us with fruit and greens.

In the supermarket we find chicken, eggs and fish. In the streets we often buy jujubes which purify the blood, these are sold in Australia as Chinese dates after being soaked in black sugar and their seeds removed. Apples, peaches,

bananas, it is all so close and accessible. Lilly scavenges for the cheapest deal -
she has her China ways. Scurrying to our nest we keep some fruit and take
most of the shopping to Mother's house where we stay for most of the day,
pecking and preparing food.

To the east of her house below Mother's bedroom window are three train
tracks which roar a metal heat as the trains thunder through the earth. The
clickety-clack, clickety-clack of rhythmic steel heralds not one but three
approaching monsters as these dragons with the chemical breath blast through.
One hears at first their high pitched squeal of metal and asbestos agony, faint
and a long way off, growing louder and louder like an approaching violent
wind. Then suddenly the roaring monsters leap through the windows crashing
half the wall down hissing and spitting, flinging their arms everyway then at
the top of their pitch let out three loud ear piercing screams. And after the
roar subsides a gentle soft breeze laced with the distinctive perfume of diesel,
asbestos and tobacco smoke. Three trains pass every half an hour to save their
keepers time and often brake simultaneously within one hundred meters from
the high bedroom window. Hence the people emerge from these monsters all
at once which creates a definite clot of humanity as they jostle for space at the
station.

It has long been known in the medical profession that exposure to asbestos
gives one asbestosis in a very short while. This is a lung condition where all the
tiny spears of asbestos fibre infiltrate the flesh and cause extreme inflammation
and eventual death. In Australia asbestos has been banned for commercial use.

Not far from the rail lines and closer to the window is a tall electric
booster station which hisses like a snake. Hence a constant fizzing sound as
the electromagnetic rays belch forth and infiltrate the very walls of Mother's
building. It is common knowledge that radiation interferes with the body's
electricity and the stronger it is the more likely one is to contract cancer.
Similarly the simple expensive electric stove cooks food unnaturally and makes
it more difficult for the body to absorb.

Gas cooking is the best these days though if used in a confined space
releases ethylene gas which is the same gas ripening fruit releases. Long-time
exposure to ethylene makes one's body literally ripen and go rotten!

The micro-wave oven which is a higher frequency of electromagnetics is
another health disaster as it de-natures food and destroys its natural fibre. With
little fibre in the diet the body does not release toxins too well as the alimentary

system slows, rendering one more susceptible to bowel cancer. Micro-wave frequencies may also alter transcription in the genes. If one surrounds a chicken's egg with mobile phones the egg will cook the same as one's brain. Seeds exposed to mobile phones die! Experiments have been done with water which has been frequentised in a micro-wave oven then fed to plants - over time the plants died. The micro-wave was first used by sailors who placed their food in front of the radars on ships to "cook."

It is now known that the electromagnetic rays which issue from television sets, lock the brain into forgetfulness mode and distort learning capacity and memory. It was originally thought that the age of electronic imaging would increase our ability to remember and consequently think. However now with much experimentation the opposite has been found to be true.

This is the age of plasmoid weaponry for we follow the electrics of the heart into the centres of our beings. It is a fact that the pineal gland emits and creates electromagnetic radiation which "flips" the water inside its sack, thus enabling dreams. However all of the above calcifies the pineal and makes dreaming cease. Thus we cling to good health like stalactites before our dreams wash away.

Other information sources suggest that radar frequencies lowered to those of low audio transmissions can affect the sonar of whales and dolphins. The navy uses low frequency transmission waves for communication as the long waves travel further through water and Earth. Some time ago many dolphins and whales were beaching themselves, though not so much now, the navy seems to have the frequency right!

As a follow-on from those findings many radar relay stations have been built around the world to frequentise the artificial clouds governments keep producing in the name of geo-engineering and climate change. They do it for their own crops and to facilitate capturing the world grain markets by changing other countries weather cycles. Weather wars are acute, unspoken about and environmentally negligent. Silver iodide, barium, aluminium, strontium and other metal dusts are bombarded with high or low frequencies (depending on the metal) of ionizing radiation to affect weather patterns and even alter tectonic plate adhesion. If the frequency is raised and pulsed cold cloud fronts can be vaporised and warmed which makes the air rise to create upper and lower air disturbances.

The science is easy to understand. The long term consequences are not however and I suggest the normal weather patterns of the planet have been severely altered. But governments merely say it is only grandmother banging the carpet on the back steps while grandfather keeps playing with his toy car!

Big governments when they work out how to make money from so called sustainable electricity production will ramp up the climate change scenario and claim carbon from oil is killing the planet, which it is. Hence a double truth shelters these covert geo-engineering practices which often produce more cloud. In the vast sky the cloud is increasing while our minds clog and cannot see.

These services to humanity should be viewed like a "natural" addiction to plastic which is rapidly smothering the whole of the world. It is spurred on by simple sugar money. Plastic floor, plastic chairs, plastic bowels and plates, plastic curtains, plastic shoes. Then formaldehyde glues to hold it all down! Money plus greed equals oil, equals plastic, equals ill health. The gasses released when plastic is exposed to ultra-violet rays from the sun take us back beyond the stone-age to a time when we as small organisms first walked on land and found that we could only do so if we produced chlorophyll which is a shield to the ultra-violet. The equivalent in the human body is melanin. In our own skins these light changing substances enable us to counteract ultra-violet rays and assist in the production of our bony or in the case of plants, woody structures.

Fluorescent lights glare and suck vitamin A from the body everywhere throughout China. Everywhere except in the countryside. In Mother's house one of Lilly's brother's is half blind with cataracts and Mother wanders about very slowly and complains of a week heart.

The cities are like factories and we the animals of slaughter. How else to communicate? How else to live and love? We cannot love the trees and stones like the winds and the rains do.

So without nature it is natural to feel isolated and only connect with small things secreted away for a rainy day in a box or a drawer or beneath a heavy eye lid.

We need the warm touch of another human being. Like ants we are all watching and being entertained.

As the hidden sun rides the sky over Shenyang I travel to another room to explore a new ambience. This is the room with the television which is always switched on. It seems to always extoll the virtues of Chinese culture. The first image I see is a soldier killing a civilian with a sword and a loud cry. In the split second that I watch, the man vomits blood. It is revolting and disgusting. Blood is often spilled and viewed close up; it is accompanied with what I call horror. Other consistent visual displays concern the abuse of ladies. I am gob-smacked when I witness a China man beating his wife in a TV drama where it is often portrayed as a normal response. I noticed this in India as well. The overall focus on love and romance evokes an underlying message of distain. I have for instance never seen so many women crying on TV.

If young children see this what will they dream? In America it is the same, that is why children massacre the public and young men throw bombs at their fellow man. Even the American government conspires and massacres those individuals who are not Jews – such as 9:11, the World Trade Centre and re-writes the truth about Pearl Harbour in their history books to satisfy their glowing egos!

But I digress. Chinese people are innocent and beautiful, all borne from love just the same as the rest of us. From nature to nature - the one big happy family!

One of Lilly's brothers watches the TV constantly. As soon as he wakes in the morning the TV is switched on. The machine invades like an insidious weed. It entrains the brain the same as a fly that wants to settle in your meal. It fogs the mind with a quivering numbness which is not rest but an internal vibration akin to a seductive drug.

The expense of the electricity to run these machines is a huge drain on natural resources. And much of the coal used to generate it comes from Australia. Their meat is imported, milk and steel the same. Their own milk according to Lilly is poisonous. The cranium of children who drink it expands beyond normal she says. Their honey has rice syrup in it as they poisoned all their bees by spraying the hives for fungi. And many of their exports such as solar panels are flimsy and have no guarantee. However their women are beautiful and those exports are well trained to create little Chinese people all over the globe.

In a matter of days a new machine will be birthed on the global market. It creates energy from the ionosphere and produces no pollution. China is closing her black-fire power stations. She is leading the way. Soon we will all have unlimited energy and the Earth will not be burnt in the cooking.

On the early morning TV screen I see a huge government celebration where hundreds if not thousands of balloons are released into the air. Immediately I write to the three editors at the China Daily Newspaper in Beijing that these balloons, if they enter the sea will kill marine turtles young and old if eaten. For the turtles mistake them for jelly-fish, their natural food.

The message bounces back with the excuse that it is too long!

Dear Editor,

I am from Australia visiting my fiancée's family in Shenyang I just saw on television a celebration marking the end of the Second World War which released hundreds maybe thousands of balloons in the air.

It is well known in my country that the marine turtle eats these balloons

If they enter the sea and when the balloons break up smaller turtles mistake the particles for their natural food also.

These bits are lethal too!

Since Chinese people and many other countries eat turtles it is important to stop reducing turtle numbers by not releasing helium balloons into our skies.

The letter does not get through, it is too long. So I reduce it to a bare minimum, writing in Chinglish. Still the mail does not go – very frustrating!

One day perhaps the whole world will talk about the beauty of nature with rivers in their eyes, with our hearts in our minds. We may become lost in a mire and will only see a glimpse of her far off in the distance rising like the ghosts of a forest, far off beyond the backs of other people's legs.

She comes on top like a flowering lily, rising in the night above my tiny sprig of soft new wood so full of sap and the need to grow and wraps her great petals around me. And there to feel, with my eyes half open – lobs a breast within my mouth. Oh China don't you know? How could you let the people sleep in these pits of ill health and not lob your own healthy breast for them to suck? But no, all your children will grow up the same and few will ever know the true delights of being alive in an organic sexual sea.

Open your heart China, open, open, open! Let the rest of the world come and see, feel and give. Your policy of segregation has split your country. So what if you change! Now we must all travel together to the stars. Your women are unhappy, do you not care? There are thousands who want to leave because you do not give! Alas they are not strong enough to call out as they, like the rest of us are transfixed by *your* hormones.

Everywhere I go people are apathetic towards doing anything to help the health prospects of China. Government this and government that, from one hand to the other, too many concerned people are flummoxed into apathetic corners believing their voice too frail.

The agricultural sector is too fragmented by archaic Western chemical science and the accompanying sales pitch has hijacked small producers who only think of money and not the quality of taste. Consequently their products are not properly food tested before they are sold or shipped abroad.

Corruption if allowed to grow flourishes like a weed once it has established a fertile soil of fear which is easily penetrated by dishonest roots. The invasion of the innocents, the rape of the people and the environment is easily done when society loses its ability to scrutinize itself. Hence freedom of speech is vital for progress. For the blind feel lost if communication is blocked and barriers become thick like canopies of weeds which reduce light and growth.

Lilly has arthritis in her left leg, back, neck and the sterno-mastoid process at the back of her head. Her leg grows cold after eating saturated fats, acid foods and protein. After scratching her soft inner-arm and smearing the damaged skin with proteins, carbohydrates, meat and the whole kitchen, fish, eggs and potato, oats, rice and many other food stuffs we were able to determine which foods were potentially causing inflammation. Over several days we found it was the acid foods which irritated and made her skin red. Already her calcium levels are dangerously low, so I encourage her to sit in the brave sunlight as much as possible.

The Chinese diet includes armfuls of boiled greens. Unfortunately too much of the accompanying oxalic acid within these greens inhibits calcium absorption and is usually consumed without vitamin C which assists calcium uptake in the small intestine. I look at other symptoms and recommend cod-liver oil and orange juice shaken and drunk last thing at night. Then as the nuts and bolts turn I realise the Chinese clearing of the throat is a sign of a lack of magnesium which is the catalyst for all metabolic reactions and without it few if any vitamins and minerals will be absorbed from the gut. For some reason a lack of magnesium in the diet increases mucus and saliva production. Boiling greens dramatically reduces the magnesium. So I dose her up on chocolate just to see if there is any reaction. To my amazement she completely stops spitting and coughing. She objects as many people grow up knowing that chocolate will make them fat - unfortunately there is no chocolate in the supermarket without sugar in it.

China
June 6
2013

We go to look at some real estate in the back streets of Shenyang it is Lilly's idea so she holds my arm and looks up sideways expectantly.

After securing a time for the agent to take us we all three set off down the busy street with me following. The agent is pushing a bicycle which has a chain dragging on the road. It makes a merry clinking sound as we all zig-zag across the busy street. Only once receiving a blast from a bus, two taxis and one car. To arrive on the other side unharmed then another "ho" from an old man as he swerves narrowly missing us on the footpath with his bicycle. The apartment has a small courtyard before its front door and a small window overlooking it. Few trees grow there and the earth has an unclean well used patina as the dust is kicked up every day by progress.

We climb the raw square spiral stairs with the metal doors and the advertising stickers on each level. Lilly looks at the walls of the flat, eyes wide, mouth turned down, then up then down. The yellow and white paint tries to hide ancient neglect as it dribbles and runs beyond its precious edge. The small window looks out west over the courtyard. One hundred such windows have eyes on three sides ensuring we all follow the same routine. In the cupboard in a corner of each kitchen runs the sewage pipe from above reminding one that we are not alone.

Perhaps we may come and live here one day. Just to stay for a holiday. While Lilly sees her mother. I could begin to dig up the courtyard and study Chinese. I could get all the young men to help me and we would plant the vegetables and fruit trees they suggest. We would encourage everybody to begin a recycling business where vegetative refuse would be placed in great black horizontal rubber balloons and the gas then taken off. The black bag would warm in the sunlight. Or large vertical cylinders of cement with inverted bell-jars floating in them, weighted down - with a one way valve in and a one way valve out, simple. Eventually Shenyang may have giant black rubber sausages full of methane gas lying around the city. People would paint happy faces on them and yellow and white stripes. And turtle faces and China would grow stronger as it mounted these bags on its strong back.

We catch a bus after breakfast. It is a kind of torture which I am getting used to. The karate stance with upstretched arms and sagging knees, it is the bob and lunge they all grow up with.

Lost again, near Chairman Mao's statue. He is alright, he knows where to go. With a great outstretched arm he shows the people where to go. But we are lost. Round and round we go, the streets all look the same. Then miraculously we have arrived. My limp hand is given to the ladies as an offering to the gods. And one in particular snaps it up and squashes it into tiny fragments like the patterns on the ceiling which I am quick to observe. I am thankful that all the women in China do not do this. I am sure they would like to mangle other bits of male anatomy sometimes.

I am chastised for not taking my special New Zealand grown organic fungus medicine tea the way they suggested and other handfuls of supplements daily. The ones which made my skin turn into a blotchy red balloon and made my body feel as though it wanted to float above Shenyang and look for a sea turtle. Those special teas which made my heart race, my fingernails pink, my eyes blood red, my liver trapped like a rat in a trap which only wanted to escape my body and call out freedom. They suggested my pink body-balloon look was my liver expelling some kind of toxin.

"Yes" I said, "Your toxin!" with much aplomb. However they did not understand English.

Lilly is forgetful and loses the way outside. She has to ask directions again. I look at her sideways. It is late and we have not eaten. I know she is thirsty as I am myself. She takes my good hand and leads me across the road. My other hand waves like a flag in the cold numbing wind and reluctantly follows. When we arrive at the hotel she is so tired she falls asleep sitting up. I put my good hand on her stomach and gently rub round and round. Her head is sore with a slight temperature. She soon breaks out in a hot sweat. She moves my hand to her leg which is cold. Then she is soon snoring like a diesel train.

The next morning she wakes early saying that she has not slept well and has to go to Mother's house for a short while. When she comes back she wants to eat little and says that we must leave the hotel and go to stay at Mother's house. She is holding her stomach, her lips are dry, I feel her brow and she repeats that she did not sleep well and has a little pain. My mind bounces from one wall to the other and I say out loud "pregnant!" She smiles and counts the days of her last period by rolling her eyes. The day moves fast and we are soon piling our bags up the cold cement steps to Mother's house.

Lilly has lived here for eleven years and given such sacrifice, it is a small secure sanctum. Through the two steel doors all those familiar things. The family like a group of mushrooms flowering prolifically from a rotting log. Cholong and Chuliwang, two brothers greet us, her sister in law with small child who is held by the hands for much of the day and encouraged to walk. His knees are not yet strong but walk he must as he is male and must work. The same would have happened to Lilly, my little mouse so strong.

Mother greets me with a small beckoning wave and provides me with indoor slippers. I feel timid and shy again as I felt the first time I met her. This time my shoes are not so tightly tied. She is wholly welcoming and Lilly's brothers dance with broad grins and a welcoming (right) hand shake. Mother has made the big bed which is as hard as nails and we have the grand room, overlooking the early morning sunrise the train lines, the power station and a tree. The horizon which is not far away is pierced by the sky-scrapers of Shenyang which come and go like memories.

Here in this bed where everybody else from the family has slept, where babies have been made, I will not dream as I venture out the window in the dark to challenge the monster mechanical turtle which threatens to invade

Shenyang and smash it all down. This time my legs seem pretty solid even though I have feathers in my heart.

The day is restless and Lilly eats little and spends much of her time asleep on the bed occasionally breaking out in menopausal hot flushes. I surmise from these that she is not pregnant. Mother goes out to the supermarket and drags her own weight in vegetables up the stairs, then sleeps after she returns. Lilly makes some food for us but eats little. Mother is ever hospitable and offers me food whenever she can. She reaches up to turn the TV on for me but I go to another room to study my ailing computer which throws blankets of images at me to hide my thoughts. In the afternoon the brothers return and switch the TV on. It is full of weaponry, blood and distraught women. Then a young girl arrives, she is part of the family and is visiting from Shandong. Then another young girl arrives, she is one of Lilly's brother's daughters who works locally in a bank and is staying here too. So nine people will sleep in these three bedrooms tonight. All the windows on the western side of the house are closed, ours is the only one open and I gasp for air.

My computer groans, it has swallowed a thousand Chinese snakes. I stamp out some hopeful words and mails to send after all its hiccups have cleared a little.

The morning roar of the trains awakes us. After another night of no sleep and much heavy breathing. Lilly's breath is rank, from the drains like the trains. Her brow knotted like an angry river. Her eyes darting this way and that. I feel her pulse and her blood is racing.

The day is not yet winking. In a restless fog she rolls her body toward me and uncompromising finds me hard. I am the strong icicle melting in the warm water, while she the mountain valley clothed in pubic hair. The tussled undergrowth has many creatures which await the flowering dawn who now collide into the arms of their companions to seek the refreshing food of eternity. But no, the cool air of the arousing day wafts unforgiving into the bed and under those voluptuous sheets finds a wretched realm to plant its seed. With a blocked nose and tingling eyes, with a semi-sore head the day begins. All night have smelt the diesel fumes – don't these people know?

Soon the table is covered in crabs and rice and greens and various meats. The breakfast is a feast as usual. Lilly eats with gusto but soon retires and lies on the bed. I begin to sense something is wrong. There is a moment when my life is moved uncontrollably and as this sense develops all faces turn to Lilly curled up like a child. I am excluded from their conversation and reach out timidly to hold her hand. It is very hot, I feel her brow and it is burning. An ocean of sweat rises and pours from her skin, dripping and running like a thousand waterfalls after rain in spring. I ask by sign language for a thermometer. Lilly holds her stomach while Mother scurries to a distant drawer.

Lilly rises as her stomach falls and goes to the phone with Mother close behind. Phone numbers skew and disappear, falling from the ceiling like chips of grey matter. After some time she is bending over still holding her stomach. Her brothers have gone off somewhere and Lilly is packing some things in a small bag. She sits with me awhile and gingerly fingers the translator, "hospital" she writes, as she crashes on the bed. I insist she drinks lots of warm water. It comes out flooding much as it went in. She looks up at me longingly with a flickering frown and tries to conceal her pain. Tears well in my eyes, I cannot see. My breath begins to hug my soul. Mother turns away, she is gathering her strength. During the day she sleeps and talks to the mountains like an eagle with whistles and wheezes and many curling questions.

That afternoon we float down the stairs slowly, Lilly step by step. She has refused to go by taxi and Cholong, with the car, is somewhere else. The air is cold, the people unmoving - cold, the buildings unloving - cold. The heavens are spitting sharp flecks like cold fingernails which bite our cheeks. The evening road is covered in ice, black water and small white clouds of snow. The cars are the enemy hiding and alive. The crossing and the lights, her sagging hot hand I hold. We walk slowly through the congested traffic, the potholes sideways. She is bent low and faltering through many crooked steps. The smear of the intrusive eye as people look our way.

Now she holds herself up high, her shoulders straight - as her mother said - and pulled back, her head proud and beautiful, as the lights turn green. The word "ho" is in the back of my mind as another bicycle swerves to miss us.

Not far across the road, in that tall white building we have passed each day, are multitudes of doctors and patients, now I realise it is a hospital. It has large blood red words written like the wings of birds on its front. It has doors and more doors, people and more people.

She has gone through the white doors and is lost immediately on entry.

I show her the way along well lit endless straight corridors sniffing my way with common sense. The solid white walls flaking from the hands of time while the surrounding railings on the stairs have the grime from a multitude of dying forms. The green middle strip on the floor resembles the ground of a forest floor it is flanked each side by two small rivers of blue, the walls are snow white clouds, all rising.

Up another flight of stairs, the people below are still waiting for the lift, she holds her belly as though it is about to fall out. She spits on the stairs accurately in a corner and I see that it is red. I do not say a word! She is dressed in black. With scorpions sequined on the thighs of her black pants. More white double doors open like the jaws of a shark and swallow us alive.

My jaw is locked, my chin clamping my teeth. The key is in my hand, turning hot with sweat, she squeezes and drops of water fall on the floor, there is no pain. She is lost again, lost in the hospital where babies are born and people die. A green cleaner with a mask on is questioned and points her mop but does not answer. We fly up some more stairs, Lilly bending evermore. And then I see her face. No other person would have the strength to walk. I hold her arm and guide her step, slowly now, breathing hard. The lift does not work; it is full of slow moving things.

Lilly goes for the stairs again. They are pale and foot polished with grime and antiseptic around their edges. The cracks are full of dead green women on their knees. We ascend forever, floating on the wings of love. Lilly pauses and I take her full weight; her face is suddenly pale like the walls, her eyes flicker, tremble. Her lips turned down. Nurses come to our aid, I release my grasp. She has to sign in and can barely write. The nurse looks at me, I know exactly what she is thinking. I am no good with other people's pain.

I wake up next to Lilly on a hospital bed, I must have passed out.

We turn to each other, neither of us can speak. She faintly smiles and looks so sad. My heart throws me from the bed and I embrace her, kissing her on the cheek and peering into her loving eyes. You will not be long here, you will be okay, there is nothing wrong I say with a half-smile. I sit on her bed and hold her hand it is so soft. The nurse is talking in Chinese quietly. And explains with difficulty that Lilly must have an x-ray. I am told to wait outside and given a glass of cold water.

Lilly looks up at me, we must part again. I want to follow her but I am not allowed. I look down and say,

"I must go."

"Miss you," she says. I release her body, her hand, her finger, her skin. I stand as she is wheeled away. But I follow grasping for her hand. I hold it and squeeze it hard. The doors close brushing me aside and I press my face to one of their small windows until the last glimpse of her fades in a smear of tears, my cheek pressed to the cold wet pain.

She has gone through the white doors, beautiful and perfect. Her shadow behind the glass slowly fades as I fill her glass with tears.

People crowd around at the end of the corridor. They peer over my shoulder as I write. Dressed in perfect order in hats and bright shoes. Thin voices twisting like vines, twirl about the airs like honey in milk, trailing off into "oohs" and "aarhs" I cannot understand. Their black raisin eyes the same as Lilly's, deep and full of concern.

The green masked cleaning lady crashes about her frilly mops just missing my eye, there is no silence in heaven. Green her clothes like a caterpillar in this bio-sphere of illness. And beyond the doors my dream is breaking down, bent double from some pain.

She will not die I tell her so. She has shown me how her lifeline extends beyond her thumb – a long life as rich as the Gondwana rainforests of Australia.

The doors open suddenly and a woman rushes out holding toilet paper to her mouth. Will Lilly be in more pain when she emerges or will her eyes be full of light?

Others begin to crowd around me as I sit on the seat like a lonely cloud above an ocean. Their eyes upon me, my hairy arms, a feature, my greying hair, my torn jeans and old tee-shirt in my Emperor's coat. My age unwrapped in China - bottled soy-sauce dug up from the forgotten clay army. All joined by our humanity we are a clot of blood before the polished doors.

I sit and I wait. I have waited two years for her already. Her tears have mingled with mine, mixed like a black fungus meal or psychedelic drink. A special meal prepared by the gods and drunk from the same cup - the water so pure.

The white butterfly doors open and close. First a shadow appears behind the frosted glass and my heart rises like a wave at sea, then it goes, the image fades and I crash on the floor and foam and splutter, grasping for more paper to write my breath again and not drown. People bite their fingernails and flick the corners of their eyes my way. All these days of China should find her behind the white doors, so close and yet so far away. The shadows fade and the artificial light pervades - cold. I begin to imagine the next few moments and live in the future and I write:

"Her shadow appears behind the door, black and faceless, the image of a ghost. And then all spring bursts forth as she emerges beautiful. Her face smooth and no longer frowning, her blotchy features void of pain. I follow her like a white rabbit in the snow, down the stairs beyond the white flecks of fallen paint. She spits in a garbage tin volumes of saliva. I watch her eyes now bright with acuity.

She loses her way outside the building and says, "Mother's house" to me so quiet. I feel my heart swell and bleed into my eyes. She spits again. The jungle traffic has blocked the road. She bravely charges through the small spaces in between. Miraculously our way is clear through the sharp roses and the sharks. She takes a wrong turn and comes back to me. These streets where she has lived for so long. Then the flight of stairs up and up to Mother's home so high above the ground. How will she climb this mountain? Up she goes, she in the lead. She wavers not once and then at the top only a little short of breath."

Her shadow appears behind the doors and suddenly she is there. But no she was not dressed in red, her eyes I cannot see. Another woman with her face in a cloth. My heart wrestles my bottom to be seated once again. A man stands to hold her arm, alas it is not me.

Another hour passes and my fingers are chewed up in pieces on the floor. The people go and new ones come. I ache so much I want to see a doctor. Why am I here? Is the baby born yet?

In slow-motion a white form comes to the door. A little face pokes out and looks at me. It says my name and I jump to attention.

"Lilly have operation," she says in English.

"Yes" comes a high voice I do not own.

"Jujube seed, stomach" she says.

I say some sound, inaudible to the world. The door closes. I go to the door, and open it slightly. There is nobody there. I creep inside and can hear soft voices beyond the partition. My heavy legs take me closer and I see. But she is not there. The nurse sees me and comes quickly. She says something in Chinese and points to the door.

"No long," she says.

"How long?" I ask.

She does not say. The door closes. My voice says something and I sit down. I stare at the white doors. The horrible white doors.

I wait and I wait, forever time drums my heart beat. Each beat an audible crunch as it slams down.

"Oh Lilly my love, my dearest precious…..."

Forever shall I wait, long into the night, the empty corridor, the silent white doors, Lilly I say out loud, over and over. It is cold so I meditate. My brain up high is rising and may explode. I remember everything as I travel back through our life together. Lilly my darling…

Very late in the night, Chuliwang arrives. I am shivering and hungry. I am beyond myself curled up in her arms. He takes my arm and drags me down the stairs. He drags me shaking and shivering across the road, and then I run. I run like no other. Lilly I ran for you.

There is only two hundred meters to go but I fly past the corner, my vision blurred, blinded by the neon lights from the hospital. I am suddenly lost, my vision smeared by running tears in the cold wind, splashing on the ground where they turn to ice. I walk on and around, my bearings confused, my breath clouds out before me. I go back, back and then around again. My hands are freezing, my nose begins to drip. There are no people, the street is dark, a garden of dead trees I do not recognise. Then a light far off at the end of the road, flashing red.

Suddenly I am back at the hospital again! Cold and shivering I find my way to Mother's house and climb the steps stamping as I rise. Cholong is there, the TV is on, the bed impossibly cold without her.

I go back, far back, to my place in Sydney Harbour by the sea. I am playing with a young dark haired girl, with black eyes, in a small oval pool we call the

Christening Pool. We are looking into its shallow depths for crabs or limpets I cannot remember. I can see my small hand feeling across the brown sea-weed on the bottom. Then a man comes from around the headland with a big fish he has speared and throws it in the pool. The water turns red and I cannot see my hand. My little friend has gone…

I am woken before dawn and from the scene deduce that I must go quickly. With Lilly's two brothers Chuliwang and Cholong, and Mother we descend the cold stairs and drive quickly to the hospital. We do not talk. My mind is still looking into the little pool.

Somehow I know, breaking down I know. Mother is crying, the two brothers, coughing and spitting. We find the lift somehow and rise like angels with leaden hearts, too slowly. The doors open and we enter the polished white doors and she is there, but she has already gone to another world.

She is sitting up in bed and has slipped into a coma. She has wires and tubes coming out everywhere. Her mouth is open. We are not allowed to go near her but we do. Her Mother falls on her daughter's legs and wails. Her two brothers weep uncontrollably. I am immediately overcome with remorse and go to her and hug her close. But I will not cry. Something in me shuts down strong and I know she is listening. I kiss her forehead, her cheek and close her mouth with its horrible plastic tube and kiss her nose with its little dark dot and whisper in her ear.

"My darling, I am with you, find a garden and make it beautiful, I will come soon and be with you forever." My strength has gone and I weep bitterly with an uncontrollable agony, an agony I cannot describe. As though my heart is being eaten alive but will not stop. I feel it shuddering and missing beats. There are no tissues to wipe my eyes, I cough and splutter into the sheets. The room is a mess of crying dilapidated souls.

I wake slowly with pain. Lilly is crashing around in the kitchen with pots banging and water running. I stare at the white ceiling the blue carpet the static cold light. Then notice that I have wires attached and a machine with bleeps like a new language of swear words.

People in white robes and heavy rimmed black glasses resembling aliens, peer into my face as though I am a breathless cockroach, stuck. They talk amongst themselves, nodding heads and eating plastic pens. My arm is puffed up with a black bag, expanding. My eyes go red and I weep.

Sometime later Cholong arrives with my passport out in front. He squeezes my arm like the bag saying something in Chinese, his face looks tired. We go, floating down the stairs on clouds of silent remorse. My legs are wobbly, there is pain in one foot, his car throws me sideways as the red eyes of the traffic lights singe.

We climb the naked cement steps to Mother's house. The whole family is there, nobody is talking, for once the TV is off. Mother offers me food and tea. I sit and begin shaking from a cold which has entered my bones.

The days grow flowers, long time exposures, opening onto fields of golden brown. The days roll like the clouds to and from impossible dreams of exquisite love. Dry of mouth and broken heart, whose fragments my arms pick up, hands try to grasp, too heavy in the shadow of her being.

Somehow, sometime, I leave China. My tail between my legs, I run.

In the plane deep in the night, my legs float out into the black air. Cold they want to go back and hold her in her grave. My mind is fleeing the Yellow Paper, the Yellow room, her reflected yellow chin, which has her name, which has her light. It comes to wrap its mortal softness around me and squeeze the daylights from me.

I see that they are all there in Mother's house with the Yellow Paper and nobody can light the flame to burn her name. It is the final custom. The match is handed to me. Lilly lights my flame.

The tears spit on my lap as I turn the TV on to forget. There before me sinks another death as the red of China runs out and pierces my eyes. I roll the paper into a tall cylinder, a tall chimney like myself and the flame encircles it rippling around its edges like her trembling lips. The flame grows tall and strong. My life, my love is turned into its ash. Bent in half it launches itself off the table and spins around to fall wasted in my hand. There I hold her in my palm, a little dark dot.

Lilly is wrapped in the waters of the Earth, purifying them and making them laugh and feel happy.

My plane, my exhausted white bird, skids into Australia, the blue world round and firm.

The ancient steel boat, the harbour and my home. To stare again into the small oval pool, the ocean which birthed my soul. The empty dream fulfilled, for the glass of love reflecting - to drink again her spirit as if risen from the dead.

Lilly passed away to another world where she now swims freely like a beautiful mermaid. A jujube seed had lodged itself in her lower stomach. It had been there for some time and septicaemia had set in. They informed the family that due to external pressure, possibly from the vibrator it had forced its way into the mesenteric artery which leads to the aorta. Jujube seeds are large with one very sharp end.

Mouse Finds the Source

Early one morning Mouse was in the garden turning over the soil when she had a thought about where the little creatures in the soil came from. She wondered how all the little animals could all get along together and how the soil was for them the best place to live. Mouse was born in the woods and Dragon used to live in a cave. They were easy places to sleep, she thought and get warm but the soil was a place where all things eventually returned and she wondered at how special a place it must be. She sat down and looked across the river and began to wonder where all the water came from. She looked at the sky and the lazy clouds and suddenly decided she wanted to find out where the source of the river was.

She went inside to talk to Dragon who was lighting the fire to cook breakfast. Mouse said she wanted to find the source of the river and Dragon said that the river began in the sea and they had just come back from a long journey there. But Mouse wanted to see the mountains and find the little stream which was the beginning of their great river.

She planned a journey and Dragon said he knew the way because he once lived deep in the mountains where it was cold and often snowed.

Mouse made herself a strong pair of shoes and collected some food from the garden. And Dragon organised his fishing lines and cleaned their new little boat which he had made.

Then one day they stretched like two old trees reaching for the morning sun and launched the boat for their journey had begun.

All that day they rowed against the current of the river. Through the tall forest and the high cliffs till the river became swifter and clearer and colder many miles upstream.

For several weeks they kept travelling till one day Dragon said they would have to hide the boat and walk the rest of the way.

Over big boulders and through deep pools they went carrying their belongings on their heads to stop them getting wet. Up and up they climbed over wet slippery stones. Occasionally waterfalls and steep cliffs stopped their way which they had to walk around. But Dragon could easily fly over the difficult ones.

Eventually the river became a small stream and Mouse began to feel the cold at night.

She noticed that in the pools were small creatures and all about them during the day were friendly birds. The clouds would sometimes come down and cover them and the trees around would drip as though they were in rain clouds.

High up on a mountain they could see a large cliff and Mouse said to Dragon that the river must begin somewhere up there. All that day they followed the sound of the little stream which often disappeared under stones and was difficult to find.

Late that evening they reached the base of the cliffs and there before them was a large crack in the rock which turned into a small cave. They camped that night on a narrow flat ledge just wide enough for the two of them. Dragon boiled some water and made tea.

Early the next morning it was very cold and Mouse was awake first. Dragon was still asleep as he was tired from all the travelling and flying. And though Mouse was freezing she crept closer to the cave and put her head inside but it was too dark to see. It smelt of old rotting wood and the sound of water echoed in her ears.

It was sometime later that they both went inside the cave to have a look. Dragon could light the way with his flame. And there before them was surely the source of the river for at the back of the cave was a large red stone which had split in two and out of the crack came a little trickle of water which fell into a small pool.

Mouse bent down to have a drink and as she did she half fell in the pool. Then she noticed something written on the stone. The writing was very hard to read as it was so old. But when Dragon saw it he said that it was written in a special language only Dragons could read.

The message read:

When we are aware that we are the river, love will flow through us and there will be no end.

Come drink from the source of the river of love.

Mouse was shivering, her teeth were rattling. Dragon warmed her hands by breathing on them until she was warm all over.

Printed in the United States
By Bookmasters

Printed in the United States
By Bookmasters